Protocols and Procedures of Cryptography and Network Security

Protocols and Procedures of Cryptography and Network Security

Edited by **Stephen Mason**

LANRYE
INTERNATIONAL

New Jersey

Published by Clanrye International,
55 Van Reypen Street,
Jersey City, NJ 07306, USA
www.clanryeinternational.com

Protocols and Procedures of Cryptography and Network Security
Edited by Stephen Mason

International Standard Book Number: 978-1-63240-423-7 (Hardback)

Contents

Preface

The world is advancing at a fast pace like never before. Therefore, the need is to keep up with the latest developments. This book was an idea that came to fruition when the specialists in the area realized the need to coordinate together and document essential themes in the subject. That's when I was requested to be the editor. Editing this book has been an honour as it brings together diverse authors researching on different streams of the field. The book collates essential materials contributed by veterans in the area which can be utilized by students and researchers alike.

This book provides an overview on various methodologies and procedures of cryptography. In the times of escalating worldwide development of electronic data storage and communications, efficient security of information has become a crucial need. The most efficient tool for the protection of information is cryptography, used in a combination with other tools for assuring the security of information in all of its applications, including user authentication, data integrity and confidentiality. This book is a compilation of in-depth research work in the field of cryptography. It describes some of the crucial challenges faced by the present computing world as well as a few techniques to defend against these challenges. It aims at serving as a useful source of reference for engineers, graduate and doctoral students, researchers, faculty members of universities, etc.

Each chapter is a sole-standing publication that reflects each author's interpretation. Thus, the book displays a multi-facetted picture of our current understanding of application, resources and aspects of the field. I would like to thank the contributors of this book and my family for their endless support.

Editor

Introduction to Quantum Cryptography

Xiaoqing Tan

Additional information is available at the end of the chapter

1. Introduction

Broadly speaking, cryptography is the problem of doing communication or computation involving two or more parties who may not trust one another. The best known cryptographic problem is the transmission of secret messages. Suppose wish to communicate in secret. For example, you may wish to give your credit card number to a merchant in exchange for goods, hopefully without any malevolent third party intercepting your credit card number. The way this is done is to use a cryptographic protocol. The most important distinction is between private key cryptosystems and public key cryptosystems.

The way a private key cryptosystem works is that two parties, 'Alice' and 'Bob', wish to communicate by sharing a private key, which only they know. The exact form of the key doesn't matter at this point – think of a string of zeroes and ones. The point is that this key is used by Alice to encrypt the information she wishes to send to Bob. After Alice encrypts she sends the encrypted information to Bob, who must now recover the original information. Exactly how Alice encrypts the message depends upon the private key, so that to recover the original message Bob needs to know the private key, in order to undo the transformation Alice applied.

Unfortunately, private key cryptosystems have some severe problems in many contexts. The most basic problem is how to distribute the keys? In many ways, the key distribution problem is just as difficult as the original problem of communicating in private – a malevolent third party may be eavesdropping on the key distribution, and then use the intercepted key to decrypt some of the message transmission.

One of the earliest discoveries in quantum computation and quantum information was that quantum mechanics can be used to do key distribution in such a way that Alice and Bob's security cannot be compromised. This procedure is known as **quantum cryptography** or **quantum key distribution** (abbreviated QKD). The basic idea is to exploit the quantum mechanical principle that observation in general disturbs the system being observed. Thus, if there is an eavesdropper listening in as Alice and Bob attempt to transmit their key, the presence of the eavesdropper will be visible as a disturbance of the communications channel Alice and Bob are using to establish the key. Alice and Bob can then throw out the key bits established while the eavesdropper was listening in, and start over.

The first quantum cryptographic ideas were proposed by Stephen Wiesner wrote "Conjugate Coding"[1], which unfortunately took more than ten years to see the light of print. In the mean time, Charles H. Bennett (who knew of Wiesner's idea) and Gilles Brassard picked up the subject and brought it to fruition in a series of papers that culminated with the demonstration of an experimental prototype that established the technological feasibility of the concept [2]. Quantum cryptographic systems take advantage of Heisenberg's uncertainty principle, according to which measuring a quantum system in general disturbs it and yields incomplete information about its state before the measurement. Eavesdropping on a quantum communication channel therefore causes an unavoidable disturbance, alerting the legitimate users. This yields a cryptographic system for the distribution of a secret random cryptographic key between two parties initially sharing no secret information that is secure against an eavesdropper having at her disposal unlimited computing power. Once this secret key is established, it can be used together with classical cryptographic techniques such as the one-time-pad (OTP) to allow the parties to communicate meaningful information in absolute secrecy.

The second major type of cryptosystem is the public key cryptosystem. Public key cryptosystem don't rely on Alice and Bob sharing a secret key in advance. Instead, Bob simply publishes a 'public key', which is made available to the general public. Alice can make use of this public key to encrypt a message which she sends to Bob. The third party cannot use Bob's public key to decrypt the message. Public key cryptography did not achieve widespread use until the mid-1970s, when it was proposed independently by Whitfield Diffie and Martin Hellman, Rivest, Adi Shamir, and Leonard Adleman developed the RSA cryptosystem, which at the time of writing is the most widely deployed public key cryptosystem, believed to offer a fine balance of security and practical usability.

The key to the security of public key cryptosystems is that it should be difficult to invert the encryption stage if only the public key is available. For example, it turns out that inverting the encryption stage of RSA is a problem closely related to factoring. Much of the presumed security of RSA comes from the belief that factoring is a problem hard to solve on a classical computer. However, Shor's fast algorithm for factoring on cryptosystems which can be broken if a fast algorithm for solving the discrete logarithm problem – like Shor's quantum algorithm for discrete logarithm – were known. This practical application of quantum computers to the breaking of cryptographic codes has excited much of the interest in quantum computation and quantum information.

In addition to key distribution, quantum techniques may also assist in the achievement of subtler cryptographic goals, important in the post-cold war world, such as protecting private information while it is being used to reach public decisions. Such techniques, pioneered by Claude Crepeau [3] [4], allow two people to compute an agreed-upon function $f(x; y)$ on private inputs x and y when one person knows x, the other knows y, and neither is willing to disclose anything about their private input to the other, except for what follows logically from one's private input and the function's output. The classic example of such discreet decision making is the "dating problem", in which two people seek a way of making a date if and only if each likes the other, without disclosing any further information. For example, if Alice likes Bob but Bob doesn't like Alice, the date should be called off without Bob finding out that Alice likes him, on the other hand, it is logically unavoidable for Alice to learn that Bob doesn't like her, because if he did the date would be on.

In general, the goal of quantum cryptography is to perform tasks that are impossible or intractable with conventional cryptography. Quantum cryptography makes use of the subtle properties of quantum mechanics such as the quantum no-cloning theorem and the Heisenberg uncertainty principle. Unlike conventional cryptography, whose security is often based on unproven computational assumptions, quantum cryptography has an important advantage in that its security is often based on the laws of physics. Thus far, proposed applications of quantum cryptography include QKD, quantum bit commitment and quantum coin tossing. These applications have varying degrees of success. The most successful and important application – QKD – has been proven to be unconditionally secure. Moreover, experimental QKD has now been performed over hundreds of kilometers over both standard commercial telecom optical fibers and open-air. In fact, commercial QKD systems are currently available on the market [5].

Classical secret sharing can be used in a number of ways besides for a joint checking account. The secret key could access a bank vault, or a computer account, or any of a variety of things. In addition, secret sharing is a necessary component for performing secure distributed computations among a number of people who do not completely trust each other. With the boom in quantum computation, it seems possible, even likely, that quantum states will become nearly as important as classical data. It might therefore be useful to have some way of sharing secret quantum states as well as secret classical data. Such a **quantum secret sharing** (abbreviated QSS) scheme might be useful for sharing quantum keys, such as those used in quantum key distribution or in other quantum cryptographic protocols. In addition, QSS might allow us to take advantage of the additional power of quantum computation in secure distributed computations.

Imagine that it is fifteen years from now and someone announces the successful construction of a large quantum computer. The New York Times runs a front-page article reporting that all of the public-key algorithms used to protect the Internet have been broken by quantum computer. Perhaps, after seeing quantum computers destroy RSA and DSA and ECDSA, Internet users will leap to the conclusion that cryptography is dead. For solving the problem, some researchers provided the idea about **post-quantum cryptography** which refers to research on cryptographic primitives (usually public-key cryptosystems) that are not breakable using quantum computers. This term came about because most currently popular public-key cryptosystems rely on the integer factorization problem or discrete logarithm problem, both of which would be easily solvable on large enough quantum computers using Shor's algorithm [6] [7]. Even though current publicly known experimental quantum computing is nowhere near powerful enough to attack real cryptosystems, many cryptographers are researching new algorithms, in case quantum computing becomes a threat in the future. This work is popularized by the PQCrypto conference series since 2006.

In the past few years, a remarkable surge of interest in the international scientific and industrial community has propelled quantum cryptography into mainstream computer science and physics. Furthermore, quantum cryptography is becoming increasingly practical at a fast pace. The first quantum key distribution prototype [2] worked over a distance of 32 centimeters in 1989. Two additional experimental demonstrations have been set up since, which work over significant lengths of optical fibre [8] [9]. The highest bit rate system currently demonstrated exchanges secure keys at 1 Mbit/s (over 20 km of optical fibre) and 10 kbit/s (over 100 km of fibre), achieved by a collaboration between the University of Cambridge and Toshiba using the BB84 protocol with decoy pulses.

As of March 2007 the longest distance over which quantum key distribution has been demonstrated using optic fibre is 148.7 km, achieved by Los Alamos National Laboratory/NIST using the BB84 protocol. Significantly, this distance is long enough for almost all the spans found in today's fibre networks. The distance record for free space QKD is 144 km between two of the Canary Islands, achieved by a European collaboration using entangled photons (the Ekert scheme) in 2006, and using BB84 enhanced with decoy states in 2007. The experiments suggest transmission to satellites is possible, due to the lower atmospheric density at higher altitudes. For example although the minimum distance from the International Space Station to the ESA Space Debris Telescope is about 400 km, the atmospheric thickness is about an order of magnitude less than in the European experiment, thus yielding less attenuation compared to this experiment.

2. Quantum cryptography fundamentals

On a wider context, quantum cryptography is a branch of quantum information processing, which includes quantum computing, quantum measurements, and quantum teleportation. Quantum computation and quantum information is the study of the information processing tasks that can be accomplished using quantum mechanical systems.

Quantum mechanics is a mathematical framework or set of rules for the construction of physical theories. The rules of quantum mechanics are simple but even experts find them counterintuitive, and the earliest antecedents of quantum computation and quantum information may be found in the long-standing desire of physicists to better understand quantum mechanics. Perhaps the most striking of these is the study of quantum entanglement. Entanglement is a uniquely quantum mechanical resource that plays a key role in many of the most interesting applications of quantum computation and quantum information; entanglement is iron to the classical world's bronze age. In recent years there has been a tremendous effort trying to better understand the properties of entanglement considered as a fundamental resource of Nature, of comparable importance to energy, information, entropy, or any other fundamental resource. Although there is as yet no complete theory of entanglement, some progress has been made in understanding this strange property of quantum mechanics. It is hoped by many researchers that further study of the properties of entanglement will yield insights that facilitate the development of new applications in quantum computation and quantum information.

As we known, it is interesting to learn that one decade before people realized that a quantum computer could be used to break public key cryptography, they had already found a solution against this quantum attack – quantum key distribution (QKD). Based on the fundamental principles in quantum physics, QKD provides an unconditionally secure way to distribute random keys through insecure channels. The secure key generated by QKD could be further applied in the OTP scheme or other encryption algorithms to enhance information security. In this chapter, we will introduce the fundamental principles behind various QKD or QSS and present the state-of-the art quantum cryptography technologies.

2.1. Entanglement state

The counterintuitive predictions of quantum mechanics about correlated systems were first discussed by Albert Einstein in 1935, in a joint paper with Boris Podolsky and Nathan Rosen [10]. They demonstrated a thought experiment that attempted to show that quantum mechanical theory was impossible.

But flowing the EPR paper, Erwin Schrodinger wrote letter (in German) to Einstein in which he used the word Verschrankung (translated by himself as entanglement) "to describe the correlations between two particles that interact and then separate, as in the EPR experiment" [11]. He shortly thereafter published a seminal paper defining and discussing the notion, and terming it "entanglement".

Entanglement is usually created by direct interactions between subatomic particles. These interactions can take numerous forms. One of the most commonly used methods is spontaneous parametric down-conversion to generate a pair of photons entangled in polarization [12]. Other methods include the use of a fiber coupler to confine and mix photons, the use of quantum dots to trap electrons until decay occurs, the use of the Hong-Ou-Mandel effect, etc. In the earliest tests of Bell's theorem, the entangled particles were generated using atomic cascades. It is also possible to create entanglement between quantum systems that never directly interacted, through the use of entanglement swapping.

Consider two noninteracting systems A and B, with respective Hilbert spaces H_A and H_B. The Hilbert space of the composite system is the tensor product $H_A \otimes H_B$. If the first system is in state $|\psi\rangle_A$ and the second in state $|\psi\rangle_B$, the state of the composite system is $|\psi\rangle_A \otimes |\psi\rangle_B$. States of the composite system which can be represented in this form are called separable states, or product states. Not all states are separable states. Fix a basis $\{|i\rangle_A\}$ for H_A and a basis $\{|j\rangle_B\}$ for H_B. The most general state in $H_A \otimes H_B$ is the form of

$$\left|\psi\right\rangle_{AB} = \sum_{i,j} C_{ij} |i\rangle_A \otimes |j\rangle_B \tag{1}$$

This state is separable if $c_{ij} = c_i^A c_j^B$ yielding $|\psi\rangle_A = \sum_i c_i^A |i\rangle_A$ and $|\phi\rangle_B = \sum_j c_j^B |j\rangle_B$. It is inseparable if $c_{ij} \neq c_i^A c_j^B$. If a state is inseparable, it is called an entangled state. For example, given two basis vectors $\{|0\rangle_A, |1\rangle_A\}$ of H_A and two basis vectors $\{|0\rangle_B, |1\rangle_B\}$ of H_B, the following is an entangled state:

$$\frac{1}{\sqrt{2}}(|0\rangle_A |0\rangle_B + |1\rangle_A |1\rangle_B) \tag{2}$$

If the composite system is in this state, it is impossible to attribute to either system A or system B a definite pure state. Another way to say this is that while the von Neumann entropy of the whole state is zero, the entropy of the subsystems is greater than zero. In this sense, the systems are "entangled". This has specific empirical ramifications for interferometry [13]. It is worthwhile to note that the above example is one of four Bell states, which are maximally entangled pure states.

2.2. One-time-pad and key distribution problem

In conventional cryptography, an unbreakable code does exist. It is called the one-time-pad and was invented by Gilbert Vernam in 1918 [14]. In the one-time-pad method, a message (traditionally called the plain text) is first converted by Alice into a binary form (a string consisting of "0"s and "1"s) by a publicly known method. A key is a binary string of the same length as the message. By combining each bit of the message with the respective bit of the key using XOR (i.e. addition modulo two), Alice converts the plain text into an encrypted form (called the cipher text). i.e. for each bit

$$c_i \equiv m_i + k_i \,(\text{mod}\quad 2). \tag{3}$$

Alice then transmits the cipher text to Bob via a broadcast channel. Anyone including an eavesdropper can get a copy of the cipher text. However, without the knowledge of the key, the cipher text is totally random and gives no information whatsoever about the plain text. For decryption, Bob, who shares the same key with Alice, can perform another XOR (i.e. addition modulo two) between each bit of the cipher text with the respective bit of the key to recover the plain text. This is because

$$c_i \equiv m_i + k_i \equiv m_i + 2k_i \equiv m_i (\text{mod}\quad 2). \tag{4}$$

The one-time-pad method is unbreakable, but it has a serious drawback: it supposes that Alice and Bob initially share a random string of secret that is as long as the message. Therefore, the one-time-pad simply shifts the problem of secure communication to the problem of key distribution. This is the key distribution problem. The one of possible solution to the key distribution problem is public key cryptography.

Quantum mechanics can provide a solution to the key distribution problem. In quantum key distribution, an encryption key is generated randomly between Alice and Bob by using non orthogonal quantum states. In quantum mechanics there is a quantum no-cloning theorem, which states that it is fundamentally impossible for anyone including an eavesdropper to make an additional copy of an unknown quantum state. Therefore, any attempt by an eavesdropper to learn information about a key in a QKD process will lead to disturbance, which can be detected by Alice and Bob who can, for example, check the bit error rate of a random sample of the raw transmission data.

2.3. Quantum no-cloning theorem

The quantum no-cloning theorem was stated by Wootters, Zurek, and Dieks in 1982, and has profound implications in quantum computing and related fields.

Theorem (Quantum no-cloning theorem) An arbitrary quantum state cannot be duplicated perfectly.

Proof: Suppose the state of a quantum system A, which we wish to copy, is $|\psi\rangle_A$. In order to make a copy, we take a system B with the same state space and initial state $|e\rangle_B$. The initial, or blank, state must be independent of $|\psi\rangle_A$, of which we have no prior knowledge. The composite system is then described by the tensor product, and its state is $|\psi\rangle_A |e\rangle_B$.

There are only two ways to manipulate the composite system. We could perform an observation, which irreversibly collapses the system into some eigenstate of the observable, corrupting the information contained in the qubit. This is obviously not what we want. Alternatively, we could control the Hamiltonian of the system, and thus the time evolution operator U (for a time independent Hamiltonian, $U(t) = e^{-iHt/\hbar}$, where $-H/\hbar$ is called the generator of translations in time) up to some fixed time interval, which yields a unitary operator. Then U acts as a copier provided that

$$U|\phi\rangle_A |e\rangle_B = |\phi\rangle_A |\phi\rangle_B,$$
(5)

for all possible states $|\phi\rangle$ in the state space (including $|\psi\rangle$). Since U is unitary, it preserves the inner product:

$$\langle e|_B \langle \phi|_A |\psi\rangle_A |e\rangle_B = \langle e|_B \langle \phi|_A U^\dagger U |\psi\rangle_A |e\rangle_B = \langle \phi|_B \langle \phi|_A |\psi\rangle_A |\psi\rangle_B,$$
(6)

and since quantum mechanical states are assumed to be normalized, it follows that $\langle \phi | \psi \rangle = \langle \phi | \psi \rangle^2$.

This implies that either $\phi = \psi$ (in which case $\langle \phi | \psi \rangle = 1$) or ϕ is orthogonal to ψ (in which case $\langle \phi | \psi \rangle = 0$). However, this is not the case for two arbitrary states. While orthogonal states in a specifically chosen basis $\{|0\rangle, |1\rangle\}$, for example, $|\phi\rangle = \frac{1}{\sqrt{2}}(|0\rangle + |1\rangle)$ and $|\psi\rangle = \frac{1}{\sqrt{2}}(|0\rangle - |1\rangle)$ fit the requirement that $\langle \phi | \psi \rangle = \langle \phi | \psi \rangle^2$, this result does not hold for more general quantum states. Apparently U cannot clone a general quantum state.

Quantum no-cloning theorem is a direct result of the linearity of quantum physics. It is closely related to another important theorem in quantum mechanics, which states: if a measurement allows one to gain information about the state of a quantum system, then in general the state of this quantum system will be disturbed, unless we know in advance that the possible states of the original quantum system are orthogonal to each other.

At first sight, the impossibility of making perfect copies of unknown quantum states seems to be a shortcoming. Surprisingly, it can also be an advantage. It turned out that by using this impossibility smartly, unconditionally secure key distribution could be achieved: any attempts by the eavesdropper to learn the information encoded quantum mechanically will disturb the quantum state and expose her existence. Specially, we can get the following characteristics about quantum no-cloning theorem:

- The no-cloning theorem prevents us from using classical error correction techniques on quantum states. For example, we cannot create backup copies of a state in the middle of a quantum computation, and use them to correct subsequent errors. Error correction is vital for practical quantum computing, and for some time this was thought to be a fatal limitation. In 1995, Shor and Steane revived the prospects of quantum computing by independently devising the first quantum error correcting codes, which circumvent the no-cloning theorem.

- Similarly, cloning would violate the no teleportation theorem, which says classical teleportation (not to be confused with entanglement-assisted teleportation) is impossible. In other words, quantum states cannot be measured reliably.

- The no-cloning theorem does not prevent superluminal communication via quantum entanglement, as cloning is a sufficient condition for such communication, but not a necessary one. Nevertheless, consider the EPR thought experiment, and suppose quantum states could be cloned. Assume parts of a maximally entangled Bell state are distributed to Alice and Bob. Alice could send bits to Bob in the following way: If Alice wishes to transmit a "0", she measures the spin of her electron in the z direction, collapsing Bob's state to either $|z+\rangle_B$ or $|z-\rangle_B$. To transmit "1", Alice does nothing to her qubit. Bob creates many copies of his electron's state, and measures the spin of each copy in the z direction. Bob will know that Alice has transmitted a "0" if all his measurements will produce the same result; otherwise, his measurements will have outcomes +1/2 and −1/2 with equal probability. This would allow Alice and Bob to communicate across space-like separations.

- The no-cloning theorem prevents us from viewing the holographic principle for black holes as meaning we have two copies of information lying at the event horizon and the black hole interior simultaneously. This leads us to more radical interpretations like black hole complementarity.

2.4. Heisenberg uncertainty principle

Heisenberg's Uncertainty Principle (abbreviated HUP) is one of the fundamental concepts of quantum physics, and is the basis for the initial realization of fundamental uncertainties in the ability of an experimenter to measure more than one quantum variable at a time. Attempting to measure an elementary particle's position to the highest degree of accuracy, for example, leads to an increasing uncertainty in being able to measure the particle's momentum to an equally high degree of accuracy.

Suppose A and B are two Hermitian operators, and $|\psi\rangle$ is a quantum state. Suppose $\langle\psi|AB|\psi\rangle = x + iy$, where x and y are real. Note that $\langle\psi|[A, B]|\psi\rangle = 2iy$ and $\langle\psi|\{A, B\}|\psi\rangle = 2x$. This implies that

$$\left|\langle\psi|[A,B]|\psi\rangle\right|^2 + \left|\langle\psi|\{A,B\}|\psi\rangle\right|^2 = 4\left|\langle\psi|AB|\psi\rangle\right|^2. \tag{7}$$

By the Cauchy-Schwarz inequality $|\langle\psi|AB|\psi\rangle|^2 \leq \langle\psi|A^2|\psi\rangle\langle\psi|B^2|\psi\rangle$, which combined with the equation (1) and dropping a non-negative term gives

$$\left|\langle\psi|[A,B]|\psi\rangle\right|^2 \leq 4\langle\psi|A^2|\psi\rangle\langle\psi|B^2|\psi\rangle. \tag{8}$$

Suppose C and D are two observables. Substituting $A = C - <C>$ and $B = D - <D>$ into the last equation, where the average value of the observable C is often written $<C> = \langle\psi|C|\psi\rangle$ and similar to D, we obtain Heisenberg's uncertainty principle as it is usually stated

$$\Delta(C)\Delta(D) \geq \frac{\left|\langle\psi|[C,D]|\psi\rangle\right|}{2}. \tag{9}$$

Quantum communication the sending of encoded messages that are un-hackable by any computer. This i allows s possible because the messages are carried by tiny particles of light called photons. If an eavesdropper attempts to read out the message in transit, they will be discovered by the disturbance their measurement causes to the particles as an inevitable consequence of the HUP. In the regime of quantum experiments, by contrast, we are uncertain about the results of experiments because the particle itself is uncertain. It has no position or speed until we measure it. We can design some protocol of quantum cryptography by using the property of quantum from HUP.

3. Quantum key distribution

The first attempt of using quantum mechanics to achieve missions impossible in classical information started in the early 70's. Stephen Wiesner proposed two communication modalities not allowed by classical physics: "quantum multiplexing" channel and counterfeit-free bank-note. Unfortunately, his paper was rejected and couldn't be published until a decade later. In 1980's, Charles H.Bennett and Gilles Brassard extended Wiesner's idea and applied it to solve the key distribution problem in classical cryptography. In 1984, the well known BB84 QKD protocol was published [15]. QKD is a new tool in the cryptographer's toolbox: it allows for secure key agreement over an untrusted channel where the output key is entirely inde-

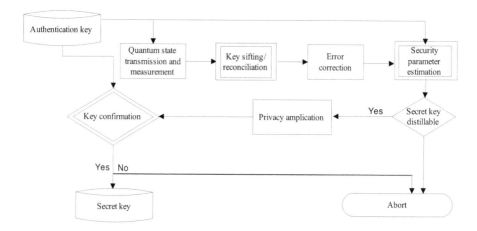

Figure 1. Flow chart of the stages of a quantum key distribution protocol. Stages with double lines require classical authentication. [18]

pendent from any input value, a task that is impossible using classical cryptography. QKD does not eliminate the need for other cryptographic primitives, such as authentication, but it can be used to build systems with new security properties.

To conquer the errors made by noise and wiretapping in the quantum channel, unconditionally secure secret-key agreement over a public channel was designed, information reconciliation and privacy amplification can be used to quantum key distribution, or otherwise, quantum entanglement purification should be used. The first general although rather complex proof of unconditional security was given by Mayers [16], which was followed by a number of other proofs. In Mayers' proof, the BB84 scheme proposed by Bennett and Brassard was proved to be unconditionally secure. Building on the quantum privacy amplification idea, Lo and Chau, proposed a conceptually simpler proof of security [17].

In QKD, two parties, Alice and Bob, obtain some quantum states and measure them. They communicate (all communication form this point onwards is classical) to determine which of their measurement results could lead to secret key bits; some are discarded in a process called sifting because the measurement settings were incompatible. They perform error correction and then estimate a security parameter which describes how much information an eavesdropper might have about their key data. If this amount is above a certain threshold, then they abort as they cannot guarantee any secrecy whatsoever. If it is below the threshold, then they can apply privacy amplification to squeeze out any remaining information the eavesdropper might have, and arrive at a shared secret key. Some of this classical communication must be authenticated to avoid man-in-the-middle attacks. Some portions of the protocol can fail with negligible probability.

A flow chart describing the stages of quantum key distribution is given in Figure 1.

Alice's bit sequence	0	1	1	1	0	1	0	0	0	1
Alice's basis	+	×	+	+	×	+	×	×	+	×
Alice's photon polarization	→	↘	↑	↑	↗	↑	↗	↗	→	↘
Bob's basis	+	+	×	+	+	×	×	+	+	×
Bob's measured polarization	→	↑	↘	↑	→	↗	↗	↑	→	↘
Bob's sifted measured polarization	→			↑			↗		→	↘
Bob's data sequence	0			1			0		0	1

Table 1. Procedure of BB84 protocol.

3.1. The BB84 QKD protocol

The best-known protocol for QKD is the Bennett and Brassard protocol (BB84). The procedure of BB84 is as follows (also shown in Table 1).

1. Quantum communication phase

    1. In BB84, Alice sends Bob a sequence of photons through an *insecure quantum channel*, each independently chosen from one of the four polarizations-vertical, horizontal, 45-degrees and 135-degrees.

    2. For each photon, Bob randomly chooses one of the two measurement bases (rectilinear and diagonal) to perform a measurement.

    3. Bob records his measurement bases and results. Bob publicly acknowledge his receipt of signals.

2. Public discussion phase

    1. Alice broadcasts her bases of measurements. Bob broadcasts his bases of measurements.

    2. Alice and Bob discard all events where they use different bases for a signal.

    3. To test for tampering, Alice randomly chooses a fraction, p, of all remaining events as test events. For those test events, she publicly broadcasts their positions and polarizations.

    4. Bob broadcasts the polarizations of the test events.

    5. Alice and Bob compute the error rate of the test events (i.e., the fraction of data for which their value disagree). If the computed error rate is larger than some prescribed threshold value, say 11%, they abort. Otherwise, they proceed to the next step.

    6. Alice and Bob each convert the polarization data of all remaining data into a binary string called a raw key (by, for example, mapping a vertical of 45-degrees photon to "0" and a horizontal or 135-degrees photon to "1"). The can perform classical postprocessing such as error correction and privacy amplification to generate a final key.

The basic idea of the BB84 QKD protocol is beautiful and its security can be intuitively understood from the quantum no-cloning theorem. On the other hand, to apply QKD in practice, Alice and Bob need to find the upper bound of Eve's information quantitatively, given the observed quantum bit error rate (abbreviated QBER) and other system parameters. This is the primary goal of various QKD security proofs and it had turned out to be extremely difficult. One major challenge comes from the fact that Eve could launch attacks way beyond today's technologies and our imaginations. Nevertheless, QKD was proved to be unconditionally secure. This is most significant achievements in quantum information.

3.2. QKD based on EPR

An essentially equivalent protocol that utilizes Einstein-Podolsky-Rosen (EPR) correlations has been worked on by Artur Ekert [19] and Bennett, Brassard, and Mermin [20]. To take advantage of EPR correlations, particles are prepared in such a way that they are "entangled". This means that although they may be separated by large distances in space, they are not independent of each other. Suppose the entangled particles are photons. If one of the particles is measured according to the rectilinear basis and found to have a vertical polarization, then the other particle will also be found to have a vertical polarization if it is measured according to the rectilinear basis. If however, the second particle is measured according to the circular basis, it may be found to have either left-circular or right-circular polarization.

In his 1991 paper, Ekert [19] suggested basing the security of this two-qubit protocol on Bell's inequality, an inequality which demonstrates that some correlations predicted by quantum mechanics cannot be reproduced by the local theory. To do this, Alice and Bob can use a third basis. In this way the probability that they might happen to choose the same basis is reduced from $\frac{1}{2}$ to $\frac{2}{9}$, but at the same time as they establish a key, they collect enough data to test Bell's inequality. They can thus check that the source really emits the entangled state and not merely product states. The following year Bennett, Brassard, and Mermin [20] criticized Ekert's letter, arguing that the violation of Bell's inequality is not necessary for the security of quantum cryptography and emphasizing the close connection between the Ekert and the BB84 schemes. This criticism quantum cryptography might be missing an important point. Although the exact relation between security and Bell's inequality is not yet fully known, there are clear results establishing fascinating connections.

The steps of the protocol for developing a secret key using EPR correlations of entangled photons are explained below.

1. Alice creates EPR pairs of polarized photons, keeping one particle for herself and sending the other particle of each pair to Bob.

2. Alice randomly measures the polarization of each particle she kept according to the rectilinear or circular basis. She records each measurement type and the polarization measured.

3. Bob randomly measures each particle he received according to the rectilinear or circular basis. He records each measurement type and the polarization measured.

4. Alice and Bob tell each other which measurement types were used, and they keep the data from all particle pairs where they both chose the same measurement type.

5. They convert the remaining data to a string of bits using a convention such as: left-circular = 0, right-circular = 1, horizontal = 0, vertical = 1.

One important difference between the BB84 and the EPR methods is that with BB84, the key created by Alice and Bob must be stored classically until it is used. Therefore, although the key was completely secure when it was created, its continued security over time is only as great as the security of its storage. Using the EPR method, Alice and Bob could potentially store the prepared entangled particles and then measure them and create the key just before they were going to use it, eliminating the problem of insecure storage.

So the idea consists in replacing the quantum channel carrying two qubits from Alice to Bob by a channel carrying two qubits from a common source, one qubit to Alice and one to Bob. A first possibility would be that the source always emits the two qubits in the same state chosen randomly among the four states of the BB84 protocol. Alice and Bob would then both measure their qubit in one of the two bases, again chosen independently and randomly. The source then announces the bases, and Alice and Bob keep the data only when they happen to have made their measurements in the compatible basis. If the source is reliable, this protocol is equivalent to that of BB84: It is as if the qubit propagates backwards in time from Alice to the source, and then forward to Bob. But better than trusting the source, which could be in Eve's hand the Ekert protocol assumes that the two qubits are emitted in a maximally entangled state like $|\phi^{+}\rangle = 1/\sqrt{2}(|00\rangle + |11\rangle)$.

Then, when Alice and Bob happen to use the same basis, either the x basis or the y basis, i.e., in about half of the cases, their results are identical, providing them with a common key.

3.3. Continuous variable QKD

In the BB84 QKD protocol, Alice's random bits are encoded in a two dimensional space like the polarization state of a single photon. More recently, QKD protocols working with continuous variables have been proposed. Among them, the Gaussian modulated coherent state (GMCS) QKD protocol has drawn special attention [21].

The protocol runs as follows. First, Alice draws two random numbers x_A and p_A from a gaussian distribution of mean zero and variance $V_A N_0$, where N_0 denotes the shot-noise variance. Then, she sends the coherent state $|x_A + ip_A\rangle$ to Bob, who randomly chooses to measure either quadrature x or p. Later, using a public authenticated channel, he informs Alice about which quadrature he measured, so she may discard the irrelevant data. After many similar exchanges, Alice and Bob (and possibly the eavesdropper Eve) share a set of correlated gaussian variables, which we call 'key elements'.

The basic scheme of the GMCS QKD protocol can be shown in Figure 2.

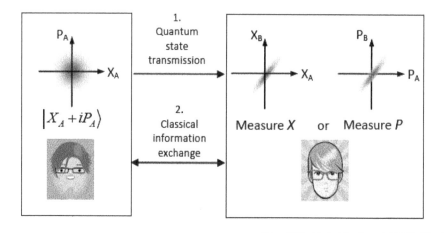

Figure 2. *The Gaussian modulated coherent state (GMCS) QKD. X: amplitude quadrature; P: phase quadrature.* [22]

Alice modulates both the amplitude quadrature and phase quadrature of a coherent state with Gaussian distributed random numbers. In classical electromagnetism, these two quadratures correspond to the in-phase and out-of-phase components of electric field, which can be conveniently modulated with optical phase and amplitude modulators. Alice sends the modulated coherent state together with a strong local oscillator (a strong laser pulse which serves as a phase reference) to Bob. Bob randomly measures one of the two quadratures with a phase modulator and a homodyne detector. After performing his measurements, Bob informs Alice which quadrature he actually measures for each pulse and Alice drops the irrelevant data. At this stage, they share a set of correlated Gaussian variables which are called the — raw key. Given the variances of the measurement results below certain thresholds, they can further work out perfectly correlated secure key by performing reconciliation and privacy amplification. Classical data processing is then necessary for Alice and Bob to obtain a fully secret binary key.

The security of the GMCS QKD can be comprehended from the uncertainty principle. In quantum optics, the amplitude quadrature and phase quadrature of a coherent state form a pair of conjugate variables, which cannot be simultaneously determined with arbitrarily high accuracies due to Heisenberg uncertainty principle. From the observed variance in one quadrature, Alice and Bob can upper bound Eve's information about the other quadrature. This provides a way to verify the security of the generated key. Recently, an unconditional security proof of the GMCS QKD appeared [23].

Different from the BB84 QKD, in GMCS QKD, homodyne detectors are employed to measure electric fields rather than photon energy. By using a strong local oscillator, high efficiency and fast photo diodes can be used to construct the homodyne detector which could result in a high secure key generation rate. However, the performance of the GMCS QKD is strongly dependent on the channel loss. Recall that in the BB84 QKD system, the channel loss plays a simple role: it reduces the communication efficiency but it will not introduce QBER. A photon is either lost in the channel, in which case Bob will not register anything, or it will reach Bob's detector intact. On the other hand, in the GMCS QKD, the channel loss will introduce vacuum noise and reduce the correlation between Alice and Bob's data. As the channel loss increases, the vacuum noise will become so high that it is impossible for Alice and Bob to resolve a small excess noise (which is used to upper bound Eve's information) on the top of a huge vacuum noise.

Comparing with the BB84 QKD, the GMCS QKD could yield a high secure key rate over short distances [24] [25].

3.4. Decoy state QKD

The security of QKD has been rigorously proven in a number of recent papers. There has been tremendous interest in experimental QKD [26] [27]. Unfortunately, all those exciting recent experiments are, in principle, insecure due to real-life imperfections. More concretely, highly attenuated lasers are often used as sources. But, these sources sometimes produce signals that contain more than one photon. Those multi-photon signals open the door to powerful new eavesdropping attacks including photon splitting attack. For example, Eve can, in principle, measure the photon number of each signal emitted by Alice and selectively suppress single photon signals. She splits multi-photon signals, keeping one copy for herself and sending one copy to Bob. Now, since Eve has an identical copy of what Bob possesses, the unconditional security of QKD is completely compromised.

In summary, in standard BB84 protocol, only signals originated from single photon pulses emitted by Alice are guaranteed to be secure. Consequently, paraphrasing GLLP (Gottesman, Lo, Lutkenhaus, Preskill [28]), the secure key generation rate (per signal state emitted by Alice) can be shown to be given by:

$$S \geq Q_\mu \{-H_2(E_\mu) + \Omega [1 - H_2(e_1)]\}, \tag{10}$$

where Q_μ and E_μ are respectively the gain and quantum bit error rate (QBER) of the signal state (Here, the gain means the ratio of the number of Bob's detection events (where Bob chooses the same basis as Alice) to Alice's number of emitted signals. QBER means the error rate of Bob's detection events for the case that Alice and Bob use the same basis), Ω and e_1 are respectively the fraction and QBER of detection events by Bob that have originated from single-photon signals emitted by Alice and H_2 is the binary Shannon entropy. It is a prior very hard to obtain a good lower bound on Ω and a good upper bound on e_1. Therefore, prior art methods (as in GLLP [28], under (semi-) realistic assumptions, if imperfections are sufficiently small, then BB84 is unconditionally secure.) make the most pessimistic assumption that all multi-photon signals emitted by Alice will be received by Bob. For this reason, until now, it has been widely believed that the demand for unconditional security will severely reduce the performance of QKD systems.

In [29], they present a simple method that will provide very good bounds to Ω and e_1. The method is based on the decoy state idea first proposed by Hwang [12]. While the idea of Hwang was highly innovative, his security analysis was heuristic. Consequently, H.K. Lo etc's method for the first time makes most of the long distance QKD experiments reported in the literature unconditionally secure. And their method has the advantage that it can be implemented with essentially the current hardware. So, unlike prior art solutions based on single-photon sources, their method does not require daunting experimental developments. The key point of the decoy state idea is that Alice prepares a set of additional states — decoy states, in addition to standard BB84 states. Those decoy states are used for the purpose of detecting eavesdropping attacks only, whereas the standard BB84 states are used for key generation only. The only difference between the decoy state and the standard BB84 states is their intensities (i.e., their photon number distributions). By measuring the yields and QBER of decoy states, Alice and Bob can obtain reliable bounds to Ω and e_1, thus allowing them to surpass all prior art results substantially [30].

At first, we recall the original decoy state QKD by Hwang [12] in detail.

Define Y_n= yield = conditional probability that a signal will be detected by Bob, given that it is emitted by Alice as an n-photon state.

To design a method to test experimentally the yield (i.e. transmittance) of multi-photons, we can use two-photon states as decoys and test their yield. For example, Alice and Bob estimate the yield $Y_2 = x / N$ if Alice sends N two-photon signals to Bob and Bob detects x signals. If Eve selectively sends multi-photons, Y_2 will be abnormally large. So Eve will be caught.

The two kinds of states are as follows for the decoy state QKD (Toy Model).

a.   Signal state: Poisson photon number distribution μ (at Alice).

b.   Decoy state: two-photon signals.

The procedure of decoy state QKD (Toy Model) is as following.

1.   Alice randomly sends either a signal state or decoy state to Bob.

2.   Bob acknowledges receipt of signals.

3.   Alice publicly announces which are signal states and which are decoy states.

4.   Alice and Bob compute the transmission probability for the signal states and for the decoy states respectively.

If Eve selectively transmits two-photons, an abnormally high fraction of the decoy state B) will be received by Bob. Eve will be caught. But the practical problem with toy model is making perfect two-photon state is hard. So the solution of Hwang's decoy state QKD is to make another mixture of good and bad photons with a different weight.

There is two kinds of states for Hwang's decoy state QKD.

a.   Signal state: Poisson photon number distribution: α (at Alice) with mixture 1.

b. Decoy state: Poisson photon number distribution: $\mu \sim 2$ (at Alice) with mixture 2.

If Eve lets an abnormally high fraction of multi-photons go to Bob, then decoy states (which has high weight of multi-photons) will have an abnormally high transmission. Therefore, Alice and Bob can catch Eve.

But there are some drawbacks of Hwang's original idea:

1. Hwang's security analysis was heuristic, rather than rigorous.

2. "Dark counts"–an important effect–are not considered.

3. Final results (distance and key generation rate) are unclear.

Suppose that a decoy state and a signal state have the same characteristics (wavelength, timing information, etc) by H.K. Lo etc's methods [29]. Therefore, Eve cannot distinguish a decoy state from a signal state and the only piece of information available to Eve is the number of photons in a signal. Therefore, the yield, Y_n (yield of an n-photon signal), and QBER, e_n (quantum bit error rate of an n-photon signal), can depend on only the photon number, n, but not which distribution (decoy or signal) the state is from. If Eve cannot treat the decoy state any differently from signal state, then

$$Y_n(signal) = Y_n(decoy) = Y_n$$
$$e_n(signal) = e_n(decoy) = e_n.$$

Let us imagine that Alice varies over all non-negative values of μ randomly and independently for each signal, Alice and Bob can experimentally measure the yield Q_μ and the QBER E_μ.

$$Q_\mu = Y_0 e^{-\mu} + Y_1 e^{-\mu} \mu + Y_2 e^{-\mu} (\mu^2/2) + ... + Y_n e^{-\mu} (\mu^n/n!) + ... \tag{11}$$

$$Q_\mu E_\mu = Y_0 e^{-\mu} e_0 + Y_1 e^{-\mu} \mu e_1 + Y_2 e^{-\mu} (\mu^2/2) e_2 + ... + Y_n e^{-\mu} (\mu^n/n!) e_n + ... \tag{12}$$

Since the relations between the variables Q_μ's and Y_n's and between E_μ's and e_n's are linear, given the set of variables Q_μ's and E_μ's measured from their experiments, Alice and Bob can deduce mathematically with high confidence the variables Y_n's and e_n's. This means that Alice and Bob can constrain simultaneously the yields, Y_n and QBER e_n simultaneously for all n. Suppose Alice and Bob know their channel property well. Then, they know what range of values of Y_n's and e_n's is acceptable. Any attack by Eve that will change the value of any one of the Y_n's and e_n's substantially will, in principle, be caught with high probability by decoy state method. Therefore, in order to avoid being detected, the eavesdropper, Eve, has very limited options in her eavesdropping attack. In summary, the ability for Alice and Bob to verify experimentally the values of Y_n and e_n's in the decoy state method greatly strengthens their

power in detecting eavesdropping, thus leading to a dramatic improvement in the performance of their QKD system. The decoy state method allows Alice and Bob to detect deviations
from the normal behavior due to eavesdropping attacks.

In [29], they also give for the first time a rigorous analysis of the security of decoy state QKD.
Moreover, they show that the decoy state idea can be combined with the prior art GLLP
analysis. And we can get the comparison results with and without decoy state as the following
Figure3.

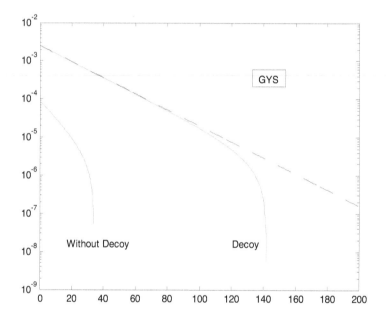

Figure 3. Compare results with and without decoy state.

4. The security of QKD

Bennett and Brassard have ever said that the most important question in quantum cryptography is to determine how secure it really is.

Security proofs are very important because a) they provide the foundation of security to a QKD
protocol, b) they provide a formula for the key generation rate of a QKD protocol and c) they

may even provide a construction for the classical post-processing protocol (for error correction and privacy amplification) that is necessary for the generation of the final key. Without security proofs, a real-life QKD system is incomplete because we can never be sure about how to generate a secure key and how secure the final key really is.

After the qubit exchange and basis reconciliation, Alice and Bob each have a sifted key. Ideally, these keys are identical. But in real life, there are always some errors, and Alice and Bob must apply some classical information processing protocols, like error correction and privacy amplification to their data. The first protocol is necessary to obtain identical keys and the second to obtain a secret key. Essentially, the problem of eavesdropping is to find protocols which, given that Alice and Bob can only measure the QBER, either provide Alice and Bob with a verifiably secure key or stop the protocol and inform the users that the key distribution has failed. This is a delicate problem at the intersection of quantum physics and information theory. Actually, it comprises several eavesdropping problems, depending on the precise protocol, the degree of idealization one admits, the technological power one assumes Eve has, and the assumed fidelity of Alice and Bob's equipment. Let us immediately stress that a complete analysis of eavesdropping on a quantum channel has yet to be achieved.

4.1. Eavesdropping attacks

In order to simplify the problem, several eavesdropping strategies of limited generality have been defined ([31-33]) and analyzed. Of particular interest is the assumption that Eve attaches independent probes to each qubit and measures her probes one after the other. They can be classified as follows:

Individual attacks: In an individual attack, Eve performs an attack on each signal independently. The intercept-resend attack is an example of an individual attack. let us consider the simple example of an intercept-resend attack by an eavesdropper Eve, who measures each photon in a randomly chosen basis and then resends the resulting state to Bob. For instance, if Eve performs a rectilinear measurement, photons prepared by Alice in the diagonal bases will be disturbed by Eve's measurement and give random answers. When Eve resends rectilinear photons to Bob, if Bob performs a diagonal measurement, then he will get random answers. Since the two bases are chosen randomly by each party, such an intercept-resend attack will give a bit error rate of $0.5 \times 0.5 + 0.5 \times 0 = 25\%$, which is readily detectable by Alice and Bob. Sophisticated attacks against QKD do exist. Fortunately, the security of QKD has now been proven.

Collective attacks: A more general class of attacks is collective attack where for each signal, Eve independently couples it with an ancillary quantum system, commonly called an ancilla, and evolves the combined signal/ancilla unitarily. She can send the resulting signals to Bob, but keep all ancillas herself. Unlike the case of individual attacks, Eve postpones her choice of measurement. Only after hearing the public discussion between Alice and Bob, does Eve decide on what measurement to perform on her ancilla to extract information about the final key.

Joint attacks: The most general class of attacks is joint attack. In a joint attack, instead of interacting with each signal independently, Eve treats all the signals as a single quantum system. She then couples the signal system with her ancilla and evolves the combined signal and ancilla system unitarily. She hears the public discussion between Alice and Bob before deciding on which measurement to perform on her ancilla.

For joint and collective attacks, the usual assumption is that Eve measures her probe only after Alice and Bob have completed all public discussion about basis reconciliation, error correction, and privacy amplification. For the more realistic individual attacks, one assumes that Eve waits only until the basis reconciliation phase of the public discussion. With today's technology, it might even be fair to assume that in individual attacks Eve must measure her probe before the basis reconciliation [34]. The motivation for this assumption is that one hardly sees what Eve could gain by waiting until after the public discussion on error correction and privacy amplification before measuring her probes, since she is going to measure them independently anyway. About practical QKD, they summary some assumptions about security of QKD in [18]. We describe them in the next subsection 4.2.

4.2. Some assumptions about security of QKD

Quantum key distribution is often described by its proponents as "unconditionally secure" to emphasize its difference with computationally secure classical cryptographic protocols. While there are still conditions that need to be satisfied for quantum key distribution to be secure, the phrase "unconditionally secure" is justified because, not only are the conditions reduced, they are in some sense minimal necessary conditions. Any secure key agreement protocol must make a few minimal assumptions, for security cannot come from nothing: we must be able to identify and authenticate the communicating parties, we must be able to have some private location to perform local operations, and all parties must operate within the laws of physics.

The following statement describes the security of quantum key distribution, and there are many formal mathematical arguments for the security of QKD.

Theorem 1 (Security statement for quantum key distribution) If 1) quantum mechanics is correct, and 2) authentication is secure, and 3) our devices are reasonably secure, then with high probability the key established by quantum key distribution is a random secret key independent (up to a negligible difference) of input values.

Assumption 1: Quantum mechanics is correct. This assumption requires that any eavesdropper be bounded by the laws of quantum mechanics, although within this realm there are no further restrictions beyond the eavesdropper's inability to access the devices. In particular, we allow the eavesdropper to have arbitrarily large quantum computing technology, far more powerful than the current state of the art. Quantum mechanics has been tested experimentally for nearly a century, to very high precision. But even if quantum mechanics is superseded by a new physical theory, it is not necessarily true that quantum key distribution would be insecure: for example, secure key distribution can be achieved in a manner similar to QKD solely based on the assumption that no faster-than-light communication is possible [35].

Assumption 2: Authentication is secure. This assumption is one of the main concerns of those evaluating quantum key distributions. In order to be protected against man-in-the-middle attack, much of the classical communication in QKD must be authenticated. Authentication can be achieved with unconditional security using short shared keys, or with computational security using public key cryptography.

Assumption 3: Our devices are secure. Constructing a QKD implementation that is verifiably secure is a substantial engineering challenge that researchers are still working on. Although the first prototype QKD system leaked key information over a side channel (it made different noises depending on the photon polarization, and thus the "prototype was unconditionally secure against any eavesdropper who happened to be deaf" [36]), experimental cryptanalysis leads to better theoretical and practical security. More sophisticated side-channel attacks continue to be proposed against particular implementations of existing systems (e.g., [37]), but so too are better theoretical methods being proposed, such as the decoy state method [38]. Device-independent security proofs [39, 40] aim to minimize the security assumptions on physical devices. It seems reasonable to expect that further theoretical and engineering advances will eventually bring us devices which have strong arguments and few assumptions for their security.

4.3. Security proofs for QKD

Proving the security of QKD against the most general attack was a very hard problem. It took more than 10 years, but the unconditional security of QKD was finally established in several papers in the 1990s. One approach by Mayers [16] was to prove the security of the BB84 directly. A simpler approach by Lo and Chau [17], mad use of the idea of entanglement distillation by Bennett, DiVincenzo, Smolin and Wootters (BDSW) [41] and quantum privacy amplification by Deutsch et al. [42] to solve the security of an entanglement-based QKD protocol. The two approaches have been unified by the work of Shor and Preskill [43], who provided a simple proof of security of BB84 using entanglement distillation idea. Other early security proofs of QKD include Biham, Boyer, Boykin, Mor, and Roychowdhury [44], and Ben-Or [45].

There are several approaches to security proof as following. [5]

4.3.1. Entanglement distillation

Entanglement distillation protocol (EDP) provides a simple approach to security proof [17, 42, 43]. The basic insight is that entanglement is a sufficient (but not necessary) condition for a secure key. In the noiseless case, suppose two distant parties, Alice and Bob, share a maximally entangled state of the form $|\phi\rangle_{AB} = \frac{1}{\sqrt{2}}(|00\rangle_{AB} + |11\rangle_{AB})$. If each of Alice and Bob measure their systems, then they will both get "0"s or "1"s, which is a shared random key. Moreover, if we consider the combined system of the three parties—Alice, Bob and an eavesdropper, Eve, we can use a pure-state description (the "Church of Larger Hilbert space") and consider a pure state $|\psi\rangle_{ABE}$. In this case, the von Neumann entropy of Eve $S(\rho_E) = S(\rho_{AB}) = 0$. This means that Eve has absolutely no information on the final key. In the noisy case, Alice and Bob may share N pairs of qubits, which are a noisy version of N maximally entangled states. Now, using the idea of entanglement distillation protocol (EDP) discussed in BDSW [41], Alice and Bob may apply local operations and classical communications (LOCCs) to distill from the N noisy pairs a smaller number, say M almost perfect pairs i.e., a state close to $| \phi \rangle_{AB}^{M}$. Once such a EDP has been performed, Alice and Bob can measure their respective system to generate an M-bit final key.

How can Alice and Bob be sure that their EDP will be successful? Whether an EDP will be successful or not depends on the initial state shared by Alice and Bob. In practice, Alice and Bob can never be sure what initial state they possess. Therefore, it is useful for them to add a verification step. By, for example, randomly testing a fraction of their pairs, they have a pretty good idea about the properties (e.g., the bit-flip and phase error rates) of their remaining pairs and are pretty confident that their EDP will be successful.

4.3.2. Communication complexity/quantum memory

The communication complexity/quantum memory approach to security proof was proposed by Ben-Or [45] and subsequently by Renner and Koenig [46]. See also [47]. They provide a formula for secure key generation rate in terms of an eavesdropper's quantum knowledge on the raw key: Let Z be a random variable with range $\mathbb{Z}$, let ρ be a random state, and let F be a two-universal function on $\mathbb{Z}$ with range $S = \{0, 1\}^s$ which is independent of Z and ρ. Then [46]

$$d(F(Z) | \{F\} \otimes \rho) \le \frac{1}{2} 2^{-\frac{1}{2}(S_2([\{Z\} \otimes \rho]) - S_0([\rho]) - s)}. \tag{13}$$

Incidentally, the quantum de Finnetti's theorem [48] is often useful for simplifying security proofs of this type.

4.3.3. Twisted state approach

What is a necessary and sufficient condition for secure key generation? From the entanglement distillation approach, we know that entanglement distillation a sufficient condition for secure key generation. For some time, it was hoped that entanglement distillation is also a necessary condition for secure key generation. However, such an idea was proven to be wrong in [49] [50], where it was found that a necessary and sufficient condition is the distillation of a private state, rather than a maximally entangled state. A private state is a "twisted" version of a maximally entangled state. They proved the following theorem in [49]: a state is private in the above sense iff it is of the following form

$$\gamma_m = U \left| \psi_{2^m}^+ \right\rangle_{AB} \left\langle \psi_{2^m}^+ \right| \otimes \rho_{A'B'} U^\dagger \tag{14}$$

Where $|\psi_d\rangle = \sum_{i=1}^{d} |ii\rangle$ and $\rho_{A'B'}$ is an arbitrary state on A', B'. U is an arbitrary unitary controlled in the computational basis

$$U = \sum_{i,j=1}^{2^m} |ij\rangle_{AB} \langle ij| \otimes U_{ij}^{A'B'}. \tag{15}$$

The operation (15) will be called "twisting" (note that only $U_{ii}^{A'B'}$ matter here, yet it will be useful to consider general twisting later).

The main new ingredient of the above theorem is the introduction of a "shield" part to Alice and Bob's system. That is, in addition to the systems A and B used by Alice and Bob for key generation, we assume that Alice and Bob also hold some ancillary systems, A' and B', often called the shield part. Since we assume that Eve has no access to the shield part, Eve is further limited in her ability to eavesdrop. Therefore, Alice and Bob can derive a higher key generation rate than the case when Eve does have access to the shield part.

4.3.4. Complementary principle

Another approach to security proof is to use the complementary principle of quantum mechanics. Such an approach is interesting because it shows the deep connection between the foundations of quantum mechanics and the security of QKD. In fact, both Mayers' proof [16] and Biham, Boyer, Boykin, Mor, and Roychowdhury's proof [44] make use of this complementary principle. A clear and rigorous discussion of the complementary principle approach to security proof has recently been achieved by Koashi [51]. The key insight of Koashi's proof is that Alice and Bob's ability to generate a random secure key in the Z-basis (by a measurement of the Pauli spin matrix σ_Z) is equivalent to the ability for Bob to help Alice prepare an eigenstate in the complementary, i.e., X-basis (σ_X), with their help of the shield. The intuition is that an X-basis eigenstate, for example, $|+\rangle_A = \frac{1}{\sqrt{2}}(|0\rangle_A + |1\rangle_A)$, when measured along the Z-basis, gives a random answer.

4.3.5. Other ideas for security proofs

Here are two other ideas for security proofs, namely, a) device-independent security proofs and b) security from the causality constraint. Unfortunately, these ideas are still very much under development and so far a complete version of a proof of unconditional security of QKD based on these ideas with a finite key rate is still missing.

Let us start with a) device-independent security proofs. So far we have assumed that Alice and Bob know what their devices are doing exactly. In practice, Alice and Bob may not know their devices for sure. Recently, there has been much interest in the idea of device independent security proofs. In other words, how to prove security when Alice and Bob's devices cannot be trusted. See, for example, [52]. The idea is to look only at the input and output variables. A handwaving argument goes as follows. Using their probability distribution, if one can demonstrate the violation of some Bell inequalities, then one cannot explain the data by a separable system. How to develop such a handwaving argument into a full proof of unconditional security is an important question.

The second idea b) security from the causality constraint is even more ambitious. The question that it tries to address is the following. How can one prove security when even quantum mechanics is wrong? In [53] and references cited therein, it was suggested that perhaps a more general physical principle such as the no-signaling requirement for space-like observables could be used to prove the security of QKD.

5. Quantum secret sharing

"Secret sharing" refers to an important family of multi-party cryptographic protocols in both the classical and the quantum contexts. A secret sharing protocol comprises a dealer and n players who are interconnected by some set of classical or quantum channels. The "secret" to be shared is a classical string or quantum state and is distributed among the players by the dealer in such a way that it can only be recovered by certain subsets of players acting collaboratively. The access structure is the set of all subsets of players who can recover the secret, and the adversary structure corresponds to those subsets that obtain no knowledge of the secret. There may, in addition, be external eavesdroppers who should also gain no knowledge of the secret.

Quantum secret sharing (abbreviated QSS) is the generalization of quantum key distribution to more than two parties [54]. In this new application of quantum communication, Alice distributes a secret key to two other users, Bob and Charlie, in such a way that neither Bob nor Charlie alone has any information about the key, but together they have full information. As in traditional QC, an eavesdropper trying to get some information about the key creates errors in the transmission data and thus reveals her presence. The motivation behind quantum secret sharing is to guarantee that Bob and Charlie cooperate—one of them might be dishonest—in order to obtain a given piece of information. In contrast with previous proposals using three particle Greenberger-Horne-Zeilinger states [55], pairs of entangled photons in so-called energy-time Bell states were used to mimic the necessary quantum correlation of three entangled qubits, although only two photons exist at the same time. This is possible because of the symmetry between the preparation device acting on the pump pulse and the devices analyzing the downconverted photons. Therefore the emission of a pump pulse can be considered as the detection of a photon with 100% efficiency, and the scheme features a much higher coincidence rate than that expected with the initially proposed "triplephoton" schemes.

QSS which is based on the laws of quantum mechanics, instead of mathematical assumptions can share the information unconditionally securely. According to the form of sharing information, QSS can be divided into QSS of classical messages and QSS of quantum information.QSS of classical messages can be divided into QSS of classical messages based on entanglement and QSS of classical messages without entanglement.

In 1999, Hillery et al. [55] used entangled three-photon GHZ states to propose the first QSS protocol, namely the HBB99 scheme. In their scheme, the dealer (Alice) prepares a three photons quantum system in the GHZ state $|\psi\rangle = \frac{1}{\sqrt{2}}(|000\rangle + |111\rangle)_{ABC}$ and sends the photon B and C to Bob and Charlie, respectively. The three parties all choose randomly one of two measuring bases to measure the photons in their hands independently. They keep the correlate results for generating the key K_A. In the same year, Cleve et al. utilized the properties of quantum error-correcting code to propose the first (k, n) threshold of QSS protocol. In a (k, n) threshold scheme, any subset of k or more parties can reconstruct the secret, while any subset of $k - 1$ or fewer parties can obtain no information [56]. In 2001, Tittel et al. used the experiment to realize quantum secret sharing for the first time [54]. In 2002, Tyc et al. developed the theory of continuous variable quantum secret sharing and propose its interferometric realization using passive and active optical elements [57]. In 2003, Gou et al. presented a quantum secret sharing scheme where only product states are employed [58]. Xiao et al. showed that in the Hillery-Bužek-Berthiaume QSS scheme [59], and the secret information is shared in the parity of binary strings formed by the measured outcomes of the participants in 2004. With the rapid development of QSS, people are researching to achieve unconditional security.

5.1. QSS based on entanglement states

Quantum entanglement is an indispensable physical resource in QSS. Many application fields of QSS such as this entanglement feature, so the study of entanglement is the core issue of quantum information theory.

Let's see the QSS based on entanglement. The entanglement states are all generated by the sender, and the order of two or more photons sent to the same agent is randomly changed. After the photons send to the receiver, for the detection mode, the order of the two photons is announced, so that the two parties detected the security of the quantum channel, for the information mode, the two receivers respectively does Bell measurement on the two photons they owned, and then communicate through classical channel to share the secret key with the sender. This protocol ensures the validity and security of the shared information.

We can see an example of QSS based on entanglement state GHZ [55].

Let us suppose that Alice, Bob, and Charlie each have one particle from a GHZ triplet that is in the state $|\psi\rangle = \frac{1}{\sqrt{2}}(|000\rangle + |111\rangle)$. They each choose at random whether to measure their particle in the x or y direction. They then announce publicly in which direction they have made a measurement, but not the results of their measurements. Half the time, Bob and Charlie, by combining the results of their measurements, can determine what the result of Alice's measurement was. This allows Alice to establish a joint key with Bob and Charlie, which she can then use to send her message. Let us see how this works in more detail. Define the x and y eigenstates

$$\left|+x\right\rangle = \tfrac{1}{\sqrt{2}}(\left|0\right\rangle + \left|1\right\rangle), \quad \left|+y\right\rangle = \tfrac{1}{\sqrt{2}}(\left|0\right\rangle + i\left|1\right\rangle),$$
$$\left|-x\right\rangle = \tfrac{1}{\sqrt{2}}(\left|0\right\rangle - \left|1\right\rangle), \quad \left|-y\right\rangle = \tfrac{1}{\sqrt{2}}(\left|0\right\rangle - i\left|1\right\rangle). \tag{16}$$

We can see the effects of measurements by Alice and Bob on the state of Charlie's particle if we express the GHZ state in different ways. Noting that

$$\left|0\right\rangle = \tfrac{1}{\sqrt{2}}(\left|+x\right\rangle + \left|-x\right\rangle), \quad \left|1\right\rangle = \tfrac{1}{\sqrt{2}}(\left|+x\right\rangle - \left|-x\right\rangle), \tag{17}$$

we can write

$$\left|\psi\right\rangle = \tfrac{1}{2\sqrt{2}}[(\left|+x\right\rangle_a \left|+x\right\rangle_b + \left|-x\right\rangle_a \left|-x\right\rangle_b)(\left|0\right\rangle_c + \left|1\right\rangle_c)$$
$$+ (\left|+x\right\rangle_a \left|-x\right\rangle_b + \left|-x\right\rangle_a \left|+x\right\rangle_b)(\left|0\right\rangle_c - \left|1\right\rangle_c)]. \tag{18}$$

This decomposition of $\left|\psi\right\rangle$ tells us what happens if both Alice and Bob make measurements in the x direction. If they both get the same result, then Charlie will have the state $\tfrac{1}{\sqrt{2}}(\left|0\right\rangle_c + \left|1\right\rangle_c)$; if they get different results, he will have the state $\tfrac{1}{\sqrt{2}}(\left|0\right\rangle_c - \left|1\right\rangle_c)$. He can determine which of these states he has by performing a measurement along the x direction. The following table summarizes the effects of Alice's and Bob's measurements on Charlie's state:

		Alice			
		+x	-x	+y	-y
Bob	+x	$\left|0\right\rangle + \left|1\right\rangle$	$\left|0\right\rangle - \left|1\right\rangle$	$\left|0\right\rangle - i\left|1\right\rangle$	$\left|0\right\rangle + i\left|1\right\rangle$
	-x	$\left|0\right\rangle - \left|1\right\rangle$	$\left|0\right\rangle + \left|1\right\rangle$	$\left|0\right\rangle + i\left|1\right\rangle$	$\left|0\right\rangle - i\left|1\right\rangle$
	+y	$\left|0\right\rangle - i\left|1\right\rangle$	$\left|0\right\rangle + i\left|1\right\rangle$	$\left|0\right\rangle - \left|1\right\rangle$	$\left|0\right\rangle + \left|1\right\rangle$
	-y	$\left|0\right\rangle + i\left|1\right\rangle$	$\left|0\right\rangle - i\left|1\right\rangle$	$\left|0\right\rangle + \left|1\right\rangle$	$\left|0\right\rangle - \left|1\right\rangle$

Table 2. QSS based on entanglement state [55].

Alice's measurements are given in the columns and Bob's are given in the rows. Charlie's state, up to normalization, appears in the boxes. From the table it is clear that if Charlie knows what measurements Alice and Bob made (that is, x or y), he can determine whether their results are the same or opposite and also that he will gain no knowledge of what their results actually are. Similarly, Bob will not be able to determine what Alice's result is without Charlie's assistance because he does not know if his result is the same as Alice's or the opposite of hers.

To improve the efficiency of QSS, a protocol share the message directly among the users was proposed. The scheme made full use of entanglement swapping of Bell states and local operations. For detection of eavesdropping, the EPR pairs were divided into two parts: the checking parts and the encoding parts. After insuring the security of the quantum channel by measuring the checking particles in conjugate bases, the sender encoded her bits via the local unitary operations on the encoding parts. And the protocol is secure, and two Bell states can be used to share two bits message. And there is a scheme for multiparty quantum secret sharing which is based on EPR entangled state. In the scheme, the secret messages are imposed on the auxiliary particles, and the transmitted particles of EPR pairs do not carry any secret messages during the whole process of transmission. After both of the communicators reliably share the EPR entangled states, all the participants can securely share the secret messages of the sender. Because there is no particles that carrying the secret message being transmitted on the quantum channel during the process of transmission, the scheme can efficiently resist the eavesdropper's attack on secret message.

So, entanglement makes an important role in quantum secret sharing and many application fields of quantum information theory such as quantum teleportation, QKD, quantum computing need to use this entanglement feature. But the quantification of the entanglement receives a better solution only for bipartite quantum system, and the quantification of multipartite entanglement is still open even for a pure multipartite state. Until now, a variety of different entanglement measures have been proposed for multipartite setting, such as the robustness of entanglement, the relative entropy of entanglement, and the geometric measure.

However, all these methods involve variable complexity problem, which make the quantification of multipartite entanglement very difficult. Fortunately, it is hopeful to obtain the exact value of the multipartite entanglement of graph states, which are very useful multipartite quantum states in quantum information processing. Graph states are the specific algorithm resources for one-way quantum computing model, and they are subsets of stabilizer states which are widely used in quantum error correction.

5.2. QSS with qudit graph states

The quantification of entanglement has attracted wide attention in recent years, but the quantification of the entanglement receives a better solution only for bipartite quantum system. And the quantification of multipartite entanglement is still open even for a pure multipartite state. Until now, a variety of different entanglement measures have been proposed for multipartite setting, such as the robustness of entanglement, the relative entropy of entanglement, and the quantification of multipartite entanglement is still open even for a pure multipartite state. Fortunately, it is hopeful to obtain the exact value of the multipartite entanglement of graph states, which are useful multipartite quantum states in quantum information processing.

The entanglement quantification of graph state is relatively simple, for it can be described by graph language. So far, the study of graph state entanglement has just started, the latest research results is determining the upper and lower bounds of graph state entanglement by using local operation and classical communication, which can only confirm the entanglement of graph states that have equal bounds. But for graph states which have unequal bounds, it can only give a range of entanglement but not the exact value.

In quantum computing, a graph state is a special type of multi-qubit state that can be represented by a graph. Each qubit is represented by a vertex of the graph, and there is an edge between every interacting pair of qubits. In particular, they are a convenient way of representing certain types of entangled states.

Given a graph $G=(V, E)$ with the set of vertices V and the set of edges E, the corresponding graph

$$|G\rangle = \prod_{(a,b)\in E} U^{\{a,b\}}|+\rangle^{\otimes V}, \tag{19}$$

where the operator $U^{\{a,b\}}$ is the controlled-Z interaction between the two vertices (qubits) a, b,

$$U^{\{a,b\}} = \begin{bmatrix} 1 & 0 & 0 & 0 \\ 0 & 1 & 0 & 0 \\ 0 & 0 & 1 & 0 \\ 0 & 0 & 0 & -1 \end{bmatrix}.$$

And $|+\rangle = \frac{1}{\sqrt{2}}(|0\rangle + |1\rangle)$. With each graph $G=(V, E)$, we associate a graph state. A graph state is a certain pure quantum state on a Hilbert space $H_V = (C^2)^{\otimes V}$.

An alternative and equivalent definition is the following. Hence each vertex labels a two-level quantum system or qubit — a notion that can be extended to quantum systems of finite dimension d. To every vertex $a \in V$ of the graph $G=(V, E)$ is attached a Hermitian operator

$$K_G^{(a)} = \sigma_x^{(a)} \prod_{b\in N_a} \sigma_z^{(b)}. \tag{20}$$

In terms of the adjacency matrix, this can be expressed as

$$K_G^{(a)} = \sigma_x^{(a)} \prod_{b\in V} (\sigma_z^{(b)})^{\Gamma_{ab}}. \tag{21}$$

As usual, the matrices $\sigma_x^{(a)}$, $\sigma_y^{(a)}$, $\sigma_z^{(a)}$ are the Pauli matrices, where the upper index specifies the Hilbert space on which the operator acts $K_G^{(a)}$ is an observable of the qubits associated with the vertex a and all of its neighbors $b \in N_a$. The graph state $|G\rangle$ is then defined as the simultaneous eigenstate of the $N = |V|$ operators $\{K_G^{(a)}\}_{a \in V}$ with eigenvalue 1:

$$K_G^{(a)}|G\rangle = |G\rangle. \tag{22}$$

Here they consider three specific varieties of such schemes previously demonstrated in graph states. They note that all existing forms of secret sharing that have been proposed fall into one of these categories. [60]

1. **CC scheme:** The secret is classical, the dealer is connected to the player via private quantum channels and all players are connected by private classical channels.

2. **CQ scheme:** The secret is classical, the dealer shares public quantum channels with each player and the players are connected to each by private classical channels.

3. **QQ scheme:** The secret is quantum, the dealer shares either private or public quantum channels with each player and the players are connected to each other by private quantum or classical channels.

Now let's see an example of QSS with graph states. It is the third scenario presented in the previous QQ scheme. This QQ scheme proposed is readily generalisable to qudits. In this scheme, the secret to be shared is a quantum state $|s\rangle$ in a d-dimensional Hilbert space now, initially possessed by the dealer, who distributes it to the other parties via a joint operation on the secret state and parties' shared graph state, in a manner analogous to quantum teleportation. We describe the general protocol explicitly below.

Denoting the dealer's secret qudit as

$$|s\rangle_D = \sum_{i=0}^{d-1} \alpha_i |i\rangle_D. \tag{23}$$

The dealer prepares the state $|s\rangle_D |G\rangle_{D,V}$. Corresponding to some graph state G for the dealer's qudit D and all the players' qudits V. The dealer distributes the player's qudits to them. The dealer then measures her two qudits in the generalized Bell basis $\{|\psi\rangle_{mn}\}$, where

$$|\psi_{mn}\rangle := \frac{1}{\sqrt{d}} \sum_j \omega^{jn} |j\rangle |j+m\rangle \tag{24}$$

If the dealer's measurement result is (m, n), corresponding to the state $|\psi\rangle_{mn}$, then it follows from the rules for projective measurement that the resultant state for all parties is

$$\begin{aligned} &|\psi_{mn}\rangle_D \langle\psi_{mn}|\,|s\rangle_D |G\rangle_{D,V} \\ &\propto\quad |\psi_{mn}\rangle_D \sum_j \alpha_j \omega^{-jn} \Big| g_{z=(j+m)(A_{D1},A_{D2},\cdots,A_{DN})}\Big\rangle_V \end{aligned} \tag{25}$$

where $|g_z\rangle$ is the encoded reduced graph state on the players $1, \cdots, n$ with labels z.

If the dealer informs the players of their measurement result (m, n), then a set of players $\in V$ can apply a correction operator

$$U_{mn} := K_a^{-nN_{D_a}^{-1}} Z^{-mA_D} \tag{26}$$

to obtain the state

$$\left|s_g\right\rangle^V = \sum_j \alpha_j \Big| g_{z=j(A_{D1},A_{D2},\cdots,A_{DN})}\Big\rangle_V . \tag{27}$$

The access properties of this final state depend on the graph state used. Qualitatively, for certain initial graph states, the state $|s_g\rangle^V$ can be regarded as a superposition of orthogonal labelled graph states whose labels have the same access structure as CC protocols. Thus, the ability to recover the quantum secret corresponds to the ability to recover these classical labels, providing a natural extension of the classical protocols to the quantum case.

6. Post-quantum cryptography

Post-quantum cryptography deals with cryptosystems that run on conventional computers and are secure against attacks by quantum computers. This field came about because most currently popular public-key cryptosystems rely on the integer factorization problem or discrete logarithm problem, both of which would be easily solvable on large enough quantum computers using Shor's algorithm. Even though current publicly known experimental quantum computing is nowhere near powerful enough to attack real cryptosystems, many cryptographers are researching new algorithms, in case quantum computing becomes a threat in the future.

In contrast, most current symmetric cryptography (symmetric ciphers and hash functions) is secure from quantum computers. The quantum Grover's algorithm can speed up attacks against symmetric ciphers, but this can be counteracted by increasing key size. Thus post-quantum cryptography does not focus on symmetric algorithms. Post-quantum cryptography is also unrelated to quantum cryptography, which refers to using quantum phenomena to achieve secrecy. Currently post-quantum cryptography is mostly focused on four different approaches:

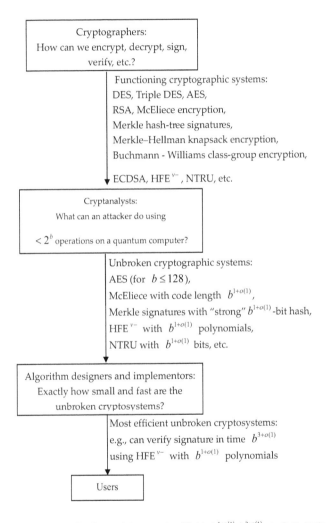

Figure 4. Post-quantum cryptography. Sizes and times are simplified to $b^{1+o(1)}$, $b^{2+o(1)}$, etc. Optimization of any specific b requires a more detailed analysis.

1. Lattice-based cryptography such as NTRU and GGH;

2. Multivariate cryptography such as unbalanced oil and vinegar;

3. Hash-based signatures such as Lamport signatures and Merkle signature scheme;

4. Code-based cryptography that relies on error-correcting codes, such McEliece encryption and Niederreiter signatures.

We can use the following figure to show the content of post-quantum cryptography clearly [7].

Post-quantum cryptography is, in general, a quite different topic from quantum cryptography:

- Post-quantum cryptography, like the rest of cryptography, covers a wide range of secure-communication tasks, ranging from secret-key operations, public-key signatures, and public-key encryption to high-level operations such as secure electronic voting. Quantum cryptography handles only one task, namely expanding a short shared secret into a long shared secret.

- Post-quantum cryptography, like the rest of cryptography, includes some systems proven to be secure, but also includes many lower-cost systems that are conjectured to be secure. Quantum cryptography rejects conjectural systems — begging the question of how Alice and Bob can securely share a secret in the first place.

- Post-quantum cryptography includes many systems that can be used for a noticeable fraction of today's Internet communication—Alice and Bob need to perform some computation and send some data but do not need any new hardware. Quantum cryptography requires new network hardware that is, at least for the moment, impossibly expensive for the vast majority of Internet users.

Acknowledgements

This work was conducted when Xiaoqing Tan visited the University of Toronto and is supported by the NSFC 61003258. She especially thanks Hoi-Kwong Lo for the hospitality during her stay at the University of Toronto.

Author details

Xiaoqing Tan*

Address all correspondence to: ttanxq@jnu.edu.cn

Dept. of Mathematics, Jinan University, Guangzhou, Guangdong, China

References

[1] Wiesner, S. Conjugate coding," *Sigact News,* (1983). , 15(1), 78-88.

[2] Bennett, C. H, Bessette, F, & Brassard, G. *et al.*, "Experimental quantum cryptography," in Proceedings of the workshop on the theory and application of cryptographic techniques on Advances in cryptology, Aarhus, Denmark, (1991). , 253-265.

[3] Bennett, C. H, Brassard, G, & Crepeau, C. *et al.*, "Practical Quantum Oblivious Transfer," in Proceedings of the 11th Annual International Cryptology Conference on Advances in Cryptology, (1992). , 351-366.

[4] Brassard, G, Crepeau, C, & Jozsa, R. *et al.*, "A quantum bit commitment scheme provably unbreakable by both parties," in Proceedings of the 1993 IEEE 34th Annual Foundations of Computer Science, (1993). , 362-371.

[5] Lo, H. -K, & Zhao, Y. Quantum Cryptography," http://arxiv.org/abs/0803.2507/.

[6] Shor, P. W. Polynomial-Time Algorithms for Prime Factorization and Discrete Logarithms on a Quantum Computer," http://arxiv.org/abs/quant-ph/9508027.

[7] Bernstein, D. J. Introduction to post-quantum cryptography " *Post-quantum cryptography*, (2009).

[8] Townsend, P. D, Rarity, J. G, & Tapster, P. R. Single photon interference in a 10 km long optical fibre interferometer," *Electronics Letters*, (1993). , 29(7), 634-635.

[9] Townsend, P. D, Rarity, J. G, & Tapster, P. R. Enhanced single photon fringe visibility in a 10 km-long prototype quantum cryptography channel," *Electronics Letters*, (1993). , 29(14), 1291-1293.

[10] Einstein, A, Podolsky, B, & Rosen, N. Can Quantum-Mechanical Description of Physical Reality Be Considered Complete?," *Physical Review*, (1935). , 47(10), 777-780.

[11] Kumar, M. *Quantum*: London : Icon books, (2009).

[12] Horodecki, R, Horodecki, P, & Horodecki, M. *et al.*, "Quantum entanglement," *Reviews of Modern Physics*, (2009). , 81(2), 865-942.

[13] Jaeger, G, Shimony, A, & Vaidman, L. Two interferometric complementarities," *Physical Review A*, (1995). , 51(1), 54-67.

[14] Vernam, G. S. Cipher Printing Telegraph Systems For Secret Wire and Radio Telegraphic Communications," *American Institute of Electrical Engineers, Transactions of the*, vol. XLV, (1926). , 295-301.

[15] Bennett, C. H, & Brassard, G. Quantum cryptography: Public key distribution and coin tossing}," in Proceedings of IEEE International Conference on Computers, Systems, and Signal Processing, India, (1984). , 175.

[16] Mayers, D. Unconditional security in quantum cryptography," *J. ACM*, (2001). , 48(3), 351-406.

[17] Lo, H. -K, & Chau, H. F. Unconditional Security of Quantum Key Distribution over Arbitrarily Long Distances," *Science*, March 26, 1999, (1999). , 283(5410), 2050-2056.

[18] Stebila, D, Mosca, M, & Lütkenhaus, N. The Case for Quantum Key Distribution," *Quantum Communication and Quantum Networking*, Lecture Notes of the Institute for Computer Sciences, Social Informatics and Telecommunications Engineering A. Sergienko, S. Pascazio and P. Villoresi, eds., Springer Berlin Heidelberg, (2010). , 283-296.

[19] Ekert, A. K. Quantum cryptography based on Bell's theorem," *Physical Review Letters*, (1991). , 67(6), 661-663.

[20] Bennett, C. H, Brassard, G, & Mermin, N. D. Quantum cryptography without Bell's theorem," *Physical Review Letters*, (1992). , 68(5), 557-559.

[21] Grosshans, F, Van Assche, G, & Wenger, J. *et al.*, "Quantum key distribution using gaussian-modulated coherent states," *Nature,* Jan 16, (2003). , 421(6920), 238-241.

[22] Bing QiLi Qian, and H.-K. Lo. "A brief introduction of quantum cryptography for engineers," http://arxiv.org/abs/1002.1237.

[23] Renner, R, & Cirac, J. I. de Finetti Representation Theorem for Infinite-Dimensional Quantum Systems and Applications to Quantum Cryptography," *Physical Review Letters,* Mar 20, (2009). , 102(11)

[24] Lodewyck, J, Bloch, M, & Garcia-patron, R. *et al.*, "Quantum key distribution over 25 km with an all-fiber continuous-variable system," *Physical Review A,* Oct, (2007). , 76(4)

[25] Qi, B, Huang, L. -L, & Qian, L. *et al.*, "Experimental study on the Gaussian-modulated coherent-state quantum key distribution over standard telecommunication fibers," *Physical Review A,* (2007). , 76(5), 052323.

[26] Ekert, A. Complex and unpredictable Cardano," *International Journal of Theoretical Physics,* Aug, (2008). , 47(8), 2101-2119.

[27] Van Dam, W, Ariano, G. M. D, & Ekert, A. *et al.*, "Optimal phase estimation in quantum networks," *Journal of Physics a-Mathematical and Theoretical,* Jul 13, (2007). , 40(28), 7971-7984.

[28] Christandl, M, Datta, N, & Ekert, A. *et al.*, "Perfect state transfer in quantum spin networks," *Physical Review Letters,* May 7, (2004). , 92(18)

[29] Lo, H. K, Ma, X. F, & Chen, K. Decoy state quantum key distribution," *Physical Review Letters,* Jun 17, (2005). , 94(23)

[30] Curty, M, Gühne, O, & Lewenstein, M. *et al.*, "Detecting two-party quantum correlations in quantum-key-distribution protocols," *Physical Review A,* (2005). , 71(2), 022306.

[31] Lütkenhaus, N. Security against eavesdropping in quantum cryptography," *Physical Review A,* (1996). , 54(1), 97-111.

[32] Biham, E, & Mor, T. Security of Quantum Cryptography against Collective Attacks," *Physical Review Letters*, (1997). , 78(11), 2256-2259.

[33] Biham, E, & Mor, T. Bounds on Information and the Security of Quantum Cryptography," *Physical Review Letters*, (1997). , 79(20), 4034-4037.

[34] Gisin, N, Ribordy, G, & Tittel, W. *et al.*, "Quantum cryptography," *Reviews of Modern Physics*, (2002). , 74(1), 145-195.

[35] Barrett, J, Hardy, L, & Kent, A. No signaling and quantum key distribution," *Physical Review Letters*, Jul 1, (2005). , 95(1)

[36] Brassard, G. Brief history of quantum cryptography: a personal perspective." , 19-23.

[37] Zhao, Y, Fung, C. -H. F, & Qi, B. *et al.*, "Quantum hacking: Experimental demonstration of time-shift attack against practical quantum-key-distribution systems," *Physical Review A*, (2008). , 78(4), 042333.

[38] Hwang, W. -Y. Quantum Key Distribution with High Loss: Toward Global Secure Communication," *Physical Review Letters*, (2003). , 91(5), 057901.

[39] Mayers, D. Unconditionally Secure Quantum Bit Commitment is Impossible," *Physical Review Letters*, (1997). , 78(17), 3414-3417.

[40] Pironio, S, Acín, A, & Brunner, N. *et al.*, "Device-independent quantum key distribution secure against collective attacks," *New Journal of Physics*, (2009). , 11(4), 045021.

[41] Bennett, C. H, & Di, D. P. . Smolin *et al.*, "Mixed-state entanglement and quantum error correction," *Physical Review A*, vol. 54, no. 5, pp. 3824-3851, 1996.

[42] Deutsch, D, Ekert, A, & Jozsa, R. *et al.*, "Quantum Privacy Amplification and the Security of Quantum Cryptography over Noisy Channels," *Physical Review Letters*, (1996). , 77(13), 2818-2821.

[43] Shor, P. W, & Preskill, J. Simple Proof of Security of the BB84 Quantum Key Distribution Protocol," *Physical Review Letters*, (2000). , 85(2), 441-444.

[44] Biham, E, Boyer, M, & Boykin, P. O. *et al.*, "A proof of the security of quantum key distribution (extended abstract)," in Proceedings of the thirty-second annual ACM symposium on Theory of computing, Portland, Oregon, United States, (2000). , 715-724.

[45] Ben-or, M. (2002). http://www.msri.org/publications/ln/msri/2002/qip/ben-or/1/index.html.

[46] Renner, R, & Koenig, R. Universally composable privacy amplification against quantum adversaries."

[47] Renner, R. Security of Quantum Key Distribution," http://arxiv.org/abs/quant-ph/0512258.

[48] Renner, R. Symmetry of large physical systems implies independence of subsystems," *Nat Phys*, (2007). , 3(9), 645-649.

[49] Horodecki, K, Horodecki, M, & Horodecki, P. *et al.*, "Secure Key from Bound Entanglement," *Physical Review Letters*, (2005). , 94(16), 160502.

[50] Karol HorodeckiMichal Horodecki, Pawel Horodecki *et al.* "Quantum key distribution based on private states: unconditional security over untrusted channels with zero quantum capacity," http://arxiv.org/abs/quant-ph/0608195.

[51] Koashi, M. Complementarity, distillable secret key, and distillable entanglement," (2007).

[52] Acín, A, Brunner, N, & Gisin, N. *et al.*, "Device-Independent Security of Quantum Cryptography against Collective Attacks," *Physical Review Letters*, (2007). , 98(23), 230501.

[53] LlMasanes, R. Renner, M. Christandl *et al.*, "Unconditional security of key distribution from causality constraints," (2006).

[54] Tittel, W, Zbinden, H, & Gisin, N. Experimental demonstration of quantum secret sharing," *Physical Review A*, (2001). , 63(4), 042301.

[55] Hillery, M, Bužek, V, & Berthiaume, A. Quantum secret sharing," *Physical Review A*, (1999). , 59(3), 1829-1834.

[56] Cleve, R, Gottesman, D, & Lo, H. -K. How to Share a Quantum Secret," *Physical Review Letters*, (1999). , 83(3), 648-651.

[57] Tyc, T, & Sanders, B. C. How to share a continuous-variable quantum secret by optical interferometry," *Physical Review A*, Apr, (2002). , 65(4)

[58] Guo, G. -P, & Guo, G. -C. Quantum secret sharing without entanglement," *Physics Letters A*, (2003). , 310(4), 247-251.

[59] Xiao, L, Lu, G, Long, F, & Deng, G. *et al.*, "Efficient multiparty quantum-secret-sharing schemes," *Physical Review A*, (2004). , 69(5), 052307.

[60] Keet, A, Fortescue, B, & Markham, D. *et al.*, "Quantum secret sharing with qudit graph states," *Physical Review A*, (2010). , 82(6), 062315.

Chapter 2

Homomorphic Encryption — Theory and Application

Jaydip Sen

Additional information is available at the end of the chapter

1. Introduction

The demand for privacy of digital data and of algorithms for handling more complex structures have increased exponentially over the last decade. This goes in parallel with the growth in communication networks and their devices and their increasing capabilities. At the same time, these devices and networks are subject to a great variety of attacks involving manipulation and destruction of data and theft of sensitive information. For storing and accessing data securely, current technology provides several methods of guaranteeing privacy such as data encryption and usage of tamper-resistant hardwares. However, the critical problem arises when there is a requirement for computing (publicly) with private data or to modify functions or algorithms in such a way that they are still executable while their privacy is ensured. This is where homomorphic cryptosystems can be used since these systems enable computations with encrypted data.

In 1978 Rivest et al. (Rivest et al, 1978a) first investigated the design of a homomorphic encryption scheme. Unfortunately, their *privacy homomorphism* was broken a couple of years later by Brickell and Yacobi (Brickell & Yacobi, 1987). The question rose again in 1991 when Feigenbaum and Merritt (Feigenbaum & Merritt, 1991) raised an important question: *is there an encryption function (E) such that both E(x + y) and E(x.y) are easy to compute from E(x) and E(y)?* Essentially, the question is intended to investigate whether there is any algebraically homomorphic encryption scheme that can be designed. Unfortunately, there has been a very little progress in determining whether such encryption schemes exist that are efficient and secure until 2009 when Craig Gentry, in his seminal paper, theoretically demonstrated the possibility of construction such an encryption system (Gentry, 2009). In this chapter, we will discuss various aspects of homomorphic encryption schemes – their definitions, requirements, applications, formal constructions, and the limitations of the current homomorphic encryption schemes. We will also briefly discuss some of the emerging trends in research in this field of computer science.

The chapter is organized as follows. In Section 2, we provide some basic and fundamental information on cryptography and various types of encryption schemes. Section 3 presents a formal discussion on homomorphic encryption schemes and discusses their various features. In Section 4, we discuss some of the most well-known and classical homomorphic encryption schemes in the literature. Section 5 provides a brief presentation on various properties and applications of homomorphic cryptosystems. Section 6 presents a discussion on fully homomorphic encryption schemes which are the most powerful encryption schemes for providing a framework for computing over encrypted data. Finally, Section 7 concludes the chapter while outlining a number of research directions and emerging trends in this exciting field of computation which has a tremendous potential of finding applications in the real-world deployments.

2. Fundamentals of cryptography

In this Section, we will recall some important concepts on encryption schemes. For more detailed information, the reader may refer to (Menezes et al., 1997; Van Tilborg, 2011). Encryption schemes are designed to preserve confidentiality. The security of encryption schemes must not rely on the obfuscation of their codes, but it should only be based on the secrecy of the key used in the encryption process. Encryption schemes are broadly of two types: *symmetric* and *asymmetric* encryption schemes. In the following, we present a very brief discussion on each of these schemes.

Symmetric encryption schemes: In these schemes, the sender and the receiver agree on the key they will use before establishing any secure communication session. Therefore, it is not possible for two persons who never met before to use such schemes directly. This also implies that in order to communicate with different persons, we must have a different key for each people. Requirement of large number of keys in these schemes make their key generation and management relatively more complex operations. However, symmetric schemes present the advantage of being very fast and they are used in applications where speed of execution is a paramount requirement. Among the existing symmetric encryption systems, AES (Daemen & Rijmen, 2000; Daemen & Rijmen, 2002), One-Time Pad (Vernam, 1926) and Snow (Ekdahl & Johansson, 2002) are very popular.

Asymmetric encryption schemes: In these schemes, every participant has a pair of keys-private and public. While the private key of a person is known to only her, the public key of each participant is known to everyone in the group. Such schemes are more secure than their symmetric counterparts and they don't need any prior agreement between the communicating parties on a common key before establishing a session of communication. RSA (Rivest et al., 1978b) and ElGamal (ElGamal, 1985) are two most popular asymmetric encryption systems.

Security of encryption schemes: Security of encryption schemes was first formalized by Shannon (Shannon, 1949). In his seminal paper, Shannon first introduced the notion of perfect secrecy/unconditional secrecy, which characterizes encryption schemes for which the knowledge of a ciphertext does not give any information about the corresponding plaintext and the encryption key. Shannon also proved that One-Time Pad (Vernam, 1926) encryption scheme is perfectly secure under certain conditions. However, no other encryption scheme has been proved to be unconditionally secure. For asymmetric schemes, we can rely on their mathematical structures to estimate their security strength in a formal way. These schemes are based on some well-identified mathematical problems which are hard to solve in general, but easy to solve for the one who knows the trapdoor – i.e., the owner of the keys. However, the estimation of the security level of these schemes may not always be correct due to several reasons. First, there may be other ways to break the system than solving the mathematical problems on which these schemes are based (Ajtai & Dwork, 1997; Nguyen & Stern, 1999). Second, most of the security proofs are performed in an idealized model called *random oracle model*, in which involved primitives, for example, hash functions, are considered truly random. This model has allowed the study of the security level of numerous asymmetric ciphers. However, we are now able to perform proofs in a more realistic model called *standard model* (Canetti et al., 1998; Paillier, 2007). This model eliminates some of the unrealistic assumptions in the random oracle model and makes the security analysis of cryptographic schemes more practical.

Usually, to evaluate the attack capacity of an adversary, we distinguish among several contexts (Diffie & Hellman, 1976): *cipher-text only attacks* (where the adversary has access only to some ciphertexts), *known-plaintext attacks* (where the adversary has access to some pairs of plaintext messages and their corresponding ciphertexts), *chosen-plaintext attacks* (the adversary has access to a decryption oracle that behaves like a black-box and takes a ciphertext as its input and outputs the corresponding plaintexts). The first context is the most frequent in real-world since it can happen when some adversary eavesdrops on a communication channel. The other cases may seem difficult to achieve, and may arise when the adversary is in a more powerful position; he may, for example, have stolen some plaintexts or an encryption engine. The *chosen* one exists in adaptive versions, where the opponents can wait for a computation result before choosing the next input (Fontaine & Galand, 2007).

Probabilistic encryption: Almost all the well-known cryptosystems are *deterministic*. This means that for a fixed encryption key, a given plaintext will always be encrypted into the same ciphertext under these systems. However, this may lead to some security problems. RSA scheme is a good example for explaining this point. Let us consider the following points with reference to the RSA cryptosystem:

- A particular plaintext may be encrypted in a too much structured way. With RSA, messages 0 and 1 are always encrypted as 0 and 1, respectively.

- It may be easy to compute some partial information about the plaintext: with RSA, the ciphertext c leaks one bit of information about the plaintext m, namely, the so called Jacobi symbol (Fontaine & Galand, 2007).

- When using a deterministic encryption scheme, it is easy to detect when the same message is sent twice while being processed with the same key.

In view of the problems stated above, we prefer encryption schemes to be probabilistic. In case of symmetric schemes, we introduce a random vector in the encryption process (e.g., in the pseudo-random generator for stream ciphers, or in the operating mode for block ciphers) – generally called *initial vector* (IV). This vector may be public and it may be transmitted in a clear-text form. However, the IV must be changed every time we encrypt a message. In case of asymmetric ciphers, the security analysis is more mathematical and formal, and we want the randomized schemes to remain analyzable in the same way as the deterministic schemes. Researchers have proposed some models to randomize the existing deterministic schemes, as the *optimal asymmetric encryption padding* (OAEP) for RSA (or any scheme that is based on a trapdoor one-way permutation) (Bellare & Rogaway, 1995). In the literature, researchers have also proposed some other randomized schemes (ElGamal, 1985; Goldwasser & Micali, 1982; Blum & Goldwasser, 1985).

A simple consequence of this requirement of the encryption schemes to be preferably probabilistic appears in the phenomenon called *expansion*. Since, for a plaintext, we require the existence of several possible ciphertexts, the number of ciphertexts is greater than the number of possible plaintexts. This means that the ciphertexts cannot be as short as the plaintexts; they have to be strictly longer. The ratio of the length of the ciphertext and the corresponding plaintext (in bits) is called expansion. The value of this parameter is of paramount importance in determining *security and efficiency tradeoff* of a probabilistic encryption scheme. In Paillier's scheme, an efficient probabilistic encryption mechanism has been proposed with the value of expansion less than 2 (Paillier, 1997). We will see the significance of expansion in other homomorphic encryption systems in the subsequent sections of this chapter.

3. Homomorphic encryption schemes

During the last few years, homomorphic encryption schemes have been studied extensively since they have become more and more important in many different cryptographic protocols such as, e.g., voting protocols. In this Section, we introduce homomorphic cryptosystems in three steps: *what*, *how* and *why* that reflects the main aspects of this interesting encryption technique. We start by defining *homomorphic cryptosystems* and *algebraically homomorphic cryptosystems*. Then we develop a method to construct algebraically homomorphic schemes given special homomorphic schemes. Finally, we describe applications of homomorphic schemes.

Definition: Let the message space (M, o) be a finite (semi-)group, and let σ be the security parameter. A *homomorphic public-key encryption scheme* (or *homomorphic cryptosystem*) on M is a quadruple (K, E, D, A) of probabilistic, expected polynomial time algorithms, satisfying the following functionalities:

- **Key Generation:** On input 1^σ the algorithm K outputs an encryption/decryption key pair $(k_e, k_d)=k \in \mathcal{K}$, where $\mathcal{K}$ denotes the key space.

- **Encryption:** On inputs $1^\sigma, k_e$, and an element $m \in M$ the encryption algorithm E outputs a ciphertext $c \in C$, where C denotes the ciphertext space.

- **Decryption:** The decryption algorithm D is deterministic. On inputs $1^\sigma, k$, and an element $c \in C$ it outputs an element in the message space M so that for all $m \in M$ it holds: if

$c = E\left(11^{\sigma}, k_{e_i} m\right)$ then $Prob[D(1^{\sigma}, k, c) \neq m]$ is negligible, i.e., it holds that $Prob[D(1^{\sigma}, k, c) \neq m] \leq 2^{-\sigma}$.

- **Homomorphic Property:** A is an algorithm that on inputs 1^{σ}, k_{e}, and elements c_1, $c_2 \in C$ outputs an element $c_3 \in C$ so that for all m_1, $m_2 \in M$ it holds: if $m_3 = m_1 \, o \, m_2$ and $c_1 = E\left(1^{\sigma}, k_{e}, m_1\right)$, and $c_2 = E\left(1^{\sigma}, k_{e}, m_2\right)$, then $Prob[D(A(1^{\sigma}, k_{e}, c_1, c_2))] \neq m_3]$ is negligible.

Informally speaking, a homomorphic cryptosystem is a cryptosystem with the additional property that there exists an efficient algorithm to compute an encryption of the sum or the product, of two messages given the public key and the encryptions of the messages but not the messages themselves.

If M is an additive (semi-)group, then the scheme is called *additively homomorphic* and the algorithms A is called *Add* Otherwise, the scheme is called *multiplicatively homomorphic* and the algorithm A is called *Mult*.

With respect to the aforementioned definitions, the following points are worth noticing:

- For a homomorphic encryption scheme to be efficient, it is crucial to make sure that the size of the ciphertexts remains polynomially bounded in the security parameter σ during repeated computations.

- The security aspects, definitions, and models of homomorphic cryptosystems are the same as those for other cryptosystems.

If the encryption algorithm E gets as additional input a uniform random number r of a set Z, the encryption scheme is called *probabilistic*, otherwise, it is called *deterministic*. Hence, if a cryptosystem is probabilistic, there belong several different ciphertexts to one message depending on the random number $r \in Z$. But note that as before the decryption algorithm remains deterministic, i.e., there is just one message belonging to a given ciphertext. Furthermore, in a probabilistic, homomorphic cryptosystem the algorithm A should be probabilistic too to hide the input ciphertext. For instance, this can be realized by applying a *blinding algorithm* on a (deterministic) computation of the encryption of the product and of the sum respectively.

Notations: In the following, we will omit the security parameter σ and the public key in the description of the algorithms. We will write $E_{k_e}(m)$ or $E(m)$ for $E\left(1^{\sigma}, k_{e}, m\right)$ and $D_k(c)$ or $D(c)$ for $D(1^{\sigma}, k, c)$ when there is no possibility of any ambiguity. If the scheme is probabilistic, we will also write $E_{k_e}(m)$ or $E(m)$ as well as $E_{k_e}(m, r)$ or $E(m, r)$ for $E\left(1^{\sigma}, k_{e}, m, r\right)$. Furthermore, we will write $A(E(m), E(m')) = E(m \, o \, m')$ to denote that the algorithm A (either *Add* or *Mult*) is applied on two encryptions of the messages m, $m' \in (M, o)$ and outputs an encryption of $m \, o \, m'$, i.e., it holds that except with negligible probability:

$$D\left(A\left(1^{\sigma}, k_{e}, E_{k_e}(m), E_{k_e}(m')\right)\right) = m \, o \, m'$$

Example: In the following, we give an example of a deterministic multiplicatively homomorphic scheme and an example of a probabilistic, additively homomorphic scheme.

The RSA Scheme: The classical RSA scheme (Rivest et al., 1987b) is an example of a deterministic multiplicatively homomorphic cryptosystem on $M = (\mathbb{Z}/N\mathbb{Z}, \cdot)$, where N is the product of two large primes. As ciphertext space, we have $C = (\mathbb{Z}/N\mathbb{Z}, \cdot)$ and as key space we have $\mathcal{K} = \{(k_e, k_d) = ((N, e), d) \mid N = pq, \ ed \equiv 1 \ mod \ \varphi(N)\}$. The encryption of a message $m \in M$ is defined as $E_{k_e}(m) = m^e \ mod \ N$ for decryption of a ciphertext $E_{k_e}(m) = c \in C$ we compute $D_{k_e, k_d}(c) = c^d \ mod \ N = m \ mod \ N$. Obviously, the encryption of the product of two messages can be efficiently computed by multiplying the corresponding ciphertexts, i.e.,

$$E_{k_e}(m_1.m_2) = (m_1.m_2)^e mod \ N = \left(m_1^e \ mod \ n\right)\left(m_2^e \ mod \ N\right) = E_{k_e}(m_1). \ E_{k_e}(m_2)$$

where $m_1, \ m_2 \in M$. Therefore, the algorithm for *Mult* can be easiliy realized as follows:

$$Mult\left(E_{k_e}(m_1), \ E_{k_e}(m_2)\right) = E_{k_e}(m_1). \ E_{k_e}(m_2)$$

Usually in the RSA scheme as well as in most of the cryptosystems which are based on the difficulty of factoring the security parameter σ is the bit length of N. For instance, $\sigma = 1024$ is a common security parameter.

The Goldwasser-Micali Scheme: The Goldwasser-Micali scheme (Goldwasser & Micali, 1984) is an example of a probabilistic, additively homomorphic cryptosystem on $M = (\mathbb{Z}/2\mathbb{Z}, \ +)$ with the ciphtertext space $C = Z = (\mathbb{Z}/N\mathbb{Z})^*$ where $N = pq$ is the product of two large primes. We have.

$$K = \left\{(k_e, \ k_d) = ((N, \ a), \ (p, \ q)) \mid N = pq, \ a \in (\mathbb{Z}/N\mathbb{Z})^* : \left(\tfrac{a}{p}\right) = \left(\tfrac{a}{q}\right) = \ -1\right\}$$

Since this scheme is probabilistic, the encryption algorithm gets as additional input a random value $r \in Z$. We define $E_{k_e}(m, \ r) = a^m r^2 \ mod \ N$ and $D_{(k_e, \ k_d)} = 0$ if c is a square and $= 1$ otherwise. The following relation therefore holds good:

$$E_{k_e}(m_1, \ r_1). \ E_{k_e}(m_2, \ r_2) = E_{k_e}(m_1 + m_2, \ r_1 r_2)$$

The algorithms *Add* can, therefore, be efficiently implemented as follows:

$$Add\left(E_{k_e}(m_1, \ r_1), \ E_{k_e}(m_2, \ r_2), \ r_3\right) = E_{k_e}(m_1, \ r_1). \ E_{k_e}(m_2, \ r_2). \ r_3^2 \ mod \ N = E_{ke}(m_1 + m_2, \ r_1 r_2 r_3)$$

In the above equation, $r_3^2 \ mod \ N$ is equivalent to $E_{k_e}(0, \ r_3)$. Also, $m_1, \ m_2 \in M$ and $r_1, \ r_2, r_3 \in Z$. Note that this algorithm should be probabilistic, since it obtains a random number r_3 as an additional input.

A public-key homomorphic encryption scheme on a (semi-)ring $(M, +, .)$ can be defined in a similar manner. Such schemes consist of two algorithms: *Add* and *Mult* for the homomorphic property instead of one algorithm for A, i.e., it is additively and multiplicatively homomorphic at the same time. Such schemes are called *algebraically homomorphic*.

Definition: An additively homomorphic encryption scheme on a (semi-)ring $(M, +, .)$ is called *scalar homomorphic* if there exists a probabilistic, expected polynomial time algorithm *Mixed_Mult* that on inputs 1^σ, $k_{e'}$ $s \in M$ and an element $c \in C$ outputs an element $c^{'} \in C$ so that for all $m \in M$ it holds that: if $m^{'} = s.m$ and $c = E(1^\sigma, k_{e'} m)$ then the probability $Prob[D(Mixed\_Mult(1^\sigma, k_{e'} s, s)) \neq m^{'}]$ is negligible.

Thus in a scalar homomorphic scheme, it is possible to compute an encryption $E(1^\sigma, k_{e'} s.m) = E(1^\sigma, k_{e'} m^{'})$ of a product of two messages s, $m \in M$ given the public key k_e and an encryption $c = E(1^\sigma, k_{e'} m)$ of one message m and the other message s as a plaintext. It is clear that any scheme that is algebraically homomorphic is scalar homomorphic as well.

We will denote by $Mixed\_Mult(m, E(m^{'})) = E(mm^{'})$ if the following equation holds good except possibly with a negligible probability of not holding.

$$D(Mixed\_Mult(1^\sigma, k_{e'} m, E_{k_e}(m^{'}))) = m . m^{'}$$

Definition: A *blinding algorithm* is a probabilistic, polynomial-time algorithm which on inputs 1^σ, $k_{e'}$ and $c \in E_{k_e}(m, r)$ where $r \in Z$ is randomly chosen outputs another encryption $c^{'} \in E_{k_e}(m, r^{'})$ of m where $r^{'} \in Z$ is chosen uniformly at random.

For instance, in a probabilistic, homomorphic cryptosystem on (M, o) the blinding algorithm can be realized by applying the algorithm A on the ciphertext c and an encryption of the identity element in M.

If M is isomorphic to Z/nZ if M is finite or to Z otherwise, then the algorithm *Mixed_Mult* can easily be implemented using a double and *Add* algorithm. This is combined with a blinding algorithm is the scheme is probabilistic (Cramer et al., 2000). Hence, every additively homomorphic cryptosystem on Z/nZ or Z is also *scalar homomorphic* and the algorithm *Mixed_Mult* can be efficiently implemented (Sander & Tschudin, 1998).

Algebraically Homomorphic Cryptosystems: The existence of an efficient and secure algebraically homomorphic cryptosystem has been a long standing open question. In this Section, we first present some related work considering this problem. Thereafter, we describe the relationship between algebraically homomorphic schemes and homomorphic schemes on special non-abelian groups. More precisely, we prove that a homomorphic encryption scheme on the non-ableain group $(S_7, .)$, the symmetric group on seven elements, allows to construct an algebraically homomorphic encryption scheme on $(F_2, +, .)$. An algebraically homomorphic encryption scheme on $(F_2, +, .)$ can also be obtained from a homomorphic encryption scheme on the special linear group $(SL(3, 2), .)$ over F_2. Furthermore, using coding theory, an algebraically homomorphic encryption on an arbitrary finite ring or field could be obtained given a homomorphic encryption scheme on one of these non-abelian groups. These observations could be a first step to solve the problem whether efficient and secure algebraically homomorphic schemes exist. The research community in cryptography has spent substantial effort on this problem. In 1996, Boneh and Lipton proved that under a reasonable assumption every deterministic, algebraically homomorphic cryptosystem can be broken in sub-exponential time (Boneh & Lipton, 1996). This may be perceived as a negative result concerning the existence of an algebraically homomorphic encryption scheme, although most of the existing cryptosystems, e.g., RSA scheme or the ElGamal scheme can be also be broken in sub-exponential time. Furthermore, if we seek for algebraically homomorphic public-key schemes on small fields or rings such as $M = F_2$, obviously such a scheme has to be probabilistic in order to be secure.

Some researchers also tried to find candidates for algebraically homomorphic schemes. In 1993, Fellows and Koblitz presented an algebraic public-key cryptosystem called Polly Cracker (Fellows & Koblitz, 1993). It is algebraically homomorphic and provably secure. Unfortunately, the scheme has a number of difficulties and is not efficient concerning the ciphertext length. Firstly, Polly Cracker is a polynomial-based system. Therefore, computing an encryption of the product $E(m_1.m_2)$ of two messages m_1 and m_2 by multiplying the corresponding ciphertext polynomials $E(m_1)$ and $E(m_2)$, leads to an exponential blowup in the number of monomials. Hence, during repeated computations, there is an exponential blow up in the ciphertext length. Secondly, all existing instantiations of Polly Cracker suffer from further drawbacks (Koblitz, 1998). They are either insecure since they succumb to certain attacks, they are too inefficient to be practical, or they lose the algebraically homomorphic property. Hence, it is far from clear how such kind of schemes could be turned into efficient and secure algebraically homomorphic encryption schemes. A detailed analysis and description of these schemes can be found in (Ly, 2002).

In 2002, J. Domingo-Ferrer developed a probabilistic, algebraically homomorphic secret-key cryptosystem (Domingo-Ferrer, 2002). However, this scheme was not efficient since there was an exponential blowup in the ciphertext length during repeated multiplications that were required to be performed. Moreover, it was also broken by Wagner and Bao (Bao, 2003; Wagner, 2003).

Thus considering homomorphic encryption schemes on groups instead of rings seems more promising to design a possible algebraically homomorphic encryption scheme. It brings us closer to structures that have been successfully used in cryptography. The following theorem shows that indeed the search for algebraically homomorphic schemes can be reduced to the search for homomorphic schemes on special non-abelian groups (Rappe, 2004).

Theorem I: The following two statements are equivalent: (1) There exists an algebraically homomorphic encryption scheme on $(F_2, +,.)$. (2) There exists a homomorphic encryption scheme on the symmetric group $(S_7,.)$.

Proof: 1 → 2: This direction of proof follows immediately and it holds for an arbitrary finite group since operations of finite groups can always be implemented by Boolean circuits. Let S_7

be represented as a subset of $\{0, 1\}^l$, where e.g. $l = 21$ can be chosen, and let C be a circuit with addition and multiplication gates that takes as inputs the binary representations of elements m_1, $m_2 \in S_7$ and outputs the binary representations of $m_1 m_2$. If we have an algebraically homomorphic encryption scheme $(K, E, D, Add, Mult)$ on $(\mathbf{F}_2, +, .)$ then we can define a homomorphic encryption scheme $(\widetilde{K}, \widetilde{E}, \widetilde{D}, \widetilde{Mult})$ on S_7 by defining $\widetilde{E}(m) = (E(s_0), ...E(s_{l-1}))$ where $(s_0, ...s_{l-1})$ denotes the binary representation of m. $\widetilde{Mult}$ is constructed by substituting the addition gates in C by Add and the multiplication gates by $Mult$. $\widetilde{K}$ and $\widetilde{D}$ are defined in the obvious way.

2 → 1: The proof has two steps. First, we use a construction of Ben-Or and Cleve (Ben-Or & Cleve, 1992) to show that the field $(\mathbf{F}_2, +, .)$ can be encoded in the special linear group $(\mathbf{SL}(3,2), .)$ over $\mathbf{F}_2$. Then, we apply a theorem from projective geometry to show that $(\mathbf{SL}(3,2), .)$ is a subgroup of S_7. This proves the claim.

Homomorphic encryption schemes on groups have been extensively studied. For instance, we have homomorphic schemes on groups $(\mathbb{Z}/M\mathbb{Z}, +)$, for M being a smooth number (Goldwasser & Micali, 1984; Benaloh, 1994; Naccache & Stern, 1998) for $M = p.q$ being an RSA modulus (Paillier, 1999; Galbraith, 2002), and for groups $((\mathbb{Z}/N\mathbb{Z})^*, .)$ where N is an RSA modulus. All known efficient and secure schemes are homomorphic on abelian groups. However, S_7 and $SL(3, 2)$ are non-abelian. Sander, Young and Yung (Sander et al., 1999) investigated the possibility of existence of a homomorphic encryption scheme on non-abelain groups. Although non-abelian groups had been used to construct encryption schemes (Ko et al., 2000; Paeng et al., 2001; Wagner & Magyarik, 1985; Grigoriev & Ponomarenko, 2006), the resulting schemes are not homomorphic in the sense that we need for computing efficiently on encrypted data.

Grigoriev and Ponomarenko propose a novel definition of homomorphic cryptosystems on which they base a method to construct homomorphic cryptosystems over arbitrary finite groups including non-abelian groups (Grigoriev & Ponomarenko, 2006). Their construction method is based on the fact that every finite group is an epimorphic image of a free product of finite cyclic groups. It uses existing homomorphic encryption schemes on finite cyclic groups as building blocks to obtain homomorphic encryption schemes on arbitrary finite groups. Since the ciphertext space obtained from the encryption scheme is a free product of groups, an exponential blowup of the ciphertext lengths during repeated computations is produced as a result. The reason is that the length of the product of two elements x and y of a free product is, in general, the sum of the length of x and the length of y. Hence, the technique proposed by Grigoriev and Ponomarenko suffers from the same drawback as the earlier schemes and does not provide an efficient cryptosystem. We note that using this construction it is possible to construct a homomorphic encryption scheme on the symmetric group S_7 and on the special linear group $SL(3, 2)$. If we combine this with **Theorem 1**, we can construct an algebraically homomorphic cryptosystem on the finite field $(\mathbf{F}_2, +, .)$. Unfortunately, the exponential blowup owing to the construction method in the homomorphic encryption scheme on S_7 and on $SL(3, 2)$ respectively, would lead to an exponential blowup in $\mathbf{F}_2$ and hence leaves the question open if an efficient algebraically homomorphic cryptosystem on F_2 exists. We will come back to this issue in Section 6, where we discuss *fully homomorphic encryption schemes.*

Grigoriev and Ponomarenko propose another method to encrypt arbitrary finite groups homomorphically (Grigoriev & Ponomarenko, 2004). This method is based on the difficulty of the membership problem for groups of integer matrices, while in (Grigoriev & Ponomarenko, 2006) it is based on the difficulty of factoring. However, as before, this scheme is not efficient. Moreover, in (Grigoriev & Ponomarenko, 2004), an algebraically homomorphic cryptosystem over finite commutative rings is proposed. However, owing to its immense size, it is infeasible to implement in real-world applications.

4. Some classical homomorphic encryption systems

In this Section, we describe some classical homomorphic encryption systems which have created substantial interest among the researchers in the domain of cryptography. We start with the first probabilistic systems proposed by Goldwasser and Micali in 1982 (Goldwasser & Micali, 1982; Goldwasser & Micali, 1984) and then discuss the famous Paillier's encryption scheme (Paillier, 1999) and its improvements. Paillier's scheme and its variants are well-known for their efficiency and the high level of security that they provide for homomorphic encryption. We do not discuss their mathematical considerations in detail, but summarize their important parameters and properties.

Goldwasser-Micali scheme: This scheme (Goldwasser & Micali, 1982; Goldwasser & Micali, 1984) is historically very important since many of subsequent proposals on homomorphic encryption were largely motivated by its approach. Like in RSA, in this scheme, we use computations modulo $n = p.q$, a product of two large primes. The encryption process is simple which uses a product and a square, whereas decryption is heavier and involves exponentiation. The complexity of the decryption process is: $O(k.l(p)^2)$, where $l(p)$ denotes the number of bits in p. Unfortunately, this scheme has a limitation since its input consists of a single bit. First, this implies that encrypting k bits leads to a cost of $O(k.l(p)^2)$. This is not very efficient even if it may be considered as practical. The second concern is related to the issue of *expansion* – a single bit of plaintext is encrypted in *an integer modulo n*, that is, $l(n)$ bits. This leads to a huge blow up of ciphertext causing a serious problem with this scheme.

Goldwasser-Micali (GM) scheme can be viewed from another perspective. When looked from this angle, the basic principle of this scheme is to partition a well-chosen subset of integers modulo n into two secret parts: M_0 and M_1. The encryption process selects a random element M_b to encrypt plaintext b, and the decryption process lets the user know in which part the randomly selected element lies. The essence of the scheme lies in the mechanism to determine the subset, and to partition it into M_0 and M_1. The scheme uses group theory to achieve this goal. The subset is the group G of invertible integers modulo n with a Jacobi symbol with respect to n, equal to 1. The partition is generated by another group $H \subset G$, consisting of the elements that are invertible modulo n with a Jacobi symbol, with respect to a fixed factor n, equal to 1. With these settings of parameters, it is possible to split G into two parts – H and $G \setminus H$. The generalization schemes of GM deal with these two groups. These schemes attempt to find two groups G and H such that G can be split into more than $k = 2$ parts.

Benaloh's scheme: Benaloh (Benaloh, 1988) is a generalization of GM scheme that enables one to manage inputs of $l(k)$ bits, k being a prime satisfying some specified constraints. Encryption is similar as in GM scheme (encrypting a message $m \in \{0, \ldots, k - 1\}$ is tantamount to picking an integer $r \in Z_n^*$ and computing $c = g^m r^k \bmod n$). However, the decryption phase is more complex. If the input and output sizes are $l(k)$ and $l(n)$ bits respectively, the expansion is equal to $l(n)/l(k)$. The value of expansion obtained in this approach is less than that achieved in GM. This makes the scheme more attractive. Moreover, the encryption is not too expensive as well. The overhead in the decryption process is estimated to be $O\left(\sqrt{k}.l(k)\right)$ for pre-computation which remains constant for each dynamic decryption step. This implies that the value of k has to be taken very small, which in turn limits the gain obtained on the value of expansion.

Naccache-Stern scheme: This scheme (Naccache & Stern, 1998) is an improvement of Benaloh's scheme. Using a value of the parameter k that is greater than that used in the Benaloh's scheme, it achieves a smaller expansion and thereby attains a superior efficiency. The encryption step is precisely the same as in Benaloh's scheme. However, decryption is different. The value of expansion is same as that in Benaloh's scheme, i.e., $l(n)/l(k)$. However, the cost of decryption is less and is given by:$O\left(l(n)^5 log\ (l(n))\right)$. The authors claim that it is possible to choose the values of the parameters in the system in such a way that the achieved value of expansion is 4 (Naccache & Stern, 1998).

Okamoto-Uchiyama scheme: To improve the performance of the earlier schemes on homomorphic encryption, Okamoto and Uchiyama changed the base group G (Okamoto & Uchiyama, 1998). By taking $n = p^2 q$, p and q being two large prime numbers as usual, and the group $G = Z_{p^2}^*$, the authors achieve $k = p$. The value of the expansion obtained in the scheme is 3. One of the biggest advantages of this scheme is that its security is equivalent to the factorization of n. However, a chosen-ciphertext attack has been proposed on this scheme that can break the factorization problem. Hence, currently it has a limited applicability. However, this scheme was used to design the EPOC systems (Okamoto et al., 2000) which is accepted in the *IEEE standard specifications for public-key cryptography* (IEEE P1363).

Paillier scheme: One of the most well-known homomorphic encryption schemes is due to Paillier (Paillier, 1999). It is an improvement over the earlier schemes in the sense that it is able to decrease the value of expansion from 3 to 2. The scheme uses $n = p.q$ with gcd $(n,\ \phi(n)) = 1$. As usual p and q are two large primes. However, it considered the group $G = Z_{n^2}^*$ and a proper choice of H led to $k = l(n)$. While the cost of encryption is not too high, decryption needs one exponentiation modulo n^2 to the power $\lambda(n)$, and a multiplication modulo n. This makes decryption a bit heavyweight process. The author has shown how to manage decryption efficiently using the famous *Chinese Remainder Theorem*. With smaller expansion and lower cost compared with the other schemes, this scheme found great acceptance. In 2002, Cramer and Shoup proposed a general approach to achieve higher security against *adaptive chosen-ciphertext attacks* for certain cryptosystems with some particular algebraic properties (Cramer & Shoup, 2002). They applied their propositions on Paillier's original scheme and designed a stronger variant of homomorphic encryption. Bresson et al. proposed a slightly different version of a homomorphic encryption scheme that is more accurate for some applications (Bresson et al., 2003).

Damgard-Jurik scheme: Damgard and Jurik propose a generalization of Paillier's scheme to groups of the form $Z_{n^{s+1}}^*$ for $s > 0$ (Damgard & Jurik, 2001). In this scheme, choice of larger values of s will achieve lower values of expansion. This scheme can be used in a number of applications. For example, we can mention the adaptation of the size of the plaintext, the use of threshold cryptography, electronic voting, and so on. To encrypt a message, $m \in Z_n^*$, one picks at random $r \in Z_n^*$ and computes $g^m r^{n^s} \in Z_{n^{s+1}}$. The authors show that if one can break the scheme for a given value $s = \sigma$, then one can break it for $s = \sigma - 1$. They also show that the semantic security of this scheme is equivalent to that of Paillier's scheme. The value of expansion can be computed using: $1 + 1/s$. It is clear that expansion can attain a value close to 1 if s is sufficiently large. The ratio of the cost for encryption in this scheme over Paillier's scheme can be estimated to be: $\frac{s(s+1)(s+2)}{6}$. The same ratio for the decryption process will have value equal to: $\frac{(s+1)(s+2)}{6}$. Even if this scheme has a lower value of expansion as compared to Paillier's scheme, it is computationally more intensive. Moreover, if we want to encrypt or decrypt k blocks of $l(n)$ bits, running Paillier's scheme k times is less expensive than running Damgard-Jurik's scheme.

Galbraith scheme: This is an adaptation of the existing homomorphic encryption schemes in the context of elliptic curves (Galbraith, 2002). Its expansion is equal to 3. For $s = 1$, the ratio of the encryption cost for this scheme over that of Paillier's scheme can be estimated to be about 7, while the same ratio for the cost of decryption cost is about 14 for the same value of s. However, the most important advantage of this scheme is that the cost of encryption and decryption can be decreased using larger values of s. In addition, the security of the scheme increases with the increase in the value of s as it is the case in Damgard-Jurik's scheme.

Castagnos scheme: Castagnos explored the possibility of improving the performance of homomorphic encryption schemes using quadratic fields quotations (Castagnos, 2006; Castagnos, 2007). This scheme achieves an expansion value of 3 and the ratio of encryption/ decryption cost with $s = 1$ over Paillier's scheme can be estimated to be about 2.

5. Applications and properties of homomorphic encryption schemes

An inherent drawback of homomorphic cryptosystems is that attacks on these systems might possibly exploit their additional structural information. For instance, using plain RSA (Rivest et al., 1978b) for signing, the multiplication of two signatures yields a valid signature of the product of the two corresponding messages. Although there are many ways to avoid such attacks, for instance, by application of hash functions, the use of redundancy or probabilistic schemes, this potential weakness leads us to the question why homomorphic schemes should be used instead of conventional cryptosystems under certain situations. The main reason for the interest in homomorphic cryptosystems is its wide application scope. There are theoretical as well as practical applications in different areas of cryptography. In the following, we list some of the main applications and properties of homomorphic schemes and summarize the idea behind them.

5.1. Some applications of homomorphic encryption schemes

Protection of mobile agents: One of the most interesting applications of homomorphic encryption is its use in protection of mobile agents. As we have seen in Section 3, a homomorphic encryption scheme on a special non-abelian group would lead to an algebraically homomorphic cryptosystem on the finite field F_2. Since all conventional computer architectures are based on binary strings and only require multiplication and addition, such homomorphic cryptosystems would offer the possibility to encrypt a whole program so that it is still executable. Hence, it could be used to protect mobile agents against malicious hosts by encrypting them (Sander & Tschudin, 1998a). The protection of mobile agents by homomorphic encryption can be used in two ways: (i) *computing with encrypted functions* and (ii) *computing with encrypted data*. Computation with encrypted functions is a special case of protection of mobile agents. In such scenarios, a secret function is publicly evaluated in such a way that the function remains secret. Using homomorphic cryptosystems, the encrypted function can be evaluated which guarantees its privacy. Homomorphic schemes also work on encrypted data to compute publicly while maintaining the privacy of the secret data. This can be done encrypting the data in advance and then exploiting the homomorphic property to compute with encrypted data.

Multiparty computation: In multiparty computation schemes, several parties are interested in computing a common, public function on their inputs while keeping their individual inputs private. This problem belongs to the area of *computing with encrypted data*. Usually in multiparty computation protocols, we have a set of $n \geq 2$ players whereas in computing with encrypted data scenarios $n = 2$. Furthermore, in multi-party computation protocols, the function that should be computed is publicly known, whereas in the area of computing with encrypted data it is a private input of one party.

Secret sharing scheme: In secret sharing schemes, parties share a secret so that no individual party can reconstruct the secret form the information available to it. However, if some parties cooperate with each other, they may be able to reconstruct the secret. In this scenario, the homomorphic property implies that the composition of the shares of the secret is equivalent to the shares of the composition of the secrets.

Threshold schemes: Both secret sharing schemes and the multiparty computation schemes are examples of threshold schemes. Threshold schemes can be implemented using homomorphic encryption techniques.

Zero-knowledge proofs: This is a fundamental primitive of cryptographic protocols and serves as an example of a theoretical application of homomorphic cryptosystems. Zero-knowledge proofs are used to prove knowledge of some private information. For instance, consider the case where a user has to prove his identity to a host by logging in with her account and private password. Obviously, in such a protocol the user wants her private information (i.e., her password) to stay private and not to be leaked during the protocol operation. Zero-knowledge proofs guarantee that the protocol communicates exactly the knowledge that was intended, and no (zero) extra knowledge. Examples of zero-knowledge proofs using homomorphic property can be found in (Cramer & Damgard, 1998).

Election schemes: In election schemes, the homomorphic property provides a tool to obtain the tally given the encrypted votes without decrypting the individual votes.

Watermarking and fingerprinting schemes: Digital watermarking and fingerprinting schemes embed additional information into digital data. The homomorphic property is used to add a mark to previously encrypted data. In general, watermarks are used to identify the owner/seller of digital goods to ensure the copyright. In fingerprinting schemes, the person who buys the data should be identifiable by the merchant to ensure that data is not illegally redistributed. Further properties of such schemes can be found in (Pfitzmann & Waidner, 1997; Adelsbach et al. 2002).

Oblivious transfer: It is an interesting cryptographic primitive. Usually in a two-party 1-out-of-2 oblivious transfer protocol, the first party sends a bit to the second party in such as way that the second party receives it with probability ½, without the first party knowing whether or not the second party received the bit. An example of such a protocol that uses the homomorphic property can be found in (Lipmaa, 2003).

Commitment schemes: Commitment schemes are some fundamental cryptographic primitives. In a commitment scheme, a player makes a commitment. She is able to choose a value from some set and commit to her choice such that she can no longer change her mind. She does not have to reveal her choice although she may do so at some point later. Some commitment schemes can be efficiently implemented using homomorphic property.

Lottery protocols: Usually in a cryptographic lottery, a number pointing to the winning ticket has to be jointly and randomly chosen by all participants. Using a homomorphic encryption scheme this can be realized as follows: Each player chooses a random number which she encrypts. Then using the homomorphic property the encryption of the sum of the random values can be efficiently computed. The combination of this and a *threshold decryption scheme* leads to the desired functionality. More details about homomorphic properties of lottery schemes can be found in (Fouque et al., 2000).

Mix-nets: Mix-nets are protocols that provide anonymity for senders by collecting encrypted messages from several users. For instance, one can consider mix-nets that collect ciphertexts and output the corresponding plaintexts in a randomly permuted order. In such a scenario, privacy is achieved by requiring that the permutation that matches inputs to outputs is kept secret to anyone except the mix-net. In particular, determining a correct input/output pair, i.e., a ciphertext with corresponding plaintext, should not be more effective then guessing one at random. A desirable property to build such mix-nets is re-encryption which is achieved by using homomorphic encryption. More information about applications of homomorphic encryption in mix-nets can be found in (Golle et al., 2004; Damgard & Jurik, 2003).

5.2. Some properties of homomorphic encryption schemes

Homomorphic encryption schemes have some interesting mathematical properties. In the following, we mention some of these properties.

Re-randomizable encryption/re-encryption: Re-randomizable cryptosystems (Groth, 2004) are probabilistic cryptosystems with the additional property that given the public key k_e and an encryption $E_{k_e}(m, r)$ of a message $m \in M$ under the public key k_e and a random number $r \in Z$ it is possible to efficiently convert $E_{k_e}(m, r)$ into another encryption $E_{k_e}(m, r')$ that is perfectly indistinguishable from a *fresh* encryption of m under the public key k_e. This property is also called *re-encryption*.

It obvious that every probabilistic homomorphic cryptosystem is re-randomizable. Without loss of generality, we assume that the cryptosystem is additively homomorphic. Given $E_{k_e}(m, r)$ and the public key k_e, we can compute $E_{k_e}(0, r'')$ for a random number r'' and hence compute the following:

$$Add\left(E_{k_e}(m, r), \ E_{k_e}(0, r'')\right) = E_{k_e}(m + 0, r') = E_{k_e}(m, r')$$

where r' is an appropriate random number. We note that this is exactly what a *blinding algorithm* does.

Random self-reducibility: Along with the possibility of re-encryption comes the property of random self-reducibility concerning the problem of computing the plaintext from the ciphertext. A cryptosystem is called *random self-reducible* if any algorithm that can break a non-trivial fraction of ciphertexts can also break a random instance with significant probability. This property is discussed in detail in (Damgard et al., 2010; Sander et al., 1999).

Verifiable encryptions / fair encryptions: If an encryption is verifiable, it provides a mechanism to check the correctness of encrypted data without compromising on the secrecy of the data. For instance, this is useful in voting schemes to convince any observer that the encrypted name of a candidate, i.e., the encrypted vote is indeed in the list of candidates. A cryptosystem with this property that is based on homomorphic encryption can be found in (Poupard & Stern, 2000). Verifiable encryptions are also called *fair encryptions*.

6. Fully homomorphic encryption schemes

In 2009, Gentry described the first plausible construction of a fully homomorphic cryptosystem that supports both addition and multiplication (Gentry, 2009). Gentry's proposed fully homomorphic encryption consists of several steps: First, it constructs a *somewhat homomorphic* scheme that supports evaluating low-degree polynomials on the encrypted data. Next, it *squashes* the decryption procedure so that it can be expressed as a low-degree polynomial which is supported by the scheme, and finally, it applies a *bootstrapping transformation* to obtain a fully homomorphic scheme. The essential approach of this scheme is to derive and establish a process that can evaluate polynomials of high-enough degree using a decryption procedure that can be expressed as a polynomial of low-enough degree. Once the degree of polynomials that can be evaluated by the scheme exceeds the degree of the decryption polynomial by a factor of two, the scheme is called *bootstrappable* and it can then be converted into a fully homomorphic scheme.

For designing a bootstrappable scheme, Gentry presented a somewhat homomorphic scheme (Gentry, 2009) which is roughly a GGH (Goldreich, Goldwasser, Halevi)-type scheme (Goldreich et al., 1997; Micciancio, 2001) over ideal lattices. Gentry later proved that with an appropriate key-generation procedure, the security of that scheme can be reduced to the worst-case hardness of some lattice problems in ideal lattice constructions (Gentry, 2010). Since this somewhat homomorphic scheme is not bootstrappable, Gentry described a transformation to squash the decryption procedure, reducing the degree of the decryption polynomial (Gentry, 2009). This is done by adding to the public key, an additional hint about the secret key in the form of a *sparse subset-sum problem* (SSSP). The public key is augmented with a big set of vectors in such a way that there exists a very sparse subset of them that adds up to the secret key. A ciphertext of the underlying scheme can be *post-processed* using this additional hint and the post-processed ciphertext can be decrypted with a low-degree polynomial, thereby achieving a bootstrappable scheme.

Gentry's construction is quite involved – the secret key, even in the private key version of his scheme is a short basis of a *random ideal lattice*. Generating pairs of public and secret bases with the right distributions appropriate for the worst-case to average-case reduction is technically quite complicated. A significant research effort has been devoted to increase the efficiency of its implementation (Gentry & Halevi, 2011; Smart & Vercauteren, 2010).

A parallel line of work that utilizes ideal lattices in cryptography dates back to the NTRU cryptosystem (Hoffstein et al., 1998). This approach uses ideal lattices for efficient cryptographic constructions. The additional structure of ideal lattices, compared to ordinary lattices, makes their representation more powerful and enables faster computation. Motivated by the work of Micciancio (Micciancio, 2007), a significant number of work (Peikert & Rosen, 2006; Lyubashevsky & Micciancio, 2006; Peikert & Rosen, 2007; Lyubashevsky et al., 2008; Lyubashevsky & Micciancio, 2008) has produced efficient constructions of various cryptographic primitives whose security can formally be reduced to the hardness of short-vector problems in ideal lattices (Brakerski & Vaikuntanathan, 2011).

Lyubashevsky et al. (Lyubashevsky et al., 2010) present the *ring learning with errors* (RLWE) assumption which is the *ring counterpart* of Regev's learning with errors assumption (Regev, 2005). In a nutshell, the assumption is that given polynomially many samples over a certain ring of the form $(a_i, a_i s + e_i)$, where s is a random *secret ring element*, a_i's are distributed uniformly randomly in the ring, and e_i are *small* ring elements, it will be impossible for an adversary to distinguish this sequence of samples from random pairs of ring elements. The authors have shown that this simple assumption can be very efficiently reduced to the worst case hardness of short-vector problems on ideal lattices. They have also shown how to construct a very efficient ring counterpart to Regev's public-key encryption scheme (Regev, 2005), as well as a counterpart to the identity-based encryption scheme presented in (Gentry et al., 2008) by using the basis sampling techniques in (Regev, 2005). The scheme presented in (Lyubashevsky et al., 2010) is very elegant and efficient since it is not dependent on any complex computations over ideal lattices.

Brakerski and Vaikuntanathan raised a natural question that whether the above approaches (i.e., ideal lattices and RLWE) can be effectively exploited so that benefits of both these approaches can be achieved at the same time – namely the functional powerfulness on the one hand (i.e., the ideal lattice approach) and the simplicity and efficiency of the other (i.e., RLWE). They have shown that indeed this can be done (Brakerski & Vaikuntanathan, 2011). They have constructed a somewhat homomorphic encryption scheme based on RLWE. The scheme inherits the simplicity and efficiency, as well as the worst case relation to ideal lattices. Moreover, the scheme enjoys *key dependent message security* (KDM security, also known as *circular security*), since it can securely encrypt polynomial functions (over an appropriately defined ring) of its own secret key. The significance of this feature of the scheme in context of homomorphic encryption has been clearly explained by the authors. The authors argue that all known constructions of fully homomorphic encryption employ a bootstrapping technique that enforces the public key of the scheme to grow linearly with the maximal depth of evaluated circuits. This is a major drawback with regard to the usability and the efficiency of the scheme. However, the size of the public key can be made independent of the circuit depth if the somewhat homomorphic scheme can securely encrypt its own secret key. With the design of this scheme, the authors have solved an open problem - achieving *circular secure somewhat homomorphic encryption*. They have also computed the circular security of their scheme with respect to the representation of the secret key as a ring element, where bootstrapping requires circular security with respect to the bitwise representation of the secret key (actually, the bitwise representation of the *squashed* secret key). Since there is no prior work that studies a possible co-existence between somewhat homomorphism with any form of circular security, the work is a significant first step towards removing the assumption (Brakerski & Vaikunta-nathan, 2011). The authors have also shown how to transform the proposed scheme into a fully homomorphic encryption scheme following Gentry's blueprint of *squashing* and *bootstrap-ping*. Applying the techniques presented in (Brakerski & Vaikuntanathan, 2011a), the authors argue that *squashing* can even be avoided at the cost of relying on *sparse* version of RLWE that is not known to reduce to worst case scenarios. This greatly enhances the efficiency of the proposed scheme in practical applications. The proposed scheme is also *additively key-homomorphic*– a property that has found applications in achieving security against *key-related attacks* (Applebaum et al., 2011).

Smart and Vercauteren (Smart & Vercauteren, 2010) present a fully homomorphic encryption scheme that has smaller key and ciphertext sizes. The construction proposed by the authors follows the fully homomorphic construction based on ideal lattices proposed by Gentry

(Gentry, 2009). It produces a fully homomorphic scheme from a *somewhat homomorphic scheme*. For a somewhat homomorphic scheme, the public and the private keys consist of two large integers (one of which is shared by both the public and the private key), and the ciphertext consists of one large integer. The scheme (Smart & Vercauteren, 2010) has smaller *ciphertext blow up* and reduced key size than in Gentry's scheme based on ideal lattices. Moreover, the scheme also allows and efficient homomorphic encryption over any field of characteristics two. More specifically, it uses arithmetic of *cyclotomic number fields*. In particular, the authors have focused on the field generated by the polynomial: $F(X) = X^{2^n} + 1$. However, they also noted that the scheme could be applied with arbitrary (even non-cyclotomic) number fields as well. In spite of having many advantages, the major problem with this scheme is that the key generation method is very slow.

Gentry and Halevi presented a novel implementation approach for the variant of Smart and Vercauteren proposition (Smart & Vercauteren, 2010), which had a greatly improved key generation phase (Gentry & Halevi, 2011). In particular, the authors have noted that the key generation (for cyclotomic fields) is essentially an application of a *Discrete Fourier Transform* (DFT), followed by a small quantum of computation, and then application of the *inverse* transform. The authors then further demonstrate that it is not even required to perform the DFTs if one selects the cyclotomic field to be of the form: $X^{2^n} + 1$. The authors illustrate this by using a recursive approach to deduce two constants from the secret key which subsequently facilitates the key generation algorithm to construct a valid associated public key. The key generation method of Gentry and Halevi (Gentry & Halevi, 2011) is fast. However, the scheme appears particularly tailored to work with two-power roots of unity.

Researchers have also examined ways of improving key generation in fully homomorphic encryption schemes. For example, in (Ogura et al., 2010), a method is proposed for construction of keys for essentially random number fields by pulling random elements and analyzing *eigenvalues* of the corresponding matrices. However, this method is unable to achieve the improvement in efficiency in terms of *reduced ciphertext blow up* as done in (Smart & Vercauteren, 2010) and (Gentry & Halevi, 2011).

Stehle and Steinfield improved Gentry's fully homomorphic scheme and obtained a faster fully homomorphic scheme with $O(n^{3.5})$ bits complexity per elementary binary addition/multiplication gate (Stehle & Steinfeld, 2010). However, the hardness assumption of the security of the scheme is stronger than that of Gentry's scheme (Gentry, 2009). The improved complexity of the proposed scheme stems from two sources. First, the authors have given a more aggressive security analysis of the *sparse subset sum problem* (SSSP) against lattice attacks as compared to the analysis presented in (Gentry, 2009). The SSSP along with the ideal lattice *bounded distance decoding* (BDD) problem are the two problems underlying the security of Gentry's fully homomorphic scheme. In his security analysis of BDD, Gentry has used the best known complexity bound for the approximate *shortest vector problem* (SVP) in lattices. However, in analyzing SSSP, Gentry has assumed the availability of an exact SVP oracle. On the contrary, the finer analysis of Stehle and Steinfield for SSSP takes into account the complexity of approximate SVP, thereby making it more consistent with the assumption underlying the analysis of the BDD problem. This leads to choices of smaller parameter in the scheme.

Moreover, Stehle and Steinfield have relaxed the definition of fully homomorphic encryption to allow for a negligible but non-zero probability of decryption error. They have shown that the randomness in the *SplitKey* key generation for the *squashed decryption algorithm* (i.e., the decryption algorithms of the bootstrappable scheme) in the Gentry's scheme can be gainfully exploited to allow a negligible decryption error probability. This decryption error, although negligible in value, can lead to rounding precision used in representing the ciphertext components that is almost half the value of the precision as achieved in Gentry's scheme (Gentry, 2009), which involves zero error probability.

In (Chunsheng, 2012), Chunsheng proposed a modification of the fully homomorphic encryption scheme of Smart and Vercauteren (Smart & Vercauteren, 2010). The author has applied a *self-loop bootstrappable technique* so that the security of the modified scheme only depends on the hardness of the *polynomial coset problem* and does not require any assumption of the *sparse subset problem* as required in the original work of Smart and Vercauteren (Smart & Vercauteren, 2010). In addition, the author have constructed a *non-self-loop fully homomorphic encryption scheme* that uses *cycle keys*. In a nutshell, the security of the improved fully homomorphic encryption scheme in this work is based on use of three mathematical approaches: (i) hardness of factoring integer problem, (ii) solving Diophantine equation problem, and (iii) finding approximate greatest common divisor problem.

Boneh and Freeman propose a linearly homomorphic signature scheme that authenticates vector subspaces of a given ambient space (Boneh & Freeman, 2011). The scheme has several novel features that were not present in any of the existing similar schemes. First, the scheme is the first of its kind that enables *authentication of vectors over binary fields*; previous schemes could not authenticate vectors with large or growing coefficients. Second, the scheme is the only scheme that is based on the *problem of finding short vectors in integer lattices*, and therefore, it enjoys the worst-case security guarantee that is common to *lattice-based cryptosystems*. The scheme can be used to authenticate linear transformations of signed data, such as those arising when computing mean and Fourier transform or in networks that use *network coding* (Boneh & Freeman, 2011). The work has three major contributions in the state of the art as identified by the authors: (i) *Homomorphic signatures over F_2*: the authors have constructed the first *unforgeable linearly homomorphic signature scheme* that authenticates vectors with coordinates in F_2. It is an example of a cryptographic primitive that can be built using lattice models, but cannot be built using bilinear maps or other traditional algebraic methods based on factoring or discrete log type problems. The scheme can be modified to authenticate vectors with coefficients in other small fields, including prime fields and extension fields such as F_{2^d}.

Moreover, the scheme is private, in the sense that a derived signature on a vector **v** leaks no information about the original signed vectors beyond what is revealed by **v**. (ii) *A simple k-time signature without random oracles*: the authors have presented a stateless signature scheme and have proved that it is secure in the standard model when used to sign at most k messages, for small values of k. The public key of the scheme is significantly smaller than that of any other stateless lattice-based signature scheme that can sign multiple large messages and is secure in the standard model. The construction proposed by the authors can be viewed as *removing the random oracle* from the signature scheme of Gentry, Peikert, and Vaikuntanathan (Gentry et al.,

2008), but only for signing k messages (Boneh & Freeman, 2011). (iii) *New tools for lattice-based signatures:* the scheme is unforgeable based on a new hard problem on lattices, which the authors have called the k-*small integer solutions* (k-SIS) problem. The authors have shown that k-SIS reduces to the *small integer solution* (SIS) problem, which is known to be as hard as standard worst-case lattice problems (Micciancio & Regev, 2007).

7. Conclusion and future trends

The study of fully homomorphic encryption has led to a number of new and exciting concepts and questions, as well as a powerful tool-kit to address them. We conclude the chapter by discussing a number of research directions related to the domain of fully homomorphic encryption and more generally, on the problem of computing on encrypted data.

Applications of fully homomorphic encryption: While Gentry's original construction was considered as being infeasible for practical deployments, recent constructions and implementation efforts have drastically improved the efficiency of fully homomorphic encryption (Vaikuntanathan, 2011). The initial implementation efforts focused on Gentry's original scheme and its variants (Smart & Vercauteren, 2010; Smart & Vercauteren, 2012; Coron et al., 2011; Gentry & Halevi, 2011), which seemed to pose rather inherent efficiency bottlenecks. Later implementations leverage the recent algorithmic advances (Brakerski & Vaikunathan, 2011; Brakerski et al., 2011; Brakerski & Vaikunathan, 2011a) that result in asymptotically better fully homomorphic encryption systems, as well as new algebraic mechanisms to improve the overall efficiency of these schemes (Naehrig et al., 2011; Gentry et al., 2012; Smart & Vercauteren, 2012).

Non-malleability and homomorphic encryption: Homomorphism and *non-malleability* are two orthogonal properties of an encryption scheme. Homomorphic encryption schemes permit anyone to transform an encryption of a message m into an encryption of $f(m)$ for non-trivial functions f. Non-malleable encryption, on the other hand, prevents precisely this sort of thing- it requires that no adversary be able to transform an encryption of m into an encryption of any *related* message. Essentially, what we need is a combination of both the properties that *selectively permit homomorphic computations* (Vaikuntanathan, 2011). This implies that the evaluator should be able to homomorphically compute any function from some pre-specified class F_{hom}; however, she should not be able to transform an encryption of m into an encryption of $f(m)$ for which $f \in F_{hom}$ does not hold good (i.e., f does not belong to F_{hom}). The natural question that arises is: *whether we can control what is being (homomorphically) computed?*

Answering this question turns out to be tricky. Boneh, Segev and Waters (Boneh et al., 2011) propose the notion of *targeted malleability* – a possible formalization of such a requirement as well as formal constructions of such encryption schemes. Their encryption scheme is based on a strong *knowledge of exponent-type* assumption that allows iterative evaluation of at most t functions, where t is a suitably determined and pre-specified constant. Improving their construction as well as the underlying complexity assumptions is an important open problem (Vaikuntanathan, 2011).

It is also interesting to extend the definition of non-malleability to allow for *chosen cipher-text attacks*. As an example, we consider the problem that involves *implementing an encrypted targeted advertisement system that generates advertisements depending on the contents of a user's e-mail*. Since the e-mail is stored in an encrypted form with the user's public key, the e-mail server performs a homomorphic evaluation and computes an encrypted advertisement to be sent back to the user. The user decrypts it, performs an action depending on what she sees. If the advertisement is relevant, she might choose to click on it; otherwise, she simply discards it. However, if the e-mail server is aware to this information, namely whether the user clicked on the advertisement or not, it can use this as a restricted *decryption oracle* to break the security of the user's encryption scheme and possibly even recover her secret key. Such attacks are ubiquitous whenever we compute on encrypted data, almost to the point that CCA security seems inevitable. Yet, it is easy to see that chosen ciphertext (CCA2-secure) homomorphic encryption schemes cannot exist. Therefore, an appropriate security definition and constructions that achieve the definition is in demand.

Fully homomorphic encryption and functional decryption: Homomorphic encryption schemes permit anyone to evaluate functions on encrypted data, but the evaluators never see any information about the result. It is possible to construct an encryption scheme where a user can compute *f(m)* from an encryption of a message *m*, but she should not be able to learn any other information about *m* (including the intermediate results in the computation of *f*)? Essentially, the issue boils down to the following question: *can we control the information that the evaluator can see?* Such an encryption scheme is called a *functional encryption scheme.* The concept of functional encryption scheme was first introduced by Sahai and Waters (Sahai & Waters, 2005) and subsequently investigated in a number of intriguing works (Katz et al., 2013; Lewko et al., 2010; Boneh et al., 2011; Agrawal et al., 2011). Although the constructions in these propositions work for several interesting families of functions (such as monotone formulas and inner products), construction of a fully functional encryption scheme is still not achieved and remains as an open problem. What we need is a novel and generic encryption system that provides us with fine-grained control over what one can see and access and what one can compute on data to get a desired output.

Other problems and applications: Another important open question relates to the assumptions underlying the current fully homomorphic encryption systems. All known fully homomorphic encryption schemes are based on *hardness of lattice problems*. The natural question that arises - can we construct fully homomorphic from other approaches – say, for example, from number-theoretic assumptions? Can we bring in the issue of the hardness of factoring or discrete logarithms in this problem?

In addition to the scenarios where it is beneficial to keep all data encrypted and to perform computations on encrypted data, fully homomorphic encryption can be gainfully exploited to solve a number of practical problems in cryptography. Two such examples are the problems of *verifiably outsourcing computation* (Goldwasser et al., 2008; Gennaro et al., 2010; Chung et al., 2010; Applebaum et al., 2010) and *constructing short non-interactive zero-knowledg e proofs* (Gentry, 2009). Some of the applications of fully homomorphic encryption do not require its full power. For example, in *private information retrieval* (PIR), it is sufficient to have a somewhat homomorphic encryption scheme that is capable of evaluating simple database indexing functions. For this applications, what is needed is an optimized and less functional encryption scheme that is more efficient than a fully homomorphic encryption function. Design of such functions for different application scenarios is also a current hot topic of research.

Author details

Jaydip Sen*

Department of Computer Science, National Institute of Science & Technology, Odisha, India

References

[1] Adelsbach, A., Katzenbeisser, S., & Sadeghi, A. (2002). Cryptography Meets Watermarking: Detecting Watermarks with Minimal or Zero Knowledge Disclosure. In: Proceedings of the European Signal Processing Conference (EUSIPCO'02), Vol 1, pp. 446-449, Toulouse, France.

[2] Agrawal, S., Freeman, D. M., & Vaikuntanathan, V. (2011). Functional Encryption for Inner Product Predicates from Learning with Errors. In: Advances in Cryptology-Proceedings of ASIACRYPT'11, Lecture Notes in Computer Science (LNCS), Vol 7073, Springer-Verlag, pp. 21-40.

[3] Ajtai, M. & Dwork, C. (1997). A Public Key Cryptosystem with Worst-Case/ Average-Case Equivalence. In: Proceedings of the 29th Annual ACM International Symposium on Theory of Computing (STOC'97), pp. 284-293, ACM Press, New York, NY, USA.

[4] Applebaum, B., Ishai, Y., & Kushilevitz, E. (2010). Semantic Security under Related-Key Attacks and Applications. Innovations in Computer Science (ICS), pp. 45-55, 2011.

[5] Applebaum, B., Ishai, Y., & Kushilevitz, E. (2010). From Secrecy to Soundness: Efficient Verification via Secure Computation. In: Automata, Language and Programming - Proceedings of ICALP, Lecture Notes in Computer Science (LNCS), Vol 6198, Springer-Verlag, pp. 152-163.

[6] Bao, F. (2003). Cryptanalysis of a Provable Secure Additive and Multiplicative Privacy Homomorphism. In: Proceedings of International Workshop on Coding and Cryptography (WCC'03), Versailles, France, pp. 43-49.

[7] Bellare, M. & Rogaway, P. (1995). Optimal Asymmetric Encryption- How to Encrypt with RSA. In: Advances in Cryptology - Proceedings of EUROCRYPT'94, Lecture Notes in Computer Science (LNCS), Vol 950, Springer-Verlag, pp. 92-111.

[8] Benaloh, J. (1994). Dense Probabilistic Encryption. In: Proceedings of the Workshop on Selected Areas of Cryptography, 1994, pp. 120-128.

[9] Benaloh, J. (1988). Verifiable Secret-Ballot Elections. Doctoral Dissertation, Department of Computer Science, Yale University, New Haven, Connecticut, USA.

[10] Ben-Or, M. & Cleve, R. (1992). Computing Algebraic Formulas Using a Constant Number of Registers. SIAM Journal on Computing, Vol 21, No 1, pp. 54-58, 1992.

[11] Blum, M. & Goldwasser, S. (1985). An Efficient Probabilistic Public-Key Encryption Scheme which Hides All Partial Information. In: Advances in Cryptology – Proceedings of EUROCRYPT'84, Lecture Notes in Computer Science (LNCS), Vol 196, Springer-Verlag, pp. 289-299.

[12] Boneh, D. & Freeman, D. M. (2011). Linearly Homomorphic Signatures over Binary Fields and New Tools for Lattice-Based Signatures. In: Public Key Cryptography (PKC'11), Lecture Notes in Computer Science (LNCS), Vol 6571, Springer-Verlag, pp. 1-16.

[13] Boneh, D. & Lipton, R. (1996). Searching for Elements in Black Box Fields and Applications. In: Advances in Cryptology- Proceedings of CRYPTO'96, Lecture Notes in Computer Science (LNCS), Vol 1109, Springer-Verlag, pp. 283-297.

[14] Boneh, D., Segev, G., & Waters, B. (2012). Targeted Malleability: Homomorphic Encryption for Restricted Computations. In: Proceedings of Innovations in Theoretical Computer Science (ITCS), pp 350-366, ACM Press, New York, NY, USA, 2012.

[15] Brakerski, Z., Gentry, C., & Vaikuntanathan, V. (2011). Fully Homomorphic Encryption without Bootstrapping. In: Proceedings of the 3rd Innovations in Theoretical Computer Science Conference (ITCS'12), pp. 309-325, ACM Press, New York, NY, USA.

[16] Brakerski, Z. & Vaikuntanathan, V. (2011). Fully Homomorphic Encryption from Ring-LWE and Security for Key Dependent Messages. In: Advances in Cryptology- Proceedings of CRYPTO'11, Lecture Notes in Computer Science (LNCS), Vol 6841, Springer-Verlag, pp. 505-524.

[17] Brakerski, Z. & Vaikuntanathan, V. (2011a). Efficient Fully Homomorphic Encryption from (Standard) LWE. In: Proceedings of the IEEE 52nd Annual Symposium on Foundations of Computer Science (FOCS'11), pp. 97-106, ACM Press, New York, NY, USA.

[18] Bresson, E., Catalano, D., & Pointcheval, D. (2003). A Simple Public-Key Cryptosystem with a Double Trapdoor Decryption Mechanism and its Applications. In: Advances in Cryptology- Proceedings of ASIACRYPT'03, Lecture Notes in Computer Science (LNCS), Vol 2894, Springer-Verlag, pp. 37-54.

[19] Brickell, E. F. & Yacobi, Y. (1987). On Privacy Homomorphisms. In: Advances in Cryptology – Proceedings of EUROCRYPT 1987, Lecture Notes in Computer Science (LNCS) Vol 304, Springer-Verlag, pp. 117-125.

[20] Canetti, R., Goldreich, O., & Halevi, S. (2004). The Random Oracle Methodology, Revisited. Journal of ACM (JACM), Vol 5, Issue 4, July 2004, pp. 557-594, ACM Press, New York, NY, USA.

[21] Castagnos, G. (2007). An Efficient Probabilistic Public-Key Cryptosystem over Quadratic Fields Quotients. Finite Fields and Their Applications, Vol 13, No 3, pp. 563-576, July 2007.

[22] Castagnos, G. (2006). Quelques Schemas De Cryptographic Asymetrique Probabiliste. Doctoral Dissertation, Universite De Limoges, 2006. Available Online at: http://epublications.unilim.fr/theses/2006/castagnos-guilhem/castagnos-guilhem.pdf

[23] Chung, K.-M., Kalai, Y. & Vadhan, S. (2010). Improved Delegation of Computation Using Fully Homomorphic Encryption. In: Advances in Cryptology - Proceedings of CRYPTO'10, Lecture Notes in Computer Science (LNCS), Vol 6223, Springer-Verlag, pp. 483-501.

[24] Chunsheng, G. (2012). More Practical Fully Homomorphic Encryption. International Journal of Cloud Computing and Services Science, Vol 1, Issue 4, pp. 199-201.

[25] Coron, J.-S., Mandal, A., Naccache, D., & Tibouchi, M. (2011). Fully Homomorphic Encryption over the Integers with Shorter Public Keys. In: Advances in Cryptology - Proceedings of CRYPTO'11, Lecture Notes in Computer Science (LNCS), Vol 6841, Springer-Verlag, pp. 487-504.

[26] Cramer, R. & Damgard, I. (1998). Zero-Knowledge Proofs for Finite Field Arithmetic, Or: Can Zero-Knowledge be for Free? In: Advances in Cryptology - Proceedings of CRYPTO'98, Lecture Notes in Computer Science (LNCS), Vol 1462, Springer-Verlag, pp. 424-441.

[27] Cramer, R., Damgard, I., & Maurer, U. (2000). General Secure Multi-party Computation from any Linear Secret-Sharing Scheme. In: Advances in Cryptology – Proceedings of EUROCRYPT'00, Lecture Notes in Computer Science (LNCS), Vol 1807, Springer-Verlag, pp. 316-334.

[28] Cramer, R. & Shoup, V. (2002). Universal Hash Proofs and a Paradigm for Adaptive Chosen Ciphertext Secure Public-Key Encryption. In: Advances in Cryptology – Proceedings of EUROCRYPT'02, Lecture Notes in Computer Science (LNCS), Vol 2332, Springer-Verlag, New York, NY, USA, pp. 45-64.

[29] Daemen, J. & Rijmen, V. (2002). The Design of Rijndael: AES- The Advanced Encryption Standard. Information Security and Cryptography, Springer, New York, NY, USA, 2002.

[30] Daemen, J. & Rijmen, V. (2000). The Block Cipher Rijndael. In: Proceedings of International Conference on Smart Cards Research and Applications (CARDS'98), Lecture Notes in Computer Science (LNCS), Vol 1820, Springer-Verlag, pp. 247-256.

[31] Damgard, I. & Jurik, M. (2003). A Length-Flexible Threshold Cryptosystem with Applications. In: Proceedings of the 8th Australasian Conference on Information Security and Privacy (ACSIP'03), Lecture Notes in Computer Science (LNCS), Vol 2727, Springer-Verlag, pp 350-364.

[32] Damgard, I. & Jurik, M. (2001). A Generalisation, a Simplification and Some Applications of Paillier's Probabilistic Public-Key System. In: Proceedings of the 4th International Workshop on Practice and Theory in Public Key Cryptography (PKC'01), Lecture Notes in Computer Science (LNCS), Vol 1992, Springer-Verlag, pp. 119-136.

[33] Damgard, I., Jurik, M., & Nielsen, J. (2010). A Generalization of Paillier's Public-Key System with Applications to Electronic Voting. International Journal on Information Security (IJIS), Special Issues on Special Purpose Protocol, Vol 9, Issue 6, December 2010, pp. 371-385, Springer-Verlag, Heidelberg, Berlin, Germany.

[34] Diffie, W. & Hellman, M. (1976). New Directions in Cryptography. IEEE Transactions on Information Theory, Vol 22, No 6, November 1976, pp. 644-654.

[35] Domingo-Ferrer, J. (2002). A Provably Secure Additive and Multiplicative Privacy Homomorphism. In: Proceedings of the 5th International Conference on Information Security (ISC'02), Lecture Notes in Computer Science (LNCS), Vol 2433, Springer-Verlag, pp. 471-483.

[36] Ekdahl, E. & Johansson, T. (2002). A New Version of the Stream Cipher SNOW. In: Proceedings of the 9th International Workshop on Selected Areas of Cryptography (SAC'02), Lecture Notes in Computer Science (LNCS), Vol 2595, Springer-Verlag, pp. 47-61.

[37] ElGamal, T. (1985). A Public Key Cryptosystem and a Signature Scheme Based on Discrete Logarithms. IEEE Transactions on Information Theory, Vol 31, Issue 4, July 1985, pp. 469-472.

[38] Feigenbaum, J. & Merritt, M. (1991). Open Questions, Talk Abstracts, and Summary of Discussions. DIMACS Series in Discrete Mathematics and Theoretical Computer Science, Vol 2, pp. 1-45.

[39] Fellows, M. & Koblitz, N. (1993). Combinatorial Cryptosystems Galore! Finite Fields-Theory, Applications and Algorithms. Contemporary Mathematics, Vol. 168, Las Vegas, 1994, pp. 51-61.

[40] Fontaine, C. & Galand, F. (2007). A Survey of Homomorphic Encryption for Nonspecialists. EURASIP Journal on Information Security, Vol 2007, January 2007, Article ID 15, Hindawi Publishing Corporation, New York, NY, USA. DOI: 10.1155/2007/13801.

[41] Fouque, P., Poupard, G., & Stern, J. (2000). Sharing Decryption in the Context of Voting or Lotteries. In: Proceedings of the 4th International Conference on Financial

Cryptography (FC'00), Lecture Notes in Computer Science (LNCS), Vol 1962, Spring-er-Verlag, pp. 90-104.

[42] Galbraith, S. D. (2002). Elliptic Curve Paillier Schemes. Journal of Cryptology, Vol 15, No 2, pp. 129-138, August 2002.

[43] Gennaro, R., Gentry, C., & Parno, B. (2010). Non-Interactive Verifiable Computing: Outsourcing Computation to Untrusted Workers. In: Advances in Cryptology-Proceedings of CRYPTO'10, Lecture Notes in Computer Science (LNCS), Vol 6223, Springer-Verlag, pp. 465-482.

[44] Gentry, C. (2010). Toward Basing Fully Homomorphic Encryption on Worst-Case Hardness. In: Advances in Cryptology- Proceedings of CRYPTO'10, Lecture Notes in Computer Science (LNCS), Vol 6223, Springer-Verlag, pp. 116-137.

[45] Gentry, C. (2009). Fully Homomorphic Encryption Using Ideal Lattices. In: Proceedings of the 41st Annual ACM Symposium on Theory of Computing (STOC'09), pp. 169-178, ACM Press, New York, NY, USA.

[46] Gentry, C. & Halevi, S. (2011). Implementing Gentry's Fully-Homomorphic Encryption Scheme. In: Advances in Cryptology - Proceedings of EUROCRYPT'11, Lecture Note in Computer Science (LNCS), Vol 6632, Springer-Verlag, pp. 129-148.

[47] Gentry, C, Halevi, S., & Smart, N. (2012). Better Bootstrapping in Fully Homomorphic Encryption. In: Proceedings of the 15th International Conference on Practice and Theory in Public Key Cryptography (PKC'12), Lecture Notes in Computer Science (LNCS), Vol 7293, Springer-Verlag, pp. 1-16.

[48] Gentry, C., Peikert, C., & Vaikuntanathan, V. (2008). Trapdoors for Hard Lattices and New Cryptographic Constructions. In: Proceedings of the 40th Annual ACM Symposium on Theory of Computing (STOC'08), pp. 197-206, ACM Press, New York, NY, USA.

[49] Goldreich, O., Goldwasser, S., & Halevi, S. (1997). Public-Key Cryptosystems from Lattice Reduction Problems. In: Advances in Cryptology- Proceedings of CRYPTO'97, Lecture Notes in Computer Science (LNCS), Vol 1294, Springer-Verlag, pp. 112-131.

[50] Goldwasser, S., Kalai, Y. T., & Rothblum, G. N. (2008). Delegating Computation: Interactive Proofs for Muggles. In: Proceedings of the 40th Annual ACM Symposium on Theory of Computing (STOC'08), pp. 113-122, ACM Press, New York, NY, USA.

[51] Goldwasser, S. & Micali, S. (1982). Probabilistic Encryption and How to Play Mental Poker Keeping Secret All Partial Information. In: Proceedings of the 14th Annual ACM Symposium on Theory of Computing (STOC'82), pp. 365-377, ACM Press, New York, NY, USA.

[52] Goldwasser, S. & Micali, S. (1984). Probabilistic Encryption. Journal of Computer and System Sciences, Vol 28, Issue 2, pp. 270-299, April 1984.

[53] Golle, P., Jakobsson, M., Juels, A., & Syverson, P. (2004). Universal Re-Encryption for Mixnets. In: Topics in Cryptology - Proceedings of the RSA Conference Cryptographers' Track (CT-RSA'04), Lecture Notes in Computer Science (LNCS), Vol 2964, Springer-Verlag, pp. 163-178.

[54] Grigoriev, D. & Ponomarenko. (2006). Homomorphic Public-Key Cryptosystems and Encrypting Boolean Circuits. Applicable Algebra in Engineering, Communication and Computing, Vol 17, Issue 3-4, pp. 239-255, August 2006.

[55] Grigoriev, D. & Ponomarenko, I. (2004). Homomorphic Public-Key Cryptosystems over Groups and Rings. Quaderni di Mathematica, Vol 13, pp. 304-325, 2004.

[56] Groth, J. (2004). Rerandomizable and Replayable Adaptive Chosen Ciphertext Attack Secure Cryptosystems. In: Proceedings of the 1st Theory of Cryptography Conference (TCC'04), Lecture Notes in Computer Science (LNCS), Vol 2951, Springer-Verlag, pp. 152-170.

[57] Hoffstein, J., Pipher, J., & Silverman, J. (1998). NTRU: A Ring-Based Public Key Cryptosystem. In: Proceedings of the 3rd International Symposium on Algorithmic Number Theory (ANTS-III), ANTS'98, Lecture Notes in Computer Science (LNCS), Vol 1423, Springer-Verlag, pp. 267-288.

[58] Katz, J. Sahai, A., & Waters, B. (2013). Predicate Encryption Supporting Disjunctions, Polynomial Equations, and Inner Products. Journal of Cryptology, Vol 26, Issue 2, pp. 191-224, April 2013, Springer-Verlag, Berlin, Heidelberg, Germany.

[59] Ko, K. H., Lee, S. J. Cheon, J. H., Han, J. W., Kang, J.-S., & Park, C. (2000). New Public-Key Cryptosystem Using Braid Groups. In: Advances in Cryptology – Proceedings of CRYPTO'00, Lecture Notes in Computer Science (LNCS), Vol 1880, Springer-Verlag, pp. 166-183.

[60] Koblitz, N. (1998). Algebraic Aspects of Cryptography: Algorithms and Computation in Mathematics, Vol 3, Springer-Verlag, Berlin, Heidelberg, Germany, 1998.

[61] Lewko, A. B., Okamoto, T., Sahai, A. Takashima, K. & Waters, B. (2010). Fully Secure Functional Encryption: Attribute-Based Encryption and (Hierarchical) Inner Product Encryption. In: Advances in Cryptology- Proceedings of EUROCRYPT'10, Lecture Notes in Computer Science (LNCS), Vol 6110, Springer-Verlag, pp. 62-91.

[62] Lipmaa, H. (2003). Verifiable Homomorphic Oblivious Transfer and Private Equality Test. In: Advances in Cryptology- Proceedings of ASIACRYPT'03, Lecture Notes in Computer Science (LNCS), Vol 2894, Springer-Verlag, pp. 416-433.

[63] Ly, L. V. (2002). Polly Two - A Public-Key Cryptosystem Based on Polly Cracker. Doctoral Dissertation, Ruhr-Universitat, Bochum, Germany, October 2002.

[64] Lyubashevsky, V. & Micciancio, D. (2008). Asymptotically Efficient Lattice-Based Digital Signatures. In: Proceedings of the 5th International Conference on Theory of

Cryptography (TCC'08), Lecture Notes in Computer Science (LNCS), Vol 4948, Springer-Verlag, pp. 37-54.

[65] Lyubashevsky, V. & Micciancio, D. (2006). Generalized Compact Knapsacks are Collision Resistant. In: Proceedings of the 33rd International Conference on Automata, Languages and Programming (ICALP'06), Lecture Notes in Computer Science (LNCS), Vol 4052, Springer-Verlag, pp. 144-155.

[66] Lyubashevsky, V., Micciancio, D., Peikert, C., & Rosen, A. (2008). SWIFT: A Modest Proposal for FFT Hashing. In: Proceedings of the 15th International Workshop on Fast Software Encryption (FSE'08), Lecture Notes in Computer Science (LNCS), Vol 5068, Springer-Verlag, pp. 54-72.

[67] Lyubashevsky, V., Peikert, C., & Regev, O. (2010). On Ideal Lattices and Learning with Errors over Rings. In: Advances in Cryptology- Proceedings of EURO-CRYPT'10, Lecture Notes in Computer Science (LNCS), Vol 6110, Springer-Verlag, pp. 1-23.

[68] Menezes, A., Van Orschot, P. & Vanstone, S. (1997). Handbook of Applied Cryptography. CRC Press, USA. Available Online at: http://www.cacr.math.uwaterloo.ca/hac/.

[69] Micciancio, D. (2007). Generalized Compact Knapsacks, Cyclic Lattices, and Efficient One-Way Functions. Computational Complexity, Vol 16, No 4, pp. 365-411, December 2007.

[70] Micciancio, D. (2001). Improving Lattice Based Cryptosystems Using Hermite Normal Form. In: Cryptography and Lattices - Proceedings of the International Conference on Cryptography and Lattices (CaLC'01), Lecture Notes in Computer Science (LNCS), Vol 2146, Springer-Verlag, pp. 126-145.

[71] Micciancio, D. & Regev, O. (2007). Worst-Case to Average-Case Reductions Based on Gaussian Measures. SIAM Journal on Computing, Vol 37, Issue 1, pp. 267-302, April 2007.

[72] Naccache, D. & Stern, J. (1998). A New Public Key Cryptosystem Based on Higher Residues. In: Proceedings of the 5th ACM Conference on Computer and Communications Security (CCS'98), pp. 59-66, ACM Press, New York, NY, USA.

[73] Naehrig, M., Lauter, K., & Vaikuntanathan, V. (2011). Can Homomorphic Encryption be Practical? In: Proceedings of the 3rd ACM Workshop on Cloud Computing Security, pp. 113-124, ACM Press, New York, NY, USA.

[74] Nguyen, P. & Stern, J. (1999). Cryptanalysis of the Ajtai-Dwork Cryptosystem. In: Advances in Cryptology – Proceedings of CRYPTO'98, Lecture Notes in Computer Science (LNCS), Springer-Verlag, Vol 1462, New York, NY, USA, pp. 223-242.

[75] Ogura, N., Yamamoto, G., Kobayashi, T., & Uchiyama, S. (2010). An Improvement of Key Generation Algorithm for Gentry's Homomorphic Encryption Scheme. In: Ad-

vances in Information and Computer Security- Proceedings of the 5th International Conference on Advances in Information and Computer Security (IWSEC'10), Lecture Notes in Computer Science (LNCS), Vol 6434, Springer-Verlag, pp. 70-83.

[76] Okamoto, T. & Uchiyama, S. (1998). A New Public-Key Cryptosystem as Secure as Factoring. In: Advances in Cryptology- Proceedings of EUROCRYPT'98, Lecture Notes in Computer Science (LNCS), Vol 1403, Springer-Verlag, pp. 308-318.

[77] Okamoto, T., Uchiyama, S., & Fujisaki, E. (2000). EPOC: Efficient Probabilistic Public-Key Encryption. Technical Report, 2000, Proposal to IEEE P1363a. Available Online at: http://grouper.iee.org/groups/1363/StudyGroup/NewFam.html.

[78] Paeng, S.-H, Ha, K.-C., Kim, J. H., Chee, S., & Park, C. (2001). New Public Key Cryptosystem Using Finite Non Abelian Groups. In: Advances in Cryptology- Proceedings of CRYPTO'01, Lecture Notes in Computer Science (LNCS), Vol 2139, Springer-Verlag, pp. 470-485.

[79] Paillier, P. (2007). Impossibility Proofs for RSA Signatures in the Standard Model. In: Topics in Cryptology - Proceedings of the RSA Conference Cryptographers' Track (CT-RSA'07), Lecture Notes in Computer Science (LNCS), Vol 4377, pp. 31-48, San Francisco, California, USA.

[80] Paillier, P. (1999). Public-Key Cryptosystems Based on Composite Degree Residuosity Classes. In: Advances in Cryptology – Proceedings of EUROCRYPT'99, Lecture Notes in Computer Science (LNCS), Vol 1592, Springer-Verlag, pp. 223-238.

[81] Pfitzmann, B. & Waidner, M. (1997). Anonymous Fingerprinting. In: Advances in Cryptology- Proceedings of the EUROCRYPT'97, Lecture Notes in Computer Science (LNCS), Vol 1233, Springer-Verlag, pp. 88-102.

[82] Peikert, C. & Rosen, A. (2007). Lattices that Admit Logarithmic Worst-Case to Average-Case Connection Factors. In: Proceedings of the 39th Annual ACM Symposium on Theory of Computing (STOC'07), pp. 478-487, ACM Press, June 2007.

[83] Peikert, C. & Rosen, A. (2006). Efficient Collision-Resistant Hashing from Worst-Case Assumptions on Cyclic Lattices. In: Theory of Cryptography - Proceedings of the 3rd International Conference on Theory of Cryptography (TCC'06), Lecture Notes in Computer Science (LNCS), Vol 3876, Springer-Verlag, pp. 145-166.

[84] Poupard, G. & Stern, J. (2000). Fair Encryption of RSA Keys. In: Advances in Cryptology- Proceedings of EUROCRYPT'00, Lecture Notes in Computer Science (LNCS), Vol 1807, Springer-Verlag, pp. 172-189.

[85] Rappe, D. (2004). Homomorphic Cryptosystems and their Applications. Doctoral Dissertation. University of Dortmund, Dortmund, Germany.

[86] Regev, O. (2005). On Lattices, Learning with Errors, Random Linear Codes, and Cryptography. In: Proceedings of the 37th Annual ACM Symposium on Theory of Computing (STOC'05), pp. 84-93, ACM Press, New York, NY, USA.

[87] Rivest, R., Adleman, L., & Dertouzos, M. (1978a). On Data Banks and Privacy Homomorphisms. Foundations of Secure Communication, pp. 169-177, Academic Press.

[88] Rivest, R., Shamir, A., & Adleman, L. (1978b). A Method for Obtaining Digital Signatures and Public-Key Cryptosystems. Communications of the ACM, Vol 21, No 2, pp. 120-126.

[89] Sahai, A. & Waters, B. (2005). Fuzzy Identity-Based Encryption. In: Advances in Cryptology - Proceedings of EUROCRYPT'05, Lecture Notes in Computer Science (LNCS), Vol 3494, Springer-Verlag, pp. 457-473.

[90] Sander, T. & Tschudin, C. F. (1998). Towards Mobile Cryptography. In: Proceedings of IEEE Symposium on Security & Privacy, Oakland, California, USA, pp. 215-224, May 1998.

[91] Sander, T. & Tshudin, C. F. (1998a). Protecting Mobile Agents against Malicious Hosts. In: Proceedings of International Conference on Mobile Agents and Security, Lecture Notes in Computer Science (LNCS), Vol 1419, Springer-Verlag, pp. 44-60.

[92] Sander, T., Young, A., & Yung, M. (1999). Non-Interactive CryptoComputing for NC. In: Proceedings of the 40th Annual IEEE Symposium on Foundations of Computer Science, pp. 564-566, October 1999.

[93] Shannon, C. (1949). Communication Theory of Secrecy Systems. Bell System Technical Journal, Vol 28, Issue 4, pp. 656-715, October 1949.

[94] Smart, N. P. & Vercauteren, F. (2010). Fully Homomorphic Encryption with Relatively Small Key and Ciphertext Sizes. In: Public Key Cryptography - Proceedings of the 13th International Conference on Practice and Theory in Public Key Cryptography (PKC'10), Lecture Notes in Computer Science (LNCS), Vol 6056, Springer-Verlag, pp. 420-443.

[95] Smart, N. & Vercauteren. (2012). Fully Homomorphic SIMD Operations. Design Codes and Cryptography, Springer, USA, July 2012.

[96] Stehle, D. & Steinfeld, R. (2010). Faster Fully Homomorphic Encryption. In: Advances in Cryptology – Proceedings of ASIACRYPT'10, Lecture Notes in Computer Science (LNCS), Vol 6477, Springer-Verlag, pp. 377-394.

[97] Vaikuntanathan, V. (2011). Computing Blindfolded: New Developments in Fully Homomorphic Encryption. In: Proceedings of the IEEE 52nd Annual Symposium on Foundations of Computer Science (FOCS'11), pp. 5-16, IEEE Computer Society Press, Washington, DC, USA.

[98] Van Tilborg, H. C. A. & Jajodia, S. (Eds) (2011). Encyclopaedia of Cryptography and Security. Springer-Verlag, New York, NY, USA, 2011.

[99] Vernam, G. S. (1926). Cipher Printing Telegraph Systems for Secret Wire and Radio Telegraphic Communications. Journal of the American Institute of Electrical Engineers, Vol 45, pp. 295-301.

[100] Wagner, D. (2003). Cryptanalysis of an Algebraic Privacy Homomorphism. In: Proceedings of the 6th International Conference on Information Security (ISC'03), Lecture Notes in Computer Science (LNCS), Vol 2851, Springer-Verlag, pp.234-239.

[101] Wagner, N. R. & Magyarik, M. R. (1985). A Public Key Cryptosystem Based on the Word Problem. In: Advances in Cryptology- Proceedings of CRYPTO'84, Lecture Notes in Computer Science (LNCS), Vol 196, Springer-Verlag, pp. 19-36.

Chapter 3

Optical Communication with Weak Coherent Light Fields

Kim Fook Lee, Yong Meng Sua and
Harith B. Ahmad

Additional information is available at the end of the chapter

1. Introduction

Entanglement and superposition are foundations for the emerging field of quantum communication and information processing. These two fundamental features of quantum mechanics have made quantum key distribution unconditionally secure (Scarani et al., 2009; Weedbrook et al., 2010) compared to communication based on classical key distribution. Currently, implementation of an optical quantum communication is mainly based on discrete and continuous quantum variables. They are usually generated through nonlinear interaction processes in $\chi^{(2)}$ (Kwiat et al., 1995) and $\chi^{(3)}$ (Lee et al., 2006,2009) media. Discrete-variable qubit based implementations using polarization (Liang et al., 2006, 2007; Chen et al. 2007, 2008; Sharping et al., 2006) and time-bin (Brendel et al., 1999; Tittel et al., 1998, 1999) entanglement have difficulty to obtain unconditional-ness, and also usually have low optical data-rate because of post-selection technique with low probability of success in a low efficient single photon detector at telecom-band (Liang et al., 2005, 2006, 2007). Continuous-variable implementations using quadrature entanglement (Yonezawa et al., 2004; Bowen et al., 2003; Silberhorn et al., 2002) and polarization squeezing (Korolkova et al., 2002) can have high efficiency and high optical data-rate because of available high speed and efficient homodyne detection. However, the quality of quadrature entanglement is very sensitive to loss, which is imperfect for implementing any entanglement based quantum protocols over long distance. Continuous-variable protocols that do not rely on entanglement, for instance, coherent-state based quantum communication (Yuen, 2004; Corndorf et al., 2003; Barbosa et al., 2003; Grosshans et al., 2002, 2003; Qi et al., 2007; Wilde Qi et al., 2008), are perfect for long distance optical communication. Several experimental approaches were taken to resolve transmission loss for long distance optical communication by using coherent light source. Optical wave mechanical implementations (Lee et al., 2002, 2004) of entanglement and superposition with coherent fields have been demonstrated.

We discuss and demonstrate a new type of optical communications based on weak coherent light fields in detail in this chapter.

2. Correlation functions of two weak light fields

Two orthogonal light fields are used to implement correlation function between two distant observers. In the Stapp's approach (Grib et al., 1999; Peres, 1995) for two distant observers A and B, when analyzer A is oriented along the polarization angle θ_1, the transmitted $|\theta_1\rangle_{//}$ and reflected $|\theta_1\rangle_\perp$ polarization vectors of the light are given by,

$$|\theta_1\rangle_{//} = \cos\theta_1 |H_1\rangle + \sin\theta_1 |V_1\rangle, \tag{1}$$

$$|\theta_1\rangle_\perp = -\sin\theta_1 |H_1\rangle + \cos\theta_1 |V_1\rangle, \tag{2}$$

where the H and V are the horizontal and vertical axes. Analyzer A is a combination of half wave plate (HWP) and a polarization beam splitter (PBS) for projecting the linear polarization of the incoming photon. The operator associated with analyzer A can be represented by

$$\hat{A}_1 = |\theta_1\rangle_{//}\langle\theta_1| - |\theta_1\rangle_\perp\langle\theta_1|, \tag{3}$$

$$\hat{A}_1 = Cos2\theta_1 \left(|H_1\rangle\langle H_1| - |V_1\rangle\langle V_1| \right) + Sin2\theta_1 \left(|H_1\rangle\langle V_1| + |V_1\rangle\langle H_1| \right). \tag{4}$$

The operator A_1 has eigenvalues of ±1, such that,

$$\hat{A}_1 |\theta_1\rangle_{//} = 1 |\theta_1\rangle_{//}, \tag{5}$$

$$\hat{A}_1 |\theta_1\rangle_\perp = -1 |\theta_1\rangle_\perp. \tag{6}$$

Depending on the photon is transmitted or rejected by the analyzer. Similarly, the analyzer B oriented at θ_2 can be defined as operator B_2,

$$\hat{B}_2 = Cos2\theta_2 \left(|H_2\rangle\langle H_2| - |V_2\rangle\langle V_2| \right) + Sin2\theta_2 \left(|H_2\rangle\langle V_2| + |V_2\rangle\langle H_2| \right). \tag{7}$$

Operator $A_1(B_2)$ with eigenvalues of ±1 can be measured by using the balanced detection scheme as shown in Fig. 1. Two detectors are placed at the two output ports of a cube polarization beam splitter. Their output currents are subtracted from each other. The arrangement of this detection scheme can be used for measuring operator A_1 of Eq.(4) and B_2 of Eq.(7) that is the subtraction between the projection of the transmitted signal $D_{//}$ and the projection of the reflected signal $D_\perp$.

Let's consider a beam of photons incidents on the PBS, if one photon goes through the PBS, it will produce non-zero signal at detector $D_{//}$ and zero signal at detector $D_\perp$. Then, the subtraction yields positive signal as of $D_{//} - D_\perp \geq 0$. If a photon is reflected from the PBS, it will go to the detector $D_\perp$ and produce non-zero signal at detector $D_\perp$ and zero signal at detector $D_{//}$. Then, the subtraction yields negative signal as of $D_{//} - D_\perp \leq 0$. For a certain amount of time, the subtraction records the random positive and negative spikes corresponding to the eigenvalues of +1 and -1 of operator A_1, respectively, as shown in the inset of Fig. 1.

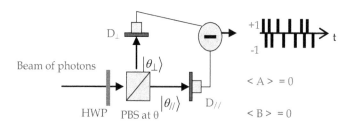

Figure 1. Detection scheme based on balanced homodyne detection for measuring operators A_1 and B_2.

If the incoming photons are in the superposition of $|\theta_1\rangle_{//}$ and $|\theta_1\rangle_\perp$, the detection scheme A records a series of discrete random values, +1 and -1. Then, the mean value of A_1 is zero, that is $\langle A_1 \rangle = 0$. Similarly, we can apply the same detection scheme for measuring operator B_2 and obtain $\langle B_2 \rangle = 0$. The expectation value of the product $\langle A_1 B_2 \rangle$ or the mean value of the product signals of A_1 and B_2 will produce correlation functions, as given by,

$$C(\theta_1,\theta_2) \propto \langle A_1 B_2 \rangle \propto \pm \cos 2(\theta_1 \pm \theta_2). \tag{8}$$

As shown in Eq.(8) above, there are 4 type of correlation functions analog to four Bell states. Theoritical prediction for the mean value measurements of $\langle A_1 B_2 \rangle$ are shown in Fig. 2.

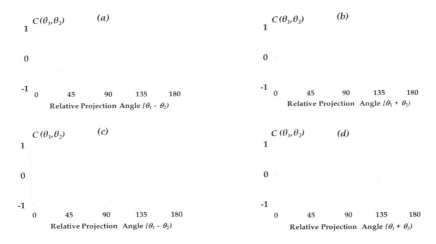

Figure 2. Theoritical prediction of correlation functions (a) $-\cos 2(\theta_1 - \theta_2)$, (b) $-\cos 2(\theta_1 + \theta_2)$, (c) $\cos 2(\theta_1 - \theta_2)$, (d) $\cos 2(\theta_1 + \theta_2)$.

3. Balanced homodyne detector

Balanced homodyne detector is utilised as the detection scheme for the weak coherent light fields for optical communication.

It consists of a 50/50 beam splitter, two photo detectors, a local oscillator field and a transimpendance amplifier. Superposed local oscillator field and weak light field will be detected by photodiodes D_1 and D_2, lead to the generation of the photocurrent I_1 and I_2. The photodiodes are connected together in such a way that the output equal to the I_1 minus I_2 as shown in Fig. 3.

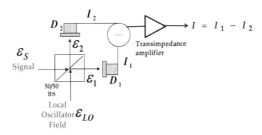

Figure 3. Balanced Homodyne detection.

The balanced detector has two input ports. The signal field and local oscillator field optically mixed at the beam splitter. The local oscillator field is a large amplitude lightwave with the same frequency as the signal and having a well-defined phase with respect to the signal field. Generally, local oscillator field can be obtained from the same laser source as the signal field. The emerging output fields ε_1 and ε_2 are the superposition of signal and local oscillator fields. The output fields ε_1 and ε_2 are given as,

$$\varepsilon_1 = \frac{1}{\sqrt{2}}(\varepsilon_{LO} + \varepsilon_s), \quad \text{(a)}$$
$$\varepsilon_2 = \frac{1}{\sqrt{2}}(\varepsilon_{LO} - \varepsilon_s). \quad \text{(b)}$$

(9)

where ε_{LO} and ε_s are the amplitude of the signal and local oscillator field respectively. Photocurrents that produced by the output fields ε_1 and ε_2 are given as

$$I_1 = |\varepsilon_1|^2 = \varepsilon_1 \varepsilon_1^*, \tag{10}$$

$$I_2 = |\varepsilon_2|^2 = \varepsilon_2 \varepsilon_2^*. \tag{11}$$

Hence, the output of the balanced homodyne detector will be given as,

$$I_1 - I_2 = 2\varepsilon_s \varepsilon_{LO}. \tag{12}$$

Since the signal and local oscillator fields are derived from the same laser source with relative phase φ. By considering only the real part of the signal and local oscillator fields, it can be described as,

$$\varepsilon_s = A\varepsilon_s Cos(\omega t), \tag{13}$$

$$\varepsilon_{LO} = A\varepsilon_{LO} Cos(\omega t + \varphi). \tag{14}$$

Where $A\varepsilon_s$ and $A\varepsilon_{LO}$ are the amplitude for signal and local oscillator fields, ω is optical frequency, φ is relative phase between the fields. Hence the output of the balanced homodyne detector is given by,

$$I_1 - I_2 = |A\varepsilon_s||A\varepsilon_{LO}|\{\cos(\varphi) + \cos(2\omega t + \varphi)\}. \tag{15}$$

The second term in the Eq.(15) is the fast varying term beyond the detection of the of the photo detector. Therefore, the output of the balanced homodyne detector is phase dependence, which is given by,

$$I_1 - I_2 \propto \left|A\varepsilon_s\right|\left|A\varepsilon_{LO}\right|\cos(\varphi). \tag{16}$$

One of the main features of the balanced homodyne detector is the high signal to noise ratio compared to a single detector. For example, classical intensity fluctuations of the laser would affect the measurement of a single detector. Contrary, any changes in intensity will be canceled by the subtraction of the photocurrent with an ideal balanced homodyne detector.

However, due to the Poissonian statistics of the coherent light and random splitting process in the 50/50 beam splitter, fluctuations in intensity cannot be completely removed. Therefore even with the presence of only local oscillator field, the balanced homodyne detector will have a shot noise level above the electronics noise level as depicted in Fig.4, limiting the signal to noise ratio.

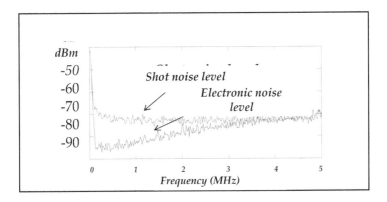

Figure 4. Frequency spectrum of balanced homodyne detector. The red line is the electronics noise of the BHD without any light while the blue line is the shot noise level of the BHD with the presence of the local oscillator field.

4. Practical demonstration of the optical communication with two weak light fields

A proof-of-principle experiment to demonstrate the correlations of two weak light fields as described in section 2 is shown in Fig.5. A continuous wave laser at telecom band wavelength (1534nm) is used to provide two orthogonal weak light fields. We use a 50/50 beam splitter to optically mix the vertically and horizontally polarized coherent light fields. The beam 1 from the output port 1 of the beam splitter is a superposition of the vertically and horizontally polarized weak light fields, similarly for beam 2 from output port 2 of the beam splitter. The balanced homodyne detectors are made of two p-i-n photodiodes (EXT500) and the signal measured by the balanced homodyne detectors will be further amplified by a transimpedance amplifier. A quarter wave plate at 45° as part of measuring device is inserted at beams 1 and 2 to transform the linearly polarized states to circularly polarized states. By using a quarter wave plate transformation matrix, the field amplitudes V_1, H_1, V_2 and H_2 are transformed as,

$$
\begin{aligned}
V_1 &\rightarrow -i\hat{H}_1 + \hat{V}_1, &\text{(a)} \\
H_1 &\rightarrow \hat{H}_1 - i\hat{V}_1, &\text{(b)} \\
V_2 &\rightarrow -i\hat{H}_2 + \hat{V}_2, &\text{(c)} \\
H_2 &\rightarrow \hat{H}_2 - i\hat{V}_2, &\text{(d)}
\end{aligned}
\qquad (17)
$$

where the phase shift due to the beam splitter is included.

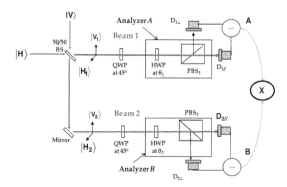

Figure 5. Experimental setup for demonstration of the optical communication with weak coherent light fields.

For simplicity we use unit vector notation and drop the amplitude of field notation. Now, analyzer A in beam 1 will experience homogeneous superposition of left circularly polarized and right circularly polarized weak light fields. Similarly for analyzer B in beam 2. Analyzer $A(B)$ is placed before the balanced homodynes detector $A(B)$ to project out the phase angle 1(2) as,

$$
\hat{e}_1 \rightarrow \cos\theta_1 \hat{H}_1 + \sin\theta_1 \hat{V}_1, \tag{18}
$$

$$
\hat{e}_2 \rightarrow \cos\theta_2 \hat{H}_2 + \sin\theta_2 \hat{V}_2. \tag{19}
$$

The superposed field in beam 1 after the $\lambda/4$ wave plate and the analyzer can be expressed as,

$$
\begin{aligned}
E_1(t) &= [(\hat{H}_1 - i\hat{V}_1)e^{-i(wt+\varphi)}] + (i\hat{H}_1 - \hat{V}_1)e^{-iwt}] \cdot \hat{e}_1 \\
&= (-\cos\theta_1 + i\sin\theta_1)e^{-i(wt-i\varphi)} \\
&\quad + (-i\cos\theta_1 + \sin\theta_1)e^{-iwt}.
\end{aligned}
\tag{20}
$$

and similarly for the superposed field in beam 2,

$$
\begin{aligned}
E_2(t) &= [(\hat{H}_2 - i\hat{V}_2)e^{-i(wt+\varphi)}] + (i\hat{H}_2 - \hat{V}_2)e^{-iwt}] \cdot \hat{e}_2 \\
&= (-\cos\theta_2 + i\sin\theta_2)e^{-i(wt+\varphi)} \\
&\quad + (-i\cos\theta_2 + \sin\theta_2)e^{-iwt},
\end{aligned}
\tag{21}
$$

where ω is optical frequency, and φ is the relative phase of the two orthogonal weak light fields. Thus, the interference signals obtained by the photodetector $D_{1//}$ in balanced homodyne detectors at beam 1 are given as,

$$
\begin{aligned}
D_{1//}(\varphi) &= -ie^{-i(2\theta_1+\varphi)} + c.c \\
&\propto \sin(2\theta_1 + \varphi). \quad\quad (a) \\
D_{1\perp}(\varphi) &= ie^{-i(2\theta_1+\pi+\varphi)} + c.c \\
&\propto -\sin(2\theta_1 + \varphi). \quad (b)
\end{aligned}
\tag{22}
$$

On the other hand, for photodetector $D_{2//}$, the reflected beat signal becomes 22b

Then, the balanced detector A measures

$$
\begin{aligned}
A_1(\varphi) &= D_{1//} - D_{1\perp} \\
&= 2\sin(2\theta_1 + \varphi).
\end{aligned}
\tag{23}
$$

Similarly, the interference signals obtained by the photodetectors in balanced homodyne detector at beam 2 can be written as,

$$
\begin{aligned}
D_{2//}(\varphi) &= ie^{-i(2\theta_2+\pi+\varphi)} + c.c \\
&\propto -\sin(2\theta_2 + \varphi), \quad\quad (a) \\
D_{2\perp}(\varphi) &= -ie^{-i(2\theta_2+\pi+\varphi)} + c.c \\
&\propto \sin(2\theta_2 + \varphi), \quad\quad (b)
\end{aligned}
\tag{24}
$$

and the balanced detector B measures

$$
\begin{aligned}
B_2(\varphi) &= D_{2//} - D_{2\perp} \\
&= -2\sin(2\theta_2 + \varphi).
\end{aligned}
\tag{25}
$$

The interference signals of Eq.(23) and Eq.(25) above for balanced detectors A and B are the measurements of operators A_1 and B_2, respectively. The interference signal in detector A is anti-correlated to detector B because of the phase shift of the beam splitter. The interference signals contain information of the projection angles of the analyzers. The average of the interference signals is zero, that is, $<A_1> = 0$ and $<B_2> = 0$. To further discuss the significant of measuring the operator A_1, the interference signals obtained in balanced detector A can be rewritten as,

$$
A_1(\varphi) = 2\{\cos(2\theta_1)\sin(\varphi) + \sin(2\theta_1)\cos(\varphi)\},
\tag{26}
$$

which is identical in structure with operator A_1 as in Eq.(4), that is

$$
\hat{A}_1 = Cos2\theta_1 \left(|H_1\rangle\langle H_1| - |V_1\rangle\langle V_1| \right) - Sin2\theta_1 \left(|H_1\rangle\langle V_1| + |V_1\rangle\langle H_1| \right).
\tag{27}
$$

The factor of 2 in Eq.(26) is due to the 3 dB gain obtained by balanced detection scheme. Note that the unit polarization projectors $\left(|H_1\rangle\langle H_1| - |V_1\rangle\langle V_1| \right)$ and $\left(|H_1\rangle\langle V_1| + |V_1\rangle\langle H_1| \right)$ in Eq.(27) can be interpreted by in-phase and out-of-phase components of the light field. Similarly for the interference signals obtained in balanced detector B.

The interference signals in detectors A and B are then multiplied to obtain the anti-correlated multiplication signal,

$$
\begin{aligned}
A_1 \times B_2 &\propto -\sin(2\theta_1 + \varphi)\sin(2\theta_2 + \varphi) \\
&\propto -\cos(2(\theta_1 - \theta_2)) - \cos(2(\theta_1 + \theta_2 + \varphi)).
\end{aligned}
\tag{28}
$$

Then, the mean value of this multiplied signal is measured. We obtain one of the correlation functions $C(\theta_1, \theta_2)$ as described in section 2,

$$
\overline{A_1 \times B_2} \propto C(\theta_1, \theta_2) \propto -\cos 2(\theta_1 - \theta_2),
\tag{29}
$$

where the second term in Eq.(26) is averaging to zero due to the slow varying relative phase φ of the two orthogonal weak light fields from 0 to 2π. We normalized the correlation function $C(\theta_1, \theta_2)$ with its maximum obtainable value that is, $\theta_1 = \theta_2$. Thus, for the setting of the analyzers at $\theta_1 = \theta_2$, the normalized correlation function $C(\theta_1, \theta_2) = -1$ shows that the two beams are anti-correlated. To generate other correlation functions, such as $C(\theta_1, \theta_2) \propto -\cos 2(\theta_1 + \theta_2)$ the $\lambda/4$ wave plate at beam 2 is rotated at -45°, then the beat signal measured by balanced homodyne detector B_2 of Eq.(25) is given by

$$B_2(\varphi) \propto D_{2//}(\varphi) - D_{2\perp}(\varphi) \propto -2\sin(2\theta_2 - \varphi). \tag{30}$$

Hence, obtaining the correlation function,

$$C(\theta_1, \theta_2) \propto -\cos 2(\theta_1 + \theta_2). \tag{31}$$

As for correlation function $C(\theta_1, \theta_2) \propto \cos 2(\theta_1 - \theta_2)$ a $\lambda/2$ plate in beam 2 is inserted, then the minus sign of beat signal B_2 of Eq.(30) is changed to positive sign, yielding the desired correlation function. Similarly, with the $\lambda/2$ wave plate at beam 2 and the $\lambda/4$ wave plate at beam 2 rotated at -45°, the beat signal B_2 of Eq.(30) is equal to $2\sin(2\theta_2 - \varphi)$. Thus, providing the last correlation function $C(\theta_1, \theta_2) \propto \cos 2(\theta_1 + \theta_2)$.

4.1. Correlation measurement of a stable field and a noise field

To verify the above analysis and measurement method for weak light fields, we present an experiment measurement of one stable coherent light field and one random noise phase modulated light field.

One stable coherent field is mixed with one noise field in a beam splitter. The experimental result has been recently published(Lee, 2009). Fig. 6(a) and (b) are the beat signals obtained at A and B, where the phase $\phi_c(t)$ is modulated with random noise through an acousto-optic modulator. The product of the beat signal at A and B is shown in Fig. 6(c). The mean-value measurement produces the bipartite correlation $-\cos2(\theta_1 - \theta_2)$, which is still classical correlation. However, it is obvious that the information of θ_1 and θ_2 are protected by classical noise not quantum noise. Classical noise is not completely random compared to quantum noise as inherited by coherent state.

In the next section, two weak coherent light fields $|\alpha\rangle$ and $|\beta\rangle$ are used for generating quantum correlation, where the quantum noise $\phi(t) = \phi_\beta - \phi_\alpha$ provided by mean photon number fluctuation.

4.2. Correlation measurement of two weak light fields

By using the experiment setup as proposed in Fig.5, we are able to generate 4 types of bipartite correlation, given as

$$C(\theta_1, \theta_2) \propto \pm\cos 2(\theta_1 \pm \theta_2). \tag{32}$$

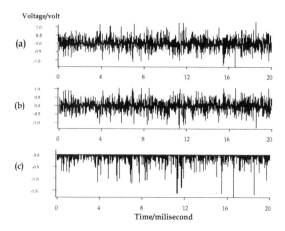

Figure 6. (a) The beat signal at balanced detector **A** (b) the beat signal at balanced detector **B** (c) the multiplied beat signal.

To verify the analysis discussed in section 2, we perform systematic studies of the proposed experiment. We use a piezoelectric transducer (PZT) to modulate the phase of a weak light field. Then, all 4 types of correlation function were obtained by manipulation of experiment setup as discussed in previous section. We normalized the correlation function $-cos\ 2(\theta_1 - \theta_2)$ with its maximum obtainable value, that is $\theta_1 = \theta_2$. Fig.7 shows the normalized correlation function $\pm cos\ 2(\theta_1 \pm \theta_2)$ as a function of the relative projection angle of the analyzer A and B. The blue line is the predicted theoretical value while the red circle with the error bar is the experimental data.

For each data point, we take ten measurements of the multiplied signal and obtain the average mean value. Each measurement was obtained by fix the projection angle of the analyzer A and rotates the projection angle of analyzer B. The error bar is mainly due to the electronic noises and temperature dependence of polarization optics.

4.3. Bit generation and measurement

After we established one of the bipartite correlation functions between observer A and B, bit generation and measurement for optical communications can be done by implementing bit correlations between them.

Lock-in-amplifier is used to measure the bit correlation of between observer A and B. Fig.8 depicts the experimental setup for bit measurement for observer A and B. To perform this measurement for the established correlation function of $-cos\ 2(\theta_1 - \theta_2)$, we ramp the Piezo-electric transducer (PZT) at one of the weak light field to obtain one period of interference signal. An example of single period of interference signal measured at observer and reference signal for the lock-in amplifier is shown in Fig.9. For practical optical communication, phase locking of the two orthogonal weak light fields are required.

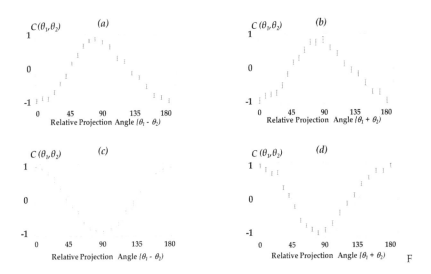

Figure 7. Experimental measurement of Bi-partite correlation functions (a)–*cos 2(θ − θ)*, (b) –*cos 2(θ + θ)*, (c) *cos 2(θ − θ)*, (d) *cos 2(θ + θ)*

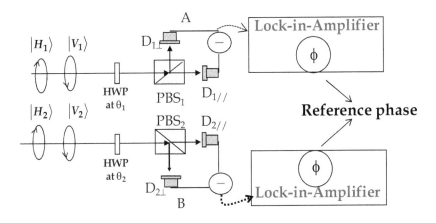

Figure 8. Experimental setup for demonstration of the bit generation and measurement

We measure quadrature phases of orthogonal weak light fields with the step size of $n\pi/2$ (n = integer) as shown in Fig. 10(a) (blue line). Using the same lock-in reference phase in the lock-in amplifier, we measure the quadrature phases of weak coherent state at detector B as shown in Fig. 10(a) (dashed red line). We have observed the bits correlation between two parties for the shared correlation function of $-cos\ 2(\theta_1 - \theta_2)$ as shown in Fig. 4(a), where the positive

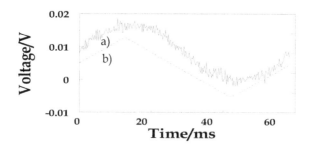

Figure 9. (a) Single period of interference signal measured at observer **A** (red line) compared to b) piezoelectric driving voltage (blue dashed line), which is used as reference phase in the lock-in amplifier.

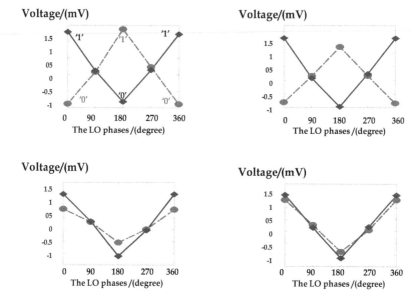

Figure 10. Bit correlation of two weak light fields (a) $-cos\ 2(\theta_1 - \theta_2)$, (b) $-cos\ 2(\theta_1 + \theta_2)$, (c) $cos\ 2(\theta_1 + \theta_2)$, and (d) $cos\ 2(\theta_1 - \theta_2)$

(negative) quadrature signal is encoded as keys/bits '1' ('0'), respectively. By using the same lock-in reference phase, we observe bits correlations for the other three types of correlation functions $-cos\ 2(\theta_1 + \theta_2)$, $cos\ 2(\theta_1 + \theta_2)$, and $cos\ 2(\theta_1 - \theta_2)$ as shown in Figs. 10(b), 10(c), and 10(d), respectively.

In real practice of long distance optical communication, we can establish one of the bit correlations for calibrating the lock-in reference phase at observer A and B. We further explore the feasibility of the scheme long distance optical communication for by performing bits correlations between two observers over a distance of 10 km through a transmission fiber. We couple one of the orthogonal weak light fields into 10 km of transmission fiber and a quarter-wave plate and a half-wave plate are used at the output of the transmission fiber to compensate the birefringence. The correlation between two observers A and B are found to be preserved over the 10 km transmission fiber (Sua et al., 2011). We managed to establish four types of correlation functions and performed bits correlations for each shared correlation function between two observers.

In short, for our proposed weak coherent light fields optical communication scheme, information is encoded onto the superposition of the vertically and horizontally polarized weak light fields; decoding involves detection of the weak light fields by balanced homodyne detector and quadrature phases measurement by lock-in amplifier. For reliable measurement of the encoded signal, both phase and polarization of the weak light field must be stable.

Apparently, stability and accurate control of phase and polarization turned out to be the main challenge for the practical implementation of weak coherent light fields optical communication. The state of polarization of the light wave is not preserved in the typical transmission fiber. Dynamic control of the state of polarization of the light is critical to ensure the reliability the proposed optical communication scheme. Each dynamic polarization controller is bulky and expensive (Noe et al., 1999), severely limits the practicality of our scheme. Phase locking is another challenging obstacle as well. Phase locking is required between the two orthogonal weak light fields that used to implement the bit correlation between two observers. Without the phase locking, quadrature phases measurement performed by lock-in amplifier is meaningless. Therefore, optical phase-locked loop must be employed for the phase locking of two weak light fields. However, for high data rate optical communication, the delays allowed in the phased-locked loop are so small that phase locking becomes an enormous challenge (Barry et al., 1992; Kazovsky, 1986).

5. Conclusion

We have experimentally demonstrated a new type of optical communication protocol based on weak coherent light fields. Coherent bipartite quantum correlations of two distant observers are generated and used to implement keys (bits) correlation over a distance of 10 km. Our scheme can be used to provide security as a supplement to the existence decoy-state Bennett-Brassard 1984 protocol and the differential phase-shift quantum key distribution (DPS-QKD) protocol. The realization of intrinsic correlation of weak coherent light fields by using the measurement method is a first step toward linear-optics quantum computing with weak light fields and single-photon source.

Acknowledgements

K.F.L and Y.M.S would like to acknowledge that this research is supported by start-up fund from Department of Physics, Michigan Technological University. H.B.A gratefully acknowledges the support from University of Malaya High Impact Research Grant UM.C/HIR/MOHE/SC/01 on this work.

Author details

Kim Fook Lee[1], Yong Meng Sua[1] and Harith B. Ahmad[2]

1 Department of Physics, Michigan Technological University, Houghton, Michigan, USA

2 Department of Physics, University of Malaya, Kuala Lumpur, Malaysia

References

[1] Barbosa, G. A.; Corndorf, E.; Kumar, P. & Yuen, H. P. (2003). Secure Communication using Mesoscopic coherent states, Phys. Rev. Lett., Vol.90, pp227901

[2] Barry, J. R. & Kahn, J. M. (1992). Carrier synchronization for homodyne and heterodyne-detection of optical quadriphase-shift keying, J. Lightwave Technol., Vol.10, pp1939–1951

[3] Bhattacharya, N.; van Linden van den Heuvell, H. B. & Spreeuw, R. J. C. (2002). Implementation of Quantum Search Algorithm using Classical Fourier Optics, Phys. Rev. Lett., Vol. 88, pp137901

[4] Bigourd, D.; Chatel, B.; Schleich, W. P. & Girard, B. (2008). Factorization of Numbers with the Temporal Talbot Effect: Optical Implementation by a Sequence of Shaped Ultrashort Pulses, Phys. Rev. Lett., Vol.100, pp030202

[5] Bowen, W. P.; Schnabel, R.; Lam, P. K.; & Ralph, T. C. (2003). Experimental Investigation of Criteria for Continuous variable entanglement, Phys. Rev. Lett., Vol.90, pp043601

[6] Brendel, J.; Gisin, N.; Tittel, W. & Zbinden, H. (1999). Pulsed energy-time entangled twin-photon source for quantum communication. Phys. Rev. Lett., Vol.82, pp2594

[7] Chen, J.; Lee, K. F.; and Kumar, P. (2007). Deterministic quantum splitter based on time-reversed Hong-Ou-Mandel interference, Phys. Rev. A, Vol.76, pp031804(R)

[8] Chen, J.; Altepeter, J. B.; Medic, M.; Lee, K. F.; Gokden, B.; Hadfield, R. H.; Nam, S. W. & Kumar, P. (2008). Demonstration of a Quantum Controlled-NOT Gate in the Telecommunications Band, Phys. Rev. Lett., Vol.100, pp133603

[9] Corndorf, E.; Barbosa, G. A.; Liang, C.; Yuen, H. P. & Kumar, P. (2003). High-speed data encryption over 25 km of fiber by two-mode coherent state quantum cryptography, Opt. Letters. Vol.28, pp2040-2042

[10] Grib, A.A.; & Rodrigues, W. A. (1999). Nonlocality in Quantum Physics, Springer, ISBN 030646182X, New York, USA

[11] Grosshans, F. & Grangier, P. (2002). Continuous variable quantum cryptography using coherent states, Phys. Rev. Lett., Vol.88, pp057902

[12] Grosshans, F.; Assche, G. V.; Wenger, J.; Brouri, R.; Cerf, N. J.; & Grangier, P. (2003). Quantum key distribution using gaussian-modulated coherent states, Nature, Vol.421, pp238

[13] Kazovsky, L. (1986). Balanced phase-locked loops for optical homodyne receivers: performance analysis, design considerations, and laser linewidth requirements, J. Lightwave Technol. ,Vol.4, pp182–195

[14] Korolkova, N.; Leuchs, G.; Loudon, R.; Ralph, T.; & Silberhorn, C. (2002). Polarization squeezing and continuous-variable polarization entanglement, Phys. Rev. A, Vol.65, pp052306

[15] Kwiat, P. G; Mattle, K.; Weinfurter, H.; Zeilinger, A.; Sergienko, A. V. & Shih, Y. (1995). New High-Intensity Source of Polarization-Entangled Photon Pairs, Phys. Rev. Lett., Vol.75, pp4337-4341

[16] Lee, K. F. & Thomas, J. E. (2002). Experimental Simulation of Two-Particle Quantum Entanglement using Classical Fields, Phys. Rev. Lett., Vol, 88, pp097902

[17] Lee, K. F.; Chen, J.; Liang, C.; Li,X.; Voss, P. L. & Kumar, P. (2006). Observation of high purity entangled photon pairs in telecom band, Optics Letters. Vol.31, pp1905

[18] Lee, K. F.; Kumar, P.; Sharping, J. E.; Foster, M. A.; Gaeta A. L.; Turner A. C.; & Lipson, M. (2008). Telecom-band entanglement generation for chipscale quantum processing, arXiv:0801.2606 (quant-ph)

[19] Lee, K. F. & Thomas, J. E. Entanglement with classical fields, (2004). Phys. Rev. A, Vol. 69, pp052311

[20] Lee, K. F. (2009). Observation of bipartite correlations using coherent light for optical communication, Optics Letters, Vol.34, pp1099-1101

[21] Liang, C.; Lee, K. F.; Voss, P. L.; Corndorf, E.; Gregory S.; Chen, J.; Li,X. & Kumar, P. (2005). Single-Photon Detector for High-Speed Quantum Communication Applications in the Fiber-optic Telecom Band, Free-Space Laser Communications V. Edited by Voelz, David G. Ricklin, Jennifer C. Proceedings of the SPIE, Vol.5893, pp282-287

[22] Liang, C.; Lee, K. F.; Chen, J. & Kumar, P. (2006). Distribution of fiber-generated polarization entangled photon-pairs over 100 km of standard fiber in OC-192 WDM environment, postdeadline paper, Optical Fiber Communications Conference and the 2006 National Fiber Optic Engineers Conference, Anaheim Convention Center, Anaheim, CA

[23] Liang, C.; Lee, K. F.; Medic, M.; Kumar, P. & Nam, S. W. (2007). Characterization of fiber-generated entangled photon pairs with superconducting single-photon detectors, Optics Express, Vol.15, pp1322

[24] Noe, R.; Sandel, D.; Yoshida-Dierolf, M.; Hinz, S.; Mirvoda, V.; Schopflin, A.; Glingener, C.; Gottwald, E.; Scheerer, C.; Fischer, G.; Weyrauch, T. & Haase, W. (1999). Polarization mode dispersion compensation at 10, 20, and 40Gb/s with various optical equalizers, J. Lightwave Technol., Vol.17, pp1602–1616

[25] Peres, A. (1995). Quantum Theory: Concepts and Methods (Fundamental Theories of Physics), Springer, ISBN 0792336321, New York, USA

[26] Qi, B.; Huang, L. L.; Qian, L. & Lo, H. K. (2007). Experimental study on the Gaussian-modulated coherent state quantum key distribution over standard telecommunication fibers, Phys. Rev. A. Vol.76, pp052323

[27] Scarani, V.; Bechmann-Pasquinucci, H.; Cerf, N. J.; Dusek, M.; Lütkenhaus, N.; & Peev, M. (2009). Rev. Mod. Phys. Vol.81, pp1301

[28] Sharping, J. E.; Lee, K. F.; Foster, M. A.; Turner, A. C.; Lipson, M.; Gaeta, A. L.; & Kumar, P. (2006). Generation of correlated photons through parametric scattering in nanoscale silicon waveguides, Optics Express, Vol.14, pp12388,

[29] Silberhorn, C.; Ralph, T. C.; Lutkenhaus, N. & Leuchs, G. (2002). Continuous variable quantum cryptography: Beating the 3 dB loss limit, Phys. Rev. Lett., Vol.89, pp167901

[30] Sua, Y. M.; Scanlon, E.; Beaulieu, T.; Bollen, V. & Lee, K. F. (2011). Intrinsic quantum correlations of weak coherent states for quantum communication, Phys. Rev. A, Vol. 83, pp030302(R)

[31] Tittel, W.; Brendel, J.; Gisin, B.; Herzog, T.; Zbinden, H & Gisin, N. (1998). Experimental demonstration of quantum correlations over more than 10 km, Phys. Rev. A. Vol.57, pp3229.

[32] Tittel, W.; Brendel, J.; Zbinden, H & Gisin, N. (1999). Long distance Bell-type tests using energy-time entangled photons, Phys. Rev. A, Vol.59, pp4150.

[33] Weedbrook, C.; Lance, A.M.; Bowen, W.P.; Symul, T.; Ralph, T.C.; & Lam, P.K. (2004). Phys. Rev. Lett., Vol.93, pp170504.

[34] Wilde, M. W.; Brun, T. A.; Dowling, J. P.; & Lee, H. (2008). Coherent communication with linear optics, Phys. Rev. A, Vol.77, pp022321

[35] Yonezawa, H.; Aoki, T. & Furusawa, A. (2004). Demonstration of a quantum teleportation network for continuous variables, Nature, Vol.431, pp 430-433

[36] Yuen, H. P. (2004). KCQ: A New Approach to quantum cryptography I. General Principles and Key generation, quant-ph/0311061 v6

A Double Cipher Scheme for Applications in Ad Hoc Networks and its VLSI Implementations

Masa-aki Fukase

Additional information is available at the end of the chapter

1. Introduction

The ubiquitous environment was described as a vision for 21st century computing [1]. In the last ten years, the ubiquitous network has become one of the remarkable trends of information and communications technology. One of the most important characteristics of the ubiquitous network is open access anytime anywhere. This corresponds to the mobility and diversity of power conscious PC processors, mobile processors, cryptography processors, RFID tags, and so forth. In view of the desire for better cost performance, simplicity, functionality, usability, and so on, the ad hoc network is an emerging technology for next generation ubiquitous computing [2]. However, these specific features involve fundamental issues as follows.

i. Currently, the promotive force of diversity is not the conventional wired network based on large servers, but convenient wireless LANs and handheld small devices, like the PDA (personal digital assistant), mobile phone and so forth. Although the diversity of various platforms is inevitable, it also causes notorious security issues such as insecurity, security threats or illegal attacks, such as tapping, intrusion and pretension. Nowadays, WEP (Wired Equivalent Privacy) is not so effective for wireless LANs. Worldwide diversity vs. the security threat are the two faces characteristic of the ubiquitous network [3]. Safety of the ubiquitous network has two aspects. One is the front-end security of the ubiquitous device and the other is the protection of the multimedia data itself, stored in the ubiquitous device. Neither approach always promises complete safety, but they complement one another. A cutting-edge technique for front-end security is the TPM (trusted platform module), commonly known as the security chip. Since the TPM implements RSA (Rivest-Shamir-Adelman), it works for short, password-size text data, and its major role is implicitly digital signing. In view of the running time, the encryption of long-length multimedia data, such as an image, is definitely outside the TPM. The other approach, back-end security, protects huge amounts of data because multimedia information, crucial for the interaction between ubiquitous devices and human beings, uses massive amounts of data. Back-end security is usually covered by common key schemes. Common key module-embedded processors are built-in cryptography processors for IC cards and portable electronic devices.

ii.   On the other hand, considering that cipher algorithms are open to third parties in the evaluation of cipher strength, hardware specifications are more important than cipher strength in developing an ad hoc network infrastructure. A fundamental issue in maintaining the mobility of the ubiquitous environment is how to achieve power-saving mobility. The power consuming factors of ubiquitous networks are large server systems controlled by network providers and small ubiquitous platform systems, handheld devices and so forth. These small systems consist of processors, memory and displays. The power dissipation of memory strongly depends on that of a memory cell and the memory space required for embedded software. LCDs (liquid crystal displays) and processors consume similar power in running mobile devices. While the LCD is turned on only when it displays some information, processors are always in the standby state to receive calls. Thus, power-saving restrictions for mobile devices are inevitably imposed on the processors.

iii.   Another issue of ubiquitous computing is its strong dependency on embedded software. This has a crucial effect on the total design of ubiquitous devices. Performable features of ubiquitous devices in processing multimedia data have mainly relied on embedded software. For example, if a new protocol appears, embedded software requires users to download an update package. Despite embedding, so far, it has rapidly increased software size due to the RTOS (real time OS), firmware, application software and so on. This results in more software costs and wider memory space. Since cutting-edge ubiquitous devices need not only sophisticated and complicated processing, but also power conscious high-speed operation, the embedded software approaches taken so far will not always continue to play key roles in ubiquitous computing.

In order to solve the fundamental issues described above, power conscious management of ubiquitous networks and cryptographic protection of massive data spreading over ubiquitous networks are required. It is really the practice of cryptography network security technologies to show optimum design for the trade-off to achieve specific features of the ubiquitous network. The double cipher scheme presented in this paper combines two cipher algorithms [4]. One is random number addressing cryptography (RAC), closely related to the internal behaviour of the processors. RAC is a transposition cipher devised from the direct connection of a built-in random number generator (RNG), a register file and a data cache. The register file plays the role of a streaming buffer. A random store, based on the direct connection, scrambles or transposes a series of multimedia data at random without any special encryption operation. The other algorithm of the double cipher is a data sealing algorithm. This is implemented during the data transfer from the register file to the data cache, by using another built-in RNG. This complements the RAC's shortcoming and enhances the security of the data information as a whole.

Since the double cipher scheme uses built-in RNGs at the micro-operation level, it is more effective than normal usage based on the processing of random number operands at the instruction level. In addition, the double cipher scheme requires no additional chip area or power dissipation. A linear feedback shift register (LFSR) is used as the RNG to achieve a longer cycle with negligible additional area. Thus, the double cipher scheme is a microarchitecture-based, software-transparent hardware cipher that offers security for the whole data with negligible hardware cost and moderate performance overhead. This is very suited to very large scale integration (VLSI) implementation. The VLSI implementation of the double cipher follows the multicore structure for bi-directional communication and multiple pipelines for multimedia processing and cipher streaming [5]. The cipher streaming is executed by the SIMD (Single Instruction stream Multiple Data stream) mode cipher and decipher codes. They do not attach operands, as is described above, but repeat instances to transfer byte-structured data from a register file to a data cache.

In this paper, we describe the double cipher scheme, hardware algorithm, architectural organization, structural aspect, internal behaviour and VLSI implementation of the double cipher in a sophisticated ubiquitous processor named HCgorilla by using a 0.18-μm standard cell CMOS chip. We evaluate the prospective specifications of the HCgorilla chip with respect to the hardware resource or cost, power dissipation, throughput and cipher strength. Potential aspects compared with the usual security techniques, cipher techniques and cryptography module-embedded processors are also described. HCgorilla is a power conscious hardware approach that provides multimedia data with practical security over a ubiquitous network.

2. Preliminaries

The problem statement and the course of the research of this study are described in more detail in this section. In addition, the area of application is also explained.

2.1. Trends and issues of ubiquitous networks

Faced with the progressive ubiquitous environment, we have experienced the alternative requirements, diversity or security [1]. Figure 1 illustrates that the diversity of the various devices has caused illegal attacks, intrusions, pretensions and so forth. When diversity is from the small mobile phone and the PDA to large traditional servers, in normal circumstances ubiquitous networks are functional and useful, but they are hard to control in abnormal circumstances. Since diversity brings about open access to ubiquitous networks anytime anywhere, this really threatens user security.

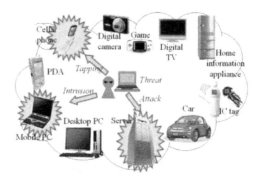

Figure 1. Diversity vs. security threat in a ubiquitous network

In order to achieve secure ubiquitous networks, both machines and data must be protected from abnormal phenomena. Table 1 surveys the current status of security techniques related to the ubiquitous network. Since tremendous network issues need complicated algorithms to detect and recognize individual phenomena, in the main, software techniques have been used. However, they are inflexible to individual demands, and are not always sufficient from the practical viewpoint. The hardware implementation of an IDS (intrusion detection system) and an IPS (intrusion prevention system) is another result we exploited independently [6]. As is clear from Table 1, cryptography is used for the protection of ubiquitous platforms. The cryptography adopted for the front-end security of an individual machine is public key cryptography to protect short, password-size text data. On the other hand, common key cryptography is used for the protection of data. Comparing the numerical values in Table 1 is irrelevant because they strongly depend on process technologies.

| Ubiquitous device | Technique | | Target | Speed | | Secureness |
	HW/SW	Cryptographic means		Running time	Transfer rate	
HCgorilla		Common key	Full text	Short	160-320 Mbps	Practical
Security chip				Out of		
Secure coprocessor		Public key	Password	account for		Large
Cryptographic core	Hardware			multimedia		
Elliptic curve processor				data		
Cryptography processor		Public key, common key	Password, biometrics	Short	2 Mbps [7]	Practical
Network processor		IDS, IPS	Sampling	Large		Medium
Server	Software					

Table 1. HCgorilla vs. regular security techniques

Table 2 shows various aspects of ubiquitous media. They are classified into discrete and streaming media. Both types are expressed by byte structure. Discrete media is still useful in the ubiquitous environment. Interactive games use many algorithmic processes for discrete data. Streaming media is more important because most ubiquitous applications use streaming media. This is further divided into two types in view of its complexity. Text data is one type of streaming data, because it is useful as refrain information in the event of a disaster. Considering endless data is hard for mobile devices; the target of this work is discrete media and stream data. Yet, they need a sophisticated and complicated process. Since streaming media is massive, it is reasonable to protect the security by a common key, which is preferable to protect large quantities of byte-structured ubiquitous information.

| | Discrete media | Streaming media | |
		Stream data	Data stream
Definition	Individual data	A sequence of similar elements	A sequence of data, which may be different from each other
Characteristic	Discrete	Stream of continuous media	
Size or quantity	Short	Long	Endless
Complexity	Low	Medium	High
Examples	Games, intelligent processes	Text, audio, video	Seismography, tsunami, traffic
Basic structure	Byte string		
Buffer storage	Respectable reregister file		
Data han- dling	Media	Algorithmic process	SIMD mode applications like signal processing, graphic rendering, data compression, etc.
	Security	Public key	Common key cryptography

Table 2. Ubiquitous media

Although the performable features of various ubiquitous devices illustrated in Figure 1 have mainly relied on embedded software, such an approach inevitably exhausts much hardware resources and results in the deterioration of speed and power, which are worsening alongside the rapid increase in ubiquitous technologies in recent years. The majority of these technologies are resource constrained in terms of chip area and battery energy available. It is very difficult for the regular techniques of the massive quantity of multimedia information to satisfy the overall demands. Thus, a drastic improvement is required for the embedded system to achieve really promising ubiquitous devices. In this respect, a practical solution will be a security aware high-performance sophisticated single VLSI chip processor [8].

2.2. Challenge and goal

The practices of an ad hoc environment require resource-constrained security. To achieve mobility, various processor chips embedded in ubiquitous platforms are designed so that the occupied area and energy budget are as small as possible [9–11]. On the other hand, the temporal formation of wireless and mobile ad hoc networks does not have the benefit of a permanent network infrastructure but relies on the connections themselves. Thus, a practical solution to achieve ad hoc security is single-chip VLSI processor built-in hardware cryptography. However, to the best of our knowledge, safety aware chips to protect multimedia data over ad hoc networks have never appeared. Thus, it is a challenging task to actualize not only the processing, but also the protection of multimedia data by unifying the role of PC processors, mobile processors, Java CPUs, cryptography processors and so on into a ubiquitous processor [5].

The goal of our study, described in this article, is the development of hardware cryptography, named the double cipher, to protect multimedia data over ad hoc networks and the implementation of the double cipher into a VLSI processor named HCgorilla. The hardware algorithm of the double cipher is based on the analysis of the internal behaviour of processors. The microarchitecture-level analysis is advantageous in achieving power-conscious multimedia data protection with high performance. Since power consumption and throughput are the basic metrics of processor specifications, careful attention is paid to them at each design step from the topmost architecture level to the transistor level. Actually, in recent years, the VLSI trend has exploited power conscious high performance not higher speed. Parallelism is really the global standard approach to the development of contemporary VLSI processors.

2.3. Application area

Figure 2 illustrates an application scenario of mobile phones which embed HCgorilla. Here, a standard image is multimedia data sent from the sender's mobile phone to the receiver's. Since the sender and receiver embed the same cipher chip, the entire encryption of the standard image is completely decrypted by the receiver. HCgorilla is able to carry out simultaneous processing of the encryption and decryption, taking into account bi-directional communication over networks. The common key is delivered ad hoc without relying on the network provider. Of course, public key infrastructure can be available for common key delivery. An electronic signature is also useful to certificate the message by using a security chip.

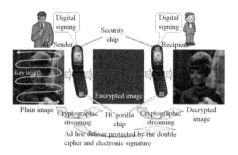

Figure 2. Application scenario

The double cipher is applicable to any multimedia data because

i.   the double cipher falls into the category of block cipher as described in Chapter 3,

ii.   multimedia data (image, audio, text) is byte structured as shown in Table 2.

Image data is expressed by PPM (portable PixMap), JPEG (joint photographic expert group), BMP (bit MaP) and so on. Figure 3 exemplifies the PPM image file of a standard image. This image has 256 lines and each line consists of 256 pixels. A PPM file consists of a header and pixel data. The header contains the PPM format ID, number of pixels in width and height and graduation. The pixel data contains all the graduation elements that are the 1-byte quantization of R-, G-, or B-elements. The 1-byte R-, G-, or B-graduation elements are the target of the double cipher process.

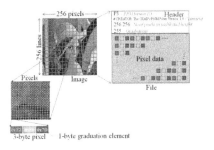

Figure 3. PPM image file

The double cipher can be applicable to cryptographic streaming. Here, the stream is a sequence of pixels, and the cryptographic streaming is the continuous encryption or decryption of a whole image and a moving picture. In view of the video display, the flame rate is 30 flames/sec. So, the resolution of the PPM format requires a bandwidth of

$$256 \times 256 \times 3 \times 30 \text{bytes} / \text{sec} \approx 6 \text{Mbytes} / \text{sec} \approx 50 \ Mbps \qquad (1)$$

On the other hand, the resolution of a QVGA (quarter video graphics array) format (320×240 pixels/flame) requires a bandwidth of

$$0.23 \times 30 \text{bytes} / \text{sec} \approx 55 \ Mbps \qquad (2)$$

Figure 4 shows the scanning modes of the image data. The continuous scan follows the exact sequence of the data format. The discontinuous scan accesses the data format in a predetermined order of discrete addresses. The mixed scan mode is also shown.

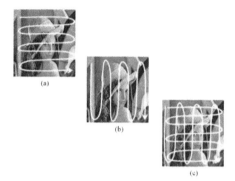

Figure 4. Scanning modes of an image (a) Continuous scan (b) Discontinuous scan (c) Mixed scan

Figure 5 illustrates the structure and encryption of audio data. This is also formed in bytes. In the case of WAV (waveform audio file) format, it consists of a header and waveform data derived by sampling and quantizing the analogue data. The quantization derives the byte form of a sampling bit at each sampling point.

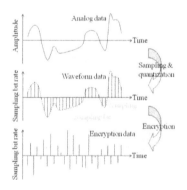

Figure 5. Audio data

3. Double cipher

The cipher strength does not merely depend on the algorithm of encryption itself, taking into account a round robin attack. It does not seek how to encrypt, but searches a key used in the encryption. Since the key is produced by an RNG, it is the essence of cipher strength. For example, the Vernam cipher lacks sealing ability, that is, the information of a plaintext is leaked by simply observing the ciphertext on the communication channel. Yet, it is assured that the Vernam cipher is ideally strong due to the use of a full length random number string.

In general, the cipher strength can be improved by increasing not only the key length but also all kinds of bit operations, which can be seen in the improvement from DES (data encryption standard) to AES (advanced encryption standard) [12]. This is based on the general rule of deciphering a secret key cryptography that seeks an unknown key or password, assuming that the plaintext, ciphertext and encryption algorithms are open [13]. According to this, the author proposes the double cipher scheme with two RNGs [4]. Consequently, this increases the key length. In practice, the double cipher approach promises strong cipher strength by providing double kinds of operations. Another advantage of this approach is power consciousness with negligible hardware cost and high throughput due to the microarchitecture-level hardware mechanism.

3.1. Proposed scheme

The hardware algorithm of the double cipher is proposed based on the analysis of the internal behaviour of the processors. The additional chip area and power dissipation required for this algorithm are negligibly small. The first scheme, RAC, is a transposition cipher devised from the direct connection of a built-in RNG (LFSR), register file (buffer of external data) and a data cache. A random store based on the direct connection scrambles or transposes a series of multimedia data at random without any special encryption operation. The second scheme is a data sealing algorithm implemented during the data transfer from the register file to the data cache. This complements the RAC's shortcoming and enhances the security of data information as a whole.

Figure 6 shows the basic algorithm of the double cipher in more detail. Here, $d_1d_2d_3d_4d_5$ exemplifies a plaintext block; d_i (i is an integer) is a 1-byte character, graduation element, and quantization of a sampling bit when the plaintext is formed into text style, image, and audio, respectively; 30241 is the corresponding key or the output of the first RNG, LFSR1; $h(d_2)h(d_5)h(d_3)h(d_1)h(d_4)$ is a ciphertext that is the result of the double encryption. In the execution of the RAC, the plaintext and LFSR1's output are synchronized according to their sequence. For example, the first data "d_1" and the first random number "3" are synchronized. During the storage in the third location of the data cache, a hidable function h works for the plaintext block. The sequence of a random addressing store like this results in the formation of a cipher in the data cache.

Double cipher encryption proceeds according to the following micro-operations.

i.   Make the LFSR1 output integer specify a register file address.

ii.   Synchronize a data cache address with the current clock count.

iii.   Transfer the specified register file's content to the synchronized data cache address. During the transfer, a hidable function works for the plaintext block by using LFSR2 output.

The sequence of a random addressing store like this results in the formation of a cipher in the data cache. Double cipher decryption similarly proceeds. These micro-operations are practiced by a simple wired logic, which is effective in maintaining usability, speed and power consciousness.

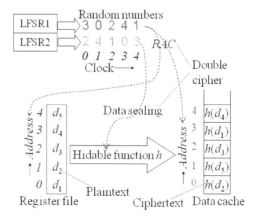

Figure 6. Double cipher

Since multimedia data is much longer than the plaintext shown in Figure 6, the adoption of block ciphers is inevitable in order to satisfy the demand for data quantity and performance. Figure 7 illustrates the relation among plaintext, blocks, dominant stages of the cipher pipeline (shortened to pipes hereafter) and the double cipher process. The relation between the cipher pipe and core is clear from Figure 8. The reason that both encryption and also decryption are shown in Figure 7 is that a single ubiquitous processor should cover bi-directional communication over networks as described in Section 2.3. A practical buffer for the external plaintext or ciphertext data is a register file whose space and speed are limited. So, the external data is divided into blocks and stored in a register file. The transfer of the block to the register file is assumed to be in DMA (direct memory access) mode, though it is not our concern in this study.

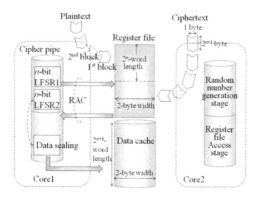

Figure 7. Double cipher mechanism within a single ubiquitous processor

Regarding the quantitative aspect of the double cipher process, the double cipher scheme regulates the block length to be the same as a buffer size. On the other hand, the block width is usually fixed to a byte because ubiquitous media takes the form of a byte-structured stream. The extensibility of the block structure is useful in high-speed processing. Another effect of the extension of the block length is to make the key length long, and thus the strength of the double cipher is expected to be strong in practice. The relation between the block, n-bit LFSR, register file and data cache is proved as follows.

$$\text{No.of blocks} = \text{plain or ciphertextsize} / \text{block size} \tag{3}$$

$$\text{Block size} = \text{logical space size} \tag{4}$$

$$\text{Block's word length} = \text{logical space length} \tag{5}$$

$$2^n = \text{register file's logical space size} = \text{data cache's logical space size} \tag{6}$$

The block transfer is subject to transposition and substitution ciphers. The interaction between the block, register file, data cache and LFSR is as follows. Core1 carries out RAC by making the LFSR1 output specify a register file address, synchronizing a data cache address with the current clock count, and transposing the specified register file's content to the synchronized data cache address. Then, LFSR2 makes the hidable function h on the data lines work for the substitution of the transferred data. The resultant content, stored in the data cache, is the encryption of the register file's content. The sequence of random addressing storage like this results in the formation of a cipher in the data cache. Double cipher decryption similarly proceeds within Core2.

3.2. VLSI implementation

According to the micro-operations shown in Figure 7, the architecture of the double cipher scheme-implemented VLSI processor is designed as shown in Figure 8. It is a ubiquitous processor named HCgorilla. The reason it is called a ubiquitous processor is due to its specific features for ubiquitous computing being power consciousness to achieve mobility, cost performance, simplicity, functionality, usability to actualize diversity and secureness to protect spreading platforms. HCgorilla is one of the most promising solutions for ubiquitous computing.

The correspondence of the double core, plaintext/ciphertext, register file and data cache is obvious in Figures 7 and 8. The double core contributes to cover both bi-directional communication and the recent trend of parallelism. Media pipes with sophisticated structures are newly added in Figure 8. This aims to cover media processing, indispensable for ubiquitous computing. Thus, HCgorilla unifies basic aspects of PC processors, mobile processors, media processors, cryptography processors and so forth and follows multicore and multiple pipelines.

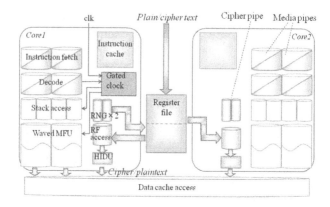

Figure 8. Architecture of HCgorilla

Each aspect specific to ubiquitous computing is achieved as follows. To begin with, secureness is achieved by the cipher pipe. The cipher pipe undertakes double encryption during the transfer from the register file to the data cache. While an LFSR controls the transposition cipher, RAC, another LFSR controls a substitution cipher or data sealing implemented by the hidable unit, HIDU (HIdable Data Unit). The double cipher executes the SIMD mode cipher and decipher codes. They do not attach operands, but repeat instances to transfer byte-structured data from a register file to a data cache. *rsw* encrypts the content stored in one half of the register file and *rlw* decrypts the content of the other half of the register file. These codes occupy the cipher pipe as long as the corresponding data stream continues. Thus, the SIMD mode sequence forms double cipher streaming.

The second aspect, power conscious resource-constrained implementation, is achieved by the design steps in the following.

i.   Architecture level parallelism: HCgorilla exploits parallelism not higher speed in order to achieve power consciousness. Parallelism at the architecture level takes a multicore and multiple pipeline structure. Each core is composed of Java-compatible media pipes and cipher pipes. In addition, the register file and data cache are shared by the double core. Following the HW/SW co-design approach, two symmetric cores run multiple threads in parallel.

ii.   Circuit module level: LFSR is used as the RNG built in the cipher pipe. LFSR falling into the category of M-sequence requires minimal additional chip area and power dissipation. A tiny n-bit LFSR produces the huge 2n-length random numbers. 1K-, 1M-, 1G-byte length texts require only 10-, 20-, and 30-bit LFSRs respectively.

iii.   Instruction level parallelism (ILP): A wave-pipelined MFU (MultiFunctional Unit) is built in the execution stage of the media pipe to achieve effective ILP. This is the combination of wave-pipelining and multifunctionalization of the arithmetic logic functions for media processing. Since the latency of the waved MFU is constant, independent of the arithmetic logic operations, the media instructions are free from scheduling [14]. The wave-pipelining is effective also in achieving power conscious high speed.

iv.   Microarchitecture level: Gated clocking is applied as described below.

Another aspect of HCgorilla, specific for ubiquitous computing, is its functionality and usability. Usability is an indispensable aspect of a multimedia mobile embedded system. Platform neutrality especially is very promising in providing multimedia entertainment such as music and games, the GPS (Global Positioning System) and so forth [15, 16]. In order to fulfil this feature, sophisticated language processing is required. In this respect, Java is expected to be useful. Thus, the media pipe shown in Figure 8 is a sort of an interpreter-type Java CPU [17]. The instruction set of HCgorilla is composed of 58 Java-compatible instructions together with two SIMD mode cipher instructions.

In Figure 8, the "Gated clock" block is a circuit module to control gated clocking [18]. Gated clocking is a cell-based approach for power saving at the microarchitecture level. It stops the clocking of such circuit blocks with low activity that waste switching power. Since leakage power is not a critical factor in the case of the 0.18-μm CMOS standard cell process used in this study, the gated clock is very effective for power saving. HCgorilla controls the clocking of the stack access and execution stages where switching probability is higher. In addition, the media pipe introduces scan logic for DFT (design for testability). This makes the pipeline register a shift register by serially connecting the FFs in order to read, write, and retrieve the pipeline stage status. The retrieval is useful for detecting and solving design errors. The scan logic is useful for the verification of the media pipe with a sophisticated structure. On the other hand, the scan logic is not applied to the cipher pipe because the cipher pipe is simpler and easier to verify. In addition, the scan logic and hardware cryptography are inconsistent with each other because the scan logic is apt to induce side-channel attack [19]. While traditional cryptographic protocols assume that only I/O signals are available to an attacker, every cryptographic circuit leaks information through other physical channels. An attack that takes advantage of these physical channels is called a side-channel attack. Side-channel attacks exploit easily accessible information, such as power consumption, running time, I/O behaviour under malfunctions and electromagnetic emissions.

Although Java is preferable as described above, in view of language processing, Java language systems are actually more complicated than regular language systems. The platform neutrality of Java applications is due to an intermediate form or class file produced by using Java compilers. This is really convenient for the JVM (Java virtual machine), but secondary for a processor itself. Since ubiquitous clients use small scale systems, the pre-processing of complicated class files should be covered by large servers with Java applications. Even Java bytecodes have a problem, that is, the running of Java bytecodes is time-consuming due to the interpreting process. Although JVM or JIT (just-in-time compilation) built-in runtime systems are common for mobile devices, like mobile phones, they need more ROM (read only memory) space. This degrades the usability, cost and performance features of small ubiquitous devices.

In order to solve the issues described above, we have so far developed the software support system for the HCgorilla chips shown in Figure 9 [20]. The system is composed of a Java interface and parallelizing compilers. For example, the software support may run on proxy servers. Web delay, installing the software support on web servers, is one of the anticipative drawbacks of this approach. Obviously, it will take some time to transfer the executable code over the Internet. However, the transfer of class files to commercial processors also takes some time. In addition, the transfer time is not so important for the evaluation of web delays [21]. The main factor in web delays is the response time of the web servers. Another concern with this approach is maintaining security during the transfer. However, transferring the executable codes over the Internet does not generate a trust problem, because Java basically seeks the global standard of the Internet.

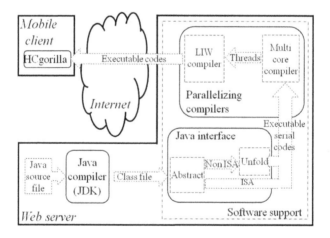

Figure 9. HCgorilla, web server, software support, and parallelizing compiler

HCgorilla, shown in Figure 8, is implemented in a 0.18-μm CMOS standard cell chip. The design environment is summarized in Table 3. Figure 10 shows the chip structure, die photo and floor planning of HCgorilla.7. This corresponds to Figure 8.

Software	
OS	Red Hat Linux 4/CentOS 5.4
Synthesis tool	Synopsys - Design Compiler D-2010.03
Simulation tool	Synopsys - VCS version Y-2006.06-SP1
Physical Implementation tool	Synopsys - IC Compiler C-2009.06
Verification tool	Mentor - Calibre v2010.02_13.12
Equivalent verification tool	Synopsys – Formality B-2008.09-SP5
Static Timing analysis tool	Synopsys – Primetime pts,vA-2007.12-SP3
Language	
Synthesis	VHDL
Simulation	Verilog-HDL
Technology	
ROHM 0.18-μm CMOS Kyoto univ. Standard Cell Library	

Table 3. Design environment of HCgorilla

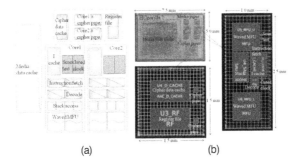

(a)   (b)

Figure 10. HCgorilla.7 (a) Structure (b) Die photo and floor planning

4. Evaluation and discussion

The overall evaluation of the HCgorilla chip ranging from the hardware cost, power dissipation, and throughput to cipher strength are described. Except for the hardware cost, quantitative measurement of the real chip and actual processor is difficult at this point. However, the simulation-based evaluation using the powerful CAD tools shown in Table 3 is reasonable enough. We prepared a DUV (design under verification) simulator and a test program run on the HCgorilla chip. Employing netlist, extracted from the chip layout, and analysing the algorithmic complexity are partly introduced. Table 4 summarizes the basic evaluation of

HCgorilla.7 compared with a previous derivative that we developed. These employ the same 0.18-μm CMOS standard cell technology. The overall aspects, chip parameters, and hardware specifications are also shown in this table.

			HCgorilla.6	HCgorilla.7
Design Rule			ROHM 0.18-μm CMOS	
Wiring			1 poly Si, 5 metal layers	
Area	Chip		2.5×5 mm	5.0 mm×7.5 mm
	Core			4.28 mm×6.94 mm
Assembly	Pad	Signal	158	
		VDD/VSS	32	
	Package		PGA257	
Power supply			1.8 V (I/O 3.3 V)	
Power consumption			275 mW	274 mW
Instruction cache			16 bits×64 words×2	
Data cache			16 bits×128 words×2	
Stack memory			16 bits×16 words×8	
Register file			16 bits×128 words	
RNG			6 bits×2	
No. of cores			2	
ILP degree			4	
Clock frequency			200 MHz	
Throughput	Media pipe		0.17 GIPS	
	Cipher pipe		0.1-0.2 GOPS	
Transfer rate			160-320 Mbps	

Table 4. Prospective specifications and potential aspects of HCgorilla chips

4.1. Hardware cost and power consumption

The hardware resource or cost is measured by the area occupied on the real chip, shown in Figure 10 (b). Figure 11 (a) shows the sharing of the occupied area. The portions denoted by "Stack access" and "Waved MFU" show the sum of four media pipes. The portion denoted by "Cipher pipes" shows the sum of four RNGs, register file and two HIDUs. The portion of the "D cache" is the sum of the media data cache and the cipher data cache. The media pipe, cipher pipe, and data cache employ 24,367, 270, and 20,625 cells, respectively. HCgorilla.7 and HCgorilla.6 have almost the same architecture. Yet, their chip areas are different. This is due to whether or not floor planning is undertaken. Since floor planning takes more area, it contradicts low resource implementation. In addition, a clear layout often withstands side-channel attacks, tampering and so forth. Nevertheless, floor planning is indispensable for local and global clock separation, effective gated clocking and so on. Figure 11 (b) demonstrates the distribution of power dissipation derived from static evaluation, which summarizes the mean value of every cell. It does not take into account the switching condition. Figure 11 (c) shows the register file length dependency of power dissipation. The register file length swings backwards and forwards from HCgorilla.7's register file length, 128 words.

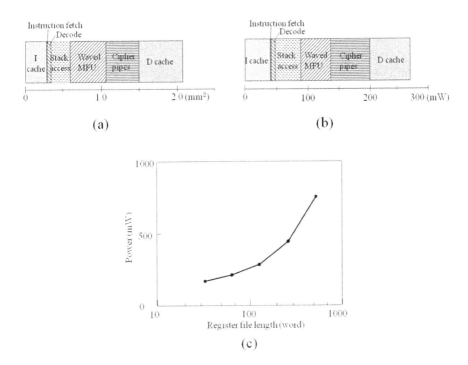

Figure 11. Overall evaluation of HCgorilla.7 (a) Occupied area (b) Power distribution (c) Power dissipation vs. register file length

4.2. Throughput

The cipher pipe's throughput, that is the mean value of the number of double cipher operations per unit of time, is derived from

$$\text{Throughput [OPS]} = \frac{\text{no.of double cipher operations}}{\text{running time [sec]}} \qquad (7)$$

Since the running in Equation (7) is the repetition of the block transfer, rewriting the register file and double cipher operation, the running time is derived from

$$\text{Running time} = m(t_1 + t_2) + t_3 \tag{8}$$

Here, m is the number of blocks. The block width is usually fixed to a byte because ubiquitous media, like pixels, takes the form of a byte-structured stream. As a consequence, the register file width is evaluated by bytes. On the other hand, the register file length is measured expediently by word as shown in Figure 7. t_1 is block access time or the latency taken to transfer a block to the register file. t_2 is the time of an SIMD mode cipher operation. t_3 is the latency taken to transfer a block from the data cache. t_2 is evaluated by the DUV simulator that simulates a test program run on the HCgorilla chip. As for t_1 and t_3, let the memory access speed of mobile phones be 208 to 532 Mbytes/s and the mean value be adopted. Although such a method based on Equation (8) compromises the analysis, simulation and measurement, it is reliable considering that the cipher streaming of media data is undertaken regularly.

The cipher pipe's transfer rate, that is the mean value of the amount of transferred data per unit of time, is given by

$$\text{Transfer rate [bps]} = \frac{\text{full text size [b]}}{\text{transfer time [sec]}} \tag{9}$$

Identifying the transfer time in the denominator of Equation (9) with the running time in Equation (8), the following relation is derived.

$$\text{Transfer rate[Mbps]} = \text{throughput[GOPS]} \times \text{register file width[b]} \times 10^3 \tag{10}$$

Figure 12 shows the register file length dependency of HCgorilla.7's throughput in running a test program as shown in Figure 13. The register file length swings similarly to Figure 11 (c). The test program is composed of the double cipher and media processing. The plaintext used in the double cipher processing is 240×320-pixel QVGA format data. Then, the time of the SIMD mode cipher operation, t_2, is derived and the throughput in GOPS is derived from Equations (8) and (7). Similarly, the throughput in GIPS is derived from

$$\text{Throughput [IPS]} = \frac{\text{no.of instructions}}{\text{running time [sec]}} \tag{11}$$

The running time of the media processing is also derived by using the DUV simulator that simulates the test program. The media pipe's throughput is almost constant in Figure 12. This is because the clock speed is kept constant in varying the length of the register file.

In order to justify the instruction scheduling the free media pipe, the media processing of the test program is coded in three ways, that is, routines A, B, and C. These are distinguished in that the variable k and loop count are integers or floating point numbers. Routine A uses only

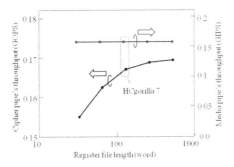

Figure 12. Throughput vs. register file length

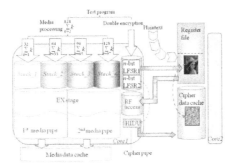

Figure 13. A test program and the internal behaviour of HCgorilla

integers and Routine B floating point numbers. Routine C uses both integer and floating point numbers. The hardware parallelism is utilized by dividing the summation into four threads and assigning them into four stacks in order to make full use of the two waved MFUs. The simulation result shows that the media pipe's throughput differs little between routines A, B, and C.

4.3. Cipher strength

Figure 14 shows how to measure the double cipher strength by experimenting with a rough-and-ready guess or round robin attack in a ubiquitous environment, where HCgorilla built-in platforms are used. The cipher strength is the degree of endurance against attack by a malicious third party. The attack is the third party's irregular action to decipher, break, or crack the cipher. This is clearly distinguished from decryption, that is, the right recipient's regular process of recovering the plaintext by using the given key.

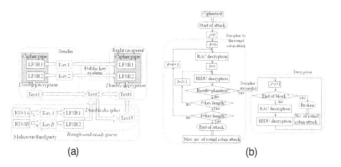

Figure 14. Measurement of double cipher strength (a) Round robin attack (b) Measurement flow

According to a normal scenario, the rules applied in deciphering the secret key cryptography in Figure 14 are as follows.

i.   A plaintext, a ciphertext and the cipher algorithm are open to third parties.

ii.   The key or the initial value of the RNG used in encryption is secret from third parties, though it is open to the right recipient.

A true key is sought out in deciphering. Sometimes it is called a password. The reason a plaintext and a ciphertext are open is because they are numerous and so, in turn, their quantity is beyond protection. In addition, it is reasonable that the cipher algorithm, or its specification, is open because its value is in its usability in the communication stages. This demands the spread of the algorithm in certain communities.

LFSR1 and LFSR2 in Figure 14 are RNGs for the double cipher built in the cipher pipes of a sender and a right recipient. They are also used by third parties according to rule (a). Key1 and Key2 are the initial values of LFSR1 and LFSR2 issued by the sender. Further encryption of these secret keys that are the target of attack is conventionally applied to maintain their confidentiality. For example, WEP cipher keys are encrypted by the RC4 cipher. In Figure 14, a public key system is available to exchange the key between a sender platform and a right recipient platform.

Text1 is a plaintext/ciphertext and Text2 is a ciphertext/plaintext derived by applying Key1 and Key2 to Text1. Key$A$ and Key$B$ are the guesses for Key1 and Key2 and are the initial values of the third party's LFSR1 and LFSR2. RNGA and RNGB, which are completely independent of LFSR1 and LFSR2, are used for rough-and-ready guesses or random guesses by the third party. Text3 is the guess of Text1 by the third party. When Text3 disagrees with Text1, one of RNGA and RNGB is forced to proceed to the next stage. If the disagreement continues by the end of the cycle of random number generation, the comparison of Text3 and Text1 is repeated by using the other RNG. Thus, the round robin attack against the double cipher undergoes nested loops.

From the discussion described above, the cipher strength is given by

$$\text{Cipher strength} = \text{time for the round robin attack} =$$
$$= \text{no.of round robin attacks} \times \text{clock cycle time} \leq 2^{\text{LFSR1 size+LFSR2 size}} \times \text{clock cycle time} \tag{12}$$

Since

$$\text{LFSR1 or LFSR2 size} \geq \log_2\left(\frac{\text{register file length}}{2}\right) \tag{13}$$

holds from Figure 13, the register file length is a critical factor of cipher strength. However, enlarging memory size surely causes an increase in power dissipation, the deterioration of clock speed, throughput and so forth. Thus, the demand of cipher strength is inevitably limited.

Figure 14 (b) shows the flow of measuring the number of round robin attacks in Equation (12). A result is achieved for every round robin attack. j is the number of blocks. The reason the measurement steps are distinguished in the cases of $j=0$ and $j>1$ is because the same random number sequence is issued for all the blocks from Figure 13. k is the number of RAC trial attacks. l is the number of HIDU trial attacks. Counting k and l through the experiment, the double cipher strength is derived from the number of nested loops or the time needed to decipher. This evaluates the degree of endurance or the strength. Actually, the cryptographic strength is the number of attack trials multiplied by the time for decryption. Each of the nested loops guesses a key at random, decrypts the ciphertext by using the key and judges if the decipher is successful.

Figure 15 shows the cipher strength achieved by practicing the method shown in Figure 14 and by using the 240×320-pixel QVGA format data, which is the same test data as is used by the test program shown in Figure 13. Note that the test data does not affect the cipher strength from Figure 13 and Figure 14 (b). It depends entirely on the block size or the half size of the register file because the blocks, after the success of the first attack, are simply decrypted by the known key. The abscissa is notched by the full length of the register file and the half size indicates a logical space. Although, from Table 3, HCgorilla.7's register file length is 128 words,

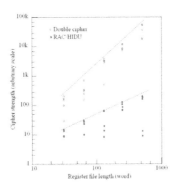

Figure 15. Cipher strength vs. register file length

to understand the dependency of the cipher strength, the register file length is varied from 32 to 512 words. Correspondingly, the size of LFSR is varied from 5 to 9 bits. The measurements are undertaken five times for each length. The dotted lines show the upper limit or the maximum number of the round robin attacks in the right hand side of Equation (11). The maximum strength of the double cipher is proportional to $2^{LFSR1\ size+LFSR2\ size}$ from Figure 14 (b). Similarly, the single cipher reaches $2^{LFSR1\ size}$.

4.4. Discussion

Overall, the discussion is based on the evaluation described above. In view of the cipher strength, Figure 15 indicates that a longer buffer size is desirable. The double cipher increases the cipher strength as the key length or the cycle of random numbers expands. Although the hardware implementation of longer cycle random number generation is very easy, it surely involves a power consuming increase in the size of the stream buffer or register file. Considering that cipher algorithms are open to third parties in the evaluation of cipher strength, hardware specifications are more important than cipher strength in developing HCgorilla. While the power dissipation rapidly increases from the 128-word length in Figure 11 (c), the cipher pipe's throughput almost saturates at the 128-word length in Figure 12. The 128-word length is the optimum buffer size because (*i*) the power dissipation of mobile processors is usually less than 1 watt, and (*ii*) the cipher pipe's transfer rate shown in Table 4 is comparable to that of an ATM.

In view of cipher streaming, 0.1 GOPS is allowable for video format, because the running time used for cipher streaming occupies a very small portion of the video processing time. Actually, 1-Mbyte of text forms 4.3 flames of QVGA format. It takes 143 msec in video processing. The running time of cipher streaming is only 3.6% of 143-msec video processing. On the other hand, a 1-minute video takes 2.2-sec running time for cipher streaming, because, as shown in Equation (2), the text size is 414 Mbytes from the bandwidth. In the case of PPM format, 1-Mbyte of text forms 5 flames. This takes 167 msec in video processing, that is, only 3%. Then, as shown in Equation (1), a 1-minute video's text size is 360 Mbytes from the bandwidth. In this case, cipher streaming takes only 1.9 sec.

However, HCgorilla's throughput in GOPS is not always reasonable in view of CPU performance. The throughput of commercial mobile processors is more than 10 GOPS, though this has the benefit of the cutting-edge technologies of process, clock and hardware parallelism. In order to further enhance HCgorilla's GOPS value, which directly affects the increase in Mbps value, the running time should be decreased from Equation (7). This is possible with respect to the following strategies.

i.   Reduce t_1 and t_3 by using a memory buffer with faster access speed.

ii.   Reduce the summation of block access and transfer times, $\sum(t_1+t_3)$, by increasing the register file size. Expanding the register file length leads to an increase in cipher strength. However, it needs to take into account the trade-off between throughput and power dissipation. Judging from Equation (7), increasing the register file size causes more power dissipation. In fact, from Figure 11 (c), the power dissipation rapidly increases from the 128-word length.

iii.   Reduce t_2 by the increase in speed of the cipher pipe's clock. Increasing the number of pipeline stages is also useful for this aim.

Table 5 summarizes various aspects of the double cipher vs. usual common key ciphers. The double cipher, especially RAC, has the following characteristic aspects.

i.   RAC simplifies the processing of multimedia data, because RAC directly handles a byte string whose structure is the same as that of the multimedia data as shown in Table 2. The effect of simplicity ranges over every aspect.

ii.   RAC allows expandable block length. Different from usual common key ciphers, RAC does not fix the block length, but regulates it to be the same as the buffer size. Although the register file's logical length is 64 words at this point, we are planning to increase it.

iii.   RAC handles wider blocks. The byte string is wider than the bit string used by other usual ciphers. At this point, the width is 2 bytes and is 16 times wider.

iv.   RAC encrypts a plaintext block without any arithmetic logic operation. The cipher mechanism due to the random transfer between a register file and a data cache is quite different from other ciphers.

		Block		Cipher means		Through-put	Running time	Cipher strength	Resource
		String unit	Length	Key	Transformation				
Double cipher	RAC	Byte	As long as a buffer (register file) length		Needless	High	Medium	Practically strong	Small
	Data sealing	Bit			Bitwise XOR				
Vernam		Bit	Full length				Short	Strong	Large
Stream	LFSR		A few bits or a character				Medi-um	Medi-um	Small
	A5								
	AES-CTR		128 bits	1-2 times length of AES key	Bitwise XOR, scramble, shift, etc.		Long	Strong	Large
Block	AES								
	DES		64 bits						

Table 5. Double cipher vs. regular common key cryptography

These aspects allow double cipher higher throughput, shorter running time and practical strength. The throughput is given by the product of block data size and clock frequency, assuming the processing of one block per clock. Thus, higher clock frequency together with expandable data size provides higher throughput. Since the block data size is the product of expandable block length and width, it is allowed to increase with ease. The expandable block length allows the double cipher to have practical cipher strength. The extension of the block length surely makes the key length long. Thus, the double cipher strength is expected to be strong in practice, because the cipher strength is closely related to the key length. The evaluation of running time is based on computational complexity and the dominant factor is the total number of iterative loops. AES has nesting loops for arithmetic, logic and functional operations. The first loop is for matrix operation and the second for rounds. However, RAC is released from such complexity.

5. Conclusion

The author has proposed a cipher scheme useful in practice for ad hoc networks with temporarily sufficient strength. The proposal is based on two cipher schemes. The first scheme is based on RAC and the second uses a data sealing algorithm. This double cipher scheme can be implemented in a security aware, power conscious and high-performance single VLSI chip processor by using built-in RNGs. Streaming the buffer size is determined from the trade-off between cipher strength, power dissipation and throughput. In practice, this is important because hardware specifications are more important than cipher strength in VLSI implementation.

HCgorilla is a sophisticated ubiquitous processor implementing the double cipher scheme. The VLSI implementation of HCgorilla is undertaken by using a 0.18-μm standard cell CMOS chip. The hardware cost, power dissipation, throughput and cipher strength of the latest HCgorilla chip are evaluated from real chip, logic synthesis and simulation by using CAD tools. Examining algorithmic complexity is partly used. The evaluation shows that HCgorilla is a power conscious, high-performance hardware approach that treats multimedia data with practical security over a ubiquitous network.

The future work of this research is the implementation of the double cipher into HCgorilla's media pipe. Although the cipher pipe and the media pipe are explicitly distinguished from each other in this study, the mixing of instruction scheduling free media processing with cipher processing at the microarchitecture level will further contribute power conscious security in ad hoc networks. Since such improvement applies the scan logic to encrypted data flow, an additional problem is raised, that is, whether the scan logic is able to avoid attacks by third parties. Apart from the disclosure of cipher algorithms, a design tolerant to side-channel attack and resistant to tamper is inevitable for VLSI implementation.

Author details

Masa-aki Fukase

Address all correspondence to: slfuka@eit.hirosaki-u.ac.jp

Graduate School of Science and Technology, Hirosaki University, Hirosaki, Japan

References

[1] Saha, D, & Mukherjee, A. Pervasive Computing: A Paradigm for the 21st Century. Computer Magazine (2003). , 36(3), 25-31.

[2] Wu, J, & Stojmenovic, I. Ad Hoc Networks. Computer Magazine (2004)., 37(2), 29–31.

[3] Satyanarayanan, M. Privacy: The Achilles Heel of Pervasive Computing? IEEE Pervasive Computing (2003). , 2(1), 2-3.

[4] Fukase, M, Uchiumi, H, Ishihara, T, Osumi, Y, & Sato, T. Cipher and Media Possibility of a Ubiquitous Processor: proceedings of International Symposium on Communications and Information Technologies, ISCIT (2009). September 2009, Incheon, Korea., 2009, 343-347.

[5] Fukase, M, & Sato, T. Double Cipher Implementation in a Ubiquitous Processor Chip. American Journal of Computer Architecture (2012). , 1(1), 6-11.

[6] Sato, T, Imaruoka, S, & Fukase, M. Hardware-Based IPS for Embedded Systems: proceedings of the 13th World Multi-Conference on Systemics, Cybernetics and Informatics, WMSCI 2009, IIII July (2009). Orlando, Florida., 74-79.

[7] Chikazawa, T, & Matui, M. Globalization of Japanese Cryptographic Technology. Journal of Digital Practice (2011). , 2(4), 267-273.

[8] Jerraya, A, Tenhunen, H, & Wolf, W. Multiprocessor Systems-on-Chips. Computer Magazine (2005). , 38(7), 36-40.

[9] Oppliger, R. Security and Privacy in an Online World. Computer Magazine (2011). , 44(9), 21-22.

[10] Stavrou, A, Voas, J, Karygiannis, T, & Quirolgico, S. Building Security into Off-the-shelf Smartphones. Computer Magazine (2012). , 45(2), 82-84.

[11] Burns, F, Bystrov, A, Koelmans, A, & Yakovlev, A. Security Evaluation of Balanced 1-of-n Circuits. IEEE Transactions on VLSI Systems (2011). , 19(11), 2135-2139.

[12] Wang, M-Y, Su, C-P, Horng, C-L, Wu, C, Huang, W, & Single- And, C. -T. Multi-core Configurable AES Architectures for Flexible Security. IEEE Transactions on VLSI Systems (2010). , 18(4), 541-552.

[13] Matsui, M. Survey of the Research and Development of MISTY Cryptography. Journal of Digital Practice (2011). , 2(4), 282-289.

[14] Fukase, M, & Sato, T. A Ubiquitous Processor Built-in a Waved Multifunctional Unit. ECTI-CIT Transactions (2010). , 4(1), 1-7.

[15] Lawton, G. Moving Java into Mobile Phones. Computer Magazine (2002). , 35(6), 17-20.

[16] Kochnev, D. S, & Terekhov, A. A. Surviving Java for Mobiles. IEEE Pervasive Computing (2003). , 2(2), 90-95.

[17] Chen, K-Y, Chang, J. M, & Hou, T-W. Multithreading in Java: Performance and Scalability on Multicore Systems. IEEE Transactions on Computers (2011). , 60(11), 1521-1534.

[18] Lee, Y, Jeong, D-K, & Kim, T. Comprehensive Analysis and Control of Design Parameters for Power Gated Circuits. IEEE Transactions on VLSI Systems (2011). , 19(3), 494-498.

[19] Alioto, M, Poli, M, & Rocchi, S. A General Power Model of Differential Power Analysis Attacks to Static Logic Circuits. IEEE Transactions on VLSI Systems (2010). , 18(5), 711-724.

[20] Fukase, M. A Ubiquitous Processor Embedded With Progressive Cipher Pipelines. International Journal of Multimedia Technology (2013)., 3(1), 31-37.

[21] Zari, M, Saiedian, H, & Naeem, M. Understanding and Reducing Web Delays. Computer Magazine (2001). , 34(12), 30-37.

Chapter 5

Efficient Computation for Pairing Based Cryptography: A State of the Art

Nadia El Mrabet

Additional information is available at the end of the chapter

1. Introduction

Cryptographic protocols are divided in two main classes, symmetric systems where keys are secret and asymmetric approaches with public keys. The security of this second category is based on algebraic problems known to be difficult to solve. Historically, in 1976, Diffie-Hellman described a protocol [26] which was one of the first crypto-systems based on the discrete logarithm problem. Later, the introduction of the elliptic curve in cryptography was promoted by V. Miller [55] and N. Koblitz [47] and a large spectrum of crypto-systems appeared. Pairings are bilinear maps which allow to transform an approach on abelian curves, such as elliptic ones, to a problem on finite fields. A first use of such maps concerns cryptanalysis and was proposed in 1993 by Menezes Okamoto and Vanstone [53] and in 1994 by G. Frey and H.G. Rück [36] they linked pairings to the discrete logarithmic problem on curves.

In 2000, A. Joux [45] had proposed a tripartite Diffie-Hellmann keys exchange using pairing. That was the beginning of a blossoming literature on the subject. In 2003, D. Boneh and M. Franklin broke a challenge given by Shamir[65] in 1984, creating an identity-based encryption scheme [19] based on pairings. The construction of the pairings is based on the algorithm proposed in 1986 by Victor Miller [54, 56]. A consequence of the rich literature on this subject [62] was the creation of a conference devoted to pairing based cryptography, Pairings [60].

With the birth of this new domain of investigation in cryptography, the problem of implementing these protocols occurs. This point is very relevant to the interest of pairings, the costs and the performances of the implementation make a cryptosystem available. Some good studies on pairings implementation are given by P. Barreto et al [13, 15], we can also refer to some books [29, 37]. We detail later what is a pairing, but at a high level: a pairing is a bilinear map between two groups G_1, G_2 into a third group G_3 all abelian groups and of the same order.

$$e : G_1 \times G_2 \longrightarrow G_3$$

The bilinearity is the property that

$$e(a \cdot A, b \cdot B) = e(A, B)^{a \cdot b}.$$

For efficient realization G_1 and G_2 are subgroups of an elliptic curve and G_3 is a subgroup of a finite field. The size of the group is fixed by security considerations and lays on the fact that the discrete logarithm problem is hard to solve over G_1, G_2 and G_3. The pairings are mainly computed with the Miller's algorithm. As a pairing evaluation can be enclosed in a smart card, the question of an efficient implementation is very important.

Several publications are dealing with the efficiency of implementation of pairings. Each of them focus on one aspect of the implementation. We want here to bring together each possible optimizations. The outline of the chapter is the following. First in Section 2 we present the necessary background for a pairing implementation. We present the two first pairings the Weil and the Tate pairings, as well as the optimizations of these, the Eta pairing, the Ate pairing, the twisted Ate pairing, which leads to the notion of optimal pairing and pairing lattices. We also give a first analysis of the arithmetic of pairings. In Section 4, we present the mathematical optimizations of pairings. The use of twisted elliptic curves which leads to the denominator elimination, the improvement of a squaring using cyclotomic subgroups. In Section 5, we present the arithmetical optimizations of a pairing implementation. We describe the different options for an efficient multiplication in Section 5.2, 5.3, 5.3.1 and 5.4. We describe as well how an original representation of a finite field can improve a pairing computation in Section 5.5. In Section 5.6, we describe how the choice of the model of elliptic curve and of its coordinates has a consequence on the implementation. Finally, we conclude in Section 6.

2. Background and notation

Let E be an elliptic curve over a finite field $\mathbb{F}_q$, with P_∞ denoting the identity element of the associated group of rational points $E(\mathbb{F}_p)$. For a positive integer $r | \#E(\mathbb{F}_p)$ coprime to p, let $\mathbb{F}_{p^k}$ be the smallest extension field of $\mathbb{F}_p$ which contains the r-th roots of unity in $\overline{\mathbb{F}}_p$; the extension degree k is called the security multiplier or embedding degree. Let $E(\mathbb{F}_p)[r]$ (respectively $E(\mathbb{F}_{p^k})[r]$) denote the subgroup of $E(\mathbb{F}_p)$ (respectively $E(\mathbb{F}_{p^k})$) of all points of order dividing r. The two groups G_1 and G_2 will be subgroups of elliptic curve groups and G_3 is a subgroup of the multiplicative group of a finite field.

2.1. The Weil, Tate and Ate pairings

2.1.1. The Miller algorithm

The Miller algorithm is the most important step for the Weil, Tate and Ate pairings computation. It is constructed like a double and add scheme using the construction of $[r]P$. Miller's algorithm is based on the notion of divisors. We only give here the essential elements for the pairing computation.

The Miller algorithm constructs the rational function $f_{r,P}$ associated to the point P, where P is a generator of $G_1 \subset E(\mathbb{F}_p)$; and at the same time, it evaluates $f_{r,P}(Q)$ for a point $Q \in G_2 \subset E(\mathbb{F}_{p^k})$.

Algorithm 1: Miller(P,Q,l)

Data: $l = (l_n \dots l_0)$(radix 2 representation), $P \in G_1(\subset E(\mathbb{F}_p))$ and $Q \in G_2(\subset E(\mathbb{F}_{p^k}))$;
Result: $F_P(Q) \in G_3(\subset \mathbb{F}_{p^k}^*)$;
1 : $T \leftarrow P$;
2 : $f_1 \leftarrow 1$;
3 : $f_2 \leftarrow 1$;
for $i = n-1$ **to** 0 **do**
$\quad$ 4 : $T \leftarrow [2]T$, 5 : $f_1 \longleftarrow f_1^2 \times h_1(Q)$, $h_1(x)$ is the equation of the tangent at the point T;
$\quad$ **if** $l_i = 1$ **then**
$\quad\quad$ 6 : $T \leftarrow T+P$;
$\quad\quad$ 7 : $f_1 \longleftarrow f_1 \times h_2(Q)$, $h_2(x)$ is the equation of the line (PT);
$\quad$ **end**
end
return f_1

2.1.2. The pairings

Definition 2.1. The Weil pairing, denoted e_W, is defined by:

$$e_W : G_1 \times G_2 \rightarrow G_3,$$
$$(P,Q) \rightarrow (-1)^r \frac{f_{r,P}(Q)}{f_{r,Q}(P)}.$$

Definition 2.2. The Tate pairing, denoted e_{Tate}, is defined by:

$$G_1 \times G_2 \mapsto G_3$$
$$(P,Q) \mapsto e_{Tate}(P,Q) = f_{r,P}(Q).$$

Here, the function $f_{r,P}$ is normalized, i.e. $(u_0^r f_{r,P})(P_\infty) = 1$ for some $\mathbb{F}_p$-rational uniformizer at P_∞. This pairing is only defined up to a representative of $(F_{p^k})^r$. In order to obtain a unique value we raise it to the power $\frac{p^k-1}{r}$, obtaining an r-th root of unity that we call the reduced Tate pairing

$$\hat{e}_{Tate}(P,Q) = f_{r,P}(Q)^{\frac{p^k-1}{r}}.$$

Let π_p be the Frobenius map over the elliptic curve: $\pi_p : E \rightarrow E : (x,y) \rightarrow (x^p, y^p)$. We denote the Frobenius trace by t. Let $T = t-1$, $G_1 := E[r] \cap \mathrm{Ker}(\pi_p - [1])$ and $G_2 := E[r] \cap \mathrm{Ker}(\pi_p - [q])$

Theorem 2.3. For $P \in G_1$ and $p \in G_2$ the following properties hold [43]:

◇ $f_{T,Q}(P)$ is a bilinear pairing called the Ate pairing.
◇ Let $N = \gcd(T^k - 1, p^k - 1)$ and $T^k - 1 = NL$, then $e_{Tate}(Q,P)^L = f_{T,Q}(P)^{c(p^k-1)/N}$, where $c = \sum_{i=0}^{k-1} T^{k-1-i} p^i \equiv kp^{k-1} \mathrm{mod}(r)$
◇ for r not dividing L, the Ate pairing is non degenerated.

We therefore obtain the reduced Ate pairing $f_{T,Q}(P)^{(p^k-1)/r}$ which is a power of the Tate pairing. As the trace t is in average of size $\sqrt{p}$, for $r \sim p$, the loop length of Miller's algorithm when computing the Ate pairing is obviously going to be two times shorter than the loop length for the Tate pairing.

2.2. The Duursma-Lee pairing

Duursma and Lee use a family of hyperelliptic curves including supersingular curves over finite fields of characteristic three and adapt it to pairing.

For $\mathbb{F}_p$ with $p = 3^m$ and $k = 6$, suitable curves are defined by an equation of the form

$$E : y^2 = x^3 - x + b,$$

with $b = \pm 1 \in \mathbb{F}_3$. If $\mathbb{F}_{p^3} = \mathbb{F}_p[\rho]/(\rho^3 - \rho - b)$, and $\mathbb{F}_{p^6} = \mathbb{F}_{p^3}[\sigma]/(\sigma^2 + 1)$ then the distortion map $\phi : E(\mathbb{F}_p) \to E(\mathbb{F}_{p^6})$ is defined by $\phi(x,y) = (\rho - x, \sigma y)$. Then, setting $G_1 = G_2 = E(\mathbb{F}_{3^m})$ and $G_3 = \mathbb{F}_{p^6}$, Algorithm 2 computes an admissible, symmetric pairing.

Algorithm 2: The Duursma-Lee pairing algorithm.

Input : $P = (x_P, y_P) \in G_1$ and $Q = (x_Q, y_Q) \in G_2$.
Output: $e(P, Q) \in G_3$.

$f \leftarrow 1$;
for $i = 1$ **upto** m **do**
    $x_P \leftarrow x_P^3, y_P \leftarrow y_P^3$;
    $\mu \leftarrow x_P + x_Q + b$;
    $\lambda \leftarrow -y_P y_Q \sigma - \mu^2$;
    $g \leftarrow \lambda - \mu\rho - \rho^2$;
    $f \leftarrow f \cdot g$;
    $x_Q \leftarrow x_Q^{1/3}, y_Q \leftarrow y_Q^{1/3}$;
end
return f^{p^3-1};

2.3. The η and η_G pairings

Barreto et al. [12] introduce the η pairing by generalising the Duursma-Lee pairing to allow use of supersingular curves over finite fields of any small characteristic; Kwon [49] independently used the same approach and in both cases characteristic two is of specific interest. The η pairing has already a simple final powering, but work done by Galbraith et al. [38] (see [59, Section 5.4]) demonstrates that it can be eliminated entirely; the crucial step is the lack of normal denominator elimination, which is enabled by evaluation of additional line functions. Interestingly, the analysis of this approach demonstrates no negative security implication in terms of pairing inversion and so on. We follow Whelan and Scott [71] by terming this approach to the η_G pairing.

For $\mathbb{F}_p$ with $p = 2^m$ and $k = 4$, suitable curves are defined by an equation of the form

$$E : y^2 + y = x^3 + x + b$$

Algorithm 3: The η pairing algorithm.

Input : $P = (x_P, y_P) \in G_1$ and $Q = (x_Q, y_Q) \in G_2$.
Output: $e(P,Q) \in G_3$.

$f \leftarrow 1;$
for $i = 1$ **upto** m **do**

    $x_P \leftarrow x_P^2, \; y_P \leftarrow y_P^2;$
    $\mu \leftarrow x_P + x_Q;$
    $\lambda \leftarrow \mu + x_P x_Q + y_P + y_Q + b;$
    $g \leftarrow \lambda + \mu t + (\mu + 1)t^2;$
    $f \leftarrow f \cdot g;$
    $x_Q \leftarrow x_Q^{1/2}, \; y_Q \leftarrow y_Q^{1/2};$

end
return $f^{p^2 - 1};$

Algorithm 4: The η_G pairing algorithm.

Input : $P = (x_P, y_P) \in G_1$ and $Q = (x_Q, y_Q) \in G_2$.
Output: $e(P,Q) \in G_3$.

---

with $b \in \mathbb{F}_2$. If $\mathbb{F}_{p^2} = \mathbb{F}_p[s]/(s^2 + s + 1)$ and $\mathbb{F}_{p^4} = \mathbb{F}_{p^2}[t]/(t^2 + t + s)$ then the distortion map $\phi : E(\mathbb{F}_p) \to E(\mathbb{F}_{p^4})$ is defined by $\phi(x,y) = (x + s^2, y + sx + t)$. Note that $s = t^5$ and that t satisfies $t^4 = t + 1$, so we can also represent $\mathbb{F}_{p^4}$ as $\mathbb{F}_p[t]/(t^4 + t + 1)$. Then, by setting $G_1 = G_2 = E(\mathbb{F}_p)$ and $G_3 = \mathbb{F}_{p^4}$, Algorithm 4 computes an admissible, symmetric pairing.

Historically, the Weil and Tate pairing was developed by mathematicians without any consideration for cryptography. As efficient implementation of pairings become an interesting question for cryptographers, they searched for improving these two pairings. The Ate and twisted Ate pairing were improvement of the Tate pairing, throught mathematical properties [43]. The notion of Optimal pairing [70] and pairing lattices [42] are the latest properties of pairing. The number of iterations is reduced to the minimum in [70]. In [42], F. Hess proves that every pairing are in relation, because the different pairings are in fact element of a lattice in which each pairing is a power of another pairing. To present the following Sections, we work over the Tate pairing, since as any optimizations of the Tate pairing can be easily adapted to others pairings.

2.4. Analysis of the arithmetic

In order to present the different existing options for the optimizations of a pairing computation, we will focus on the Miller's algorithm. Among the several algorithms which exist to compute a pairing, the most efficient implementations are obtained with the Miller's algorithm.

Let $P = (X_P, Y_P)$ be a point in affine coordinates of the set $E(\mathbb{F}_p)[r]$ (or in Jacobian coordinates with $Z_P = 1$). We consider the point p of order r in $E(\mathbb{F}_{p^k})$, also given in affine coordinates (x_Q, y_Q). Let $G_1 = <P>$ be the subgroup of order r of $E(\mathbb{F}_p)$ generated by the point P and $G_2 = <Q>$ the subgroup of order r of $E(\mathbb{F}_{p^k})$. We want to compute a pairing between G_1 and G_2, under the condition $G_1 \neq G_2$. The group G_3 is a subgroup of order r of $\mathbb{F}_{p^k}^\star$.

Let $T = (X_T, Y_T, Z_T)$ be a point of $E(\mathbb{F}_{p^k})$ in Jacobian coordinates. The main advantage of Jacobian coordinates is that there is no inversion during the arithmetical operation over the elliptic curve.

The Miller's algorithm is given in Algorithm 5.

Algorithm 5: Miller(P, Q, r)

Données: $r = (r_n \ldots r_0)$(binary representation), $P \in G_1 (\subset E(\mathbb{F}_p))$ and $Q \in G_2 (\subset E(\mathbb{F}_{p^k}))$;
Résultat: $f_{r,P}(Q) \in G_3 (\subset \mathbb{F}_{p^k}^{\star})$;

1. $T \leftarrow P$;
2. $f_1 \leftarrow 1$;
3. $f_2 \leftarrow 1$;
for $i = n - 1$ **to** 0 **do**
    4. $T \leftarrow [2]T$;
    5. $f_1 \longleftarrow f_1^2 \times l_1(Q)$, l_1 is the tangent at point T of E. ;
    6. $f_2 \longleftarrow f_2^2 \times v_1(Q)$, v_1 is the vertical line at point $[2]T$. ;
    ($Div(\frac{l_1}{v_1}) = 2(T) - ([2]T) - P_\infty$);
    if $n_i = 1$ **then**
        7. $T \leftarrow T + P$;
        8. $f_1 \longleftarrow f_1 \times l_2(Q)$, l_2 is the line (PT) ;
        9. $f_2 \longleftarrow f_2 \times v_2(Q)$, v_2 is the vertical line at $P + T$;
        ($Div(\frac{l_2}{v_2}) = (T) + D_P - ((T) \oplus D_P) - P_\infty$);
    end
    return $\frac{f_1}{f_2}$
end

The functions $l_1(Q)$, $l_2(Q)$, $v_1(Q)$ and $v_2(Q)$ occurring in Miller's algorithm have their images in $\mathbb{F}_{p^k}^{\star}$. The parameters f_1 and f_2 are elements of $\mathbb{F}_{p^k}^{\star}$.

The order r of the subgroups is chosen with a very sparse binary decomposition. In this case, the addition step in Miller's algorithm is not often executed, whereas the doubling step is computed for every iteration of the Miller's algorithm. As a consequence, we consider that the complexity of Miller's algorithm is approximately given by the doubling step. So we will only consider the computation of l_1 and v_1 in the complexity evaluation of Miller's algorithm.

In a general case, we consider that the equation of the elliptic curve is given into the Weierstrass form $E : Y^2 = X^3 + aXZ^4 + bZ^6$, with a and b elements of $\mathbb{F}_p$. In order to be very general, we consider a and b ordinary. Indeed, it is possible to consider that $a = -3$ [20] and the value of b is also a vector of optimizations, but we do not take in consideration these options. We denote $P = (X_P, Y_P)$, $T = (X_T, Y_T, Z_T)$ is the current point in the Miller's algorithm and $2T = (X_{2T}, Y_{2T}, Z_{2T})$ the doubling of T.

The formulas of the doubling in Jacobian coordinates are the following [25]

$$C = 2Y_T^2, \quad D = Z_T^2, \quad A = 4X_T Y_T^2 = 2X_T C, \quad B = (3X_T^2 + aZ_T^4) \tag{1}$$

$$X_{2T} = B^2 - 2A, \quad Y_{2T} = B(A - X_{2T}) - 2C^2, \quad Z_{2T} = 2Y_T Z_T. \tag{2}$$

In this case, the expressions of l_1 and v_1, for $Q = (x_Q, y_Q) \in E(\mathbb{F}_{p^k})$ are given by

$$l_1(x_Q, y_Q) = Z_P^2 (Z_{2T} D y_Q - B(D x_Q - X_T) - 2Y_T) \tag{3}$$

$$v_1(x_Q, y_Q) = Z_{2T}^2 Z_P x_Q + 4Y_P^2 (X_P D + X_T Z_P^2) - Z_P^2 B^2. \tag{4}$$

We could remark that some intermediary results of the previous formulas may be reused, for instance Y_T^2, Z_T^2, $4X_T Y_T^2$, $(3X_T^2 + aZ_T^4)$. This precomputation reduce the cost of the doubling step, considering the number of operations over the finite field $\mathbb{F}_p$.

Let A_{p^e} (respectively Sub_{p^e}, Sq_{p^e} and M_{p^e}) denote an addition (respectively a subtraction, a squaring and a multiplication) in the finite field $\mathbb{F}_{p^e}$, for e a natural integer. Let also M_a be the cost of a multiplication by a. The Table 1 gives the cost of each operation occurring in the computation of the doubling step. Each cost is given in number of operations over the finite fields. We optimize the computation as possible without any trick different from the one which are following. We consider that a multiplication by 2 is nothing more than a shift in binary representation and thus may be neglected. As a consequence, a multiplication by 3 can be seen as a multiplication by 2 plus an addition and then a multiplication by 3 is equivalent to an addition.

Doubling of a point over E	$4A_p + 3Sub_p + M_a + 4S_p + 4M_p$
Evaluation of l_1	$2Sub_p + Sub_{p^k} S_p + (3 + 3k)M_P$
Evaluation of v_1	$2A_p + Sub_p + 3S_p + (5 + k)M_P$
Step 1 in Algorithm 5	$6A_p + 4Sub_p + Sub_{p^k} + 8S_p + (12 + 4k)M_p + 2S_{p^k} + 2M_{p^k}$

Table 1. Cost of the doubling step in Miller's algorithm

We will present in Section 4 the optimizations related with mathematics and in Section the optimization in pairings related with the arithmetic of finite fields, in Section 4 the optimizations related with mathematics, in Section 5 the optimizations related with algorithmical breakout.

3. Pairing based cryptography

The first use of pairing in cryptography was destructive: in [53] the Weil pairing was used to shift the discrete logarithm problem from an elliptic curve to a finite field. As the discrete logarithm problem is more easily solved over a finite field than over an elliptic curve, the MOV attack consists in transfering a hard problem over a structure where the same problem is easier. The MOV attack is named after its authors Menezes Okamoto and Vanstome. Later on the pairing was used to improve existing protocols as tri-partite Diffie Hellman key exchange [45] and to construct original protocol like identity based encryption [19, 21].

The aim of identity based encryption is that a person λ, even if λ does not know anything about cryptography, is able to receive and more importantly to read an encrypted message with almost no help.

The public key of λ is its identity, its private key would be send to λ by a trusted authority T. This trusted authority will have all the private keys related with the identity based protocol.

The general scheme of identity based encryption is the following.

The public data are an elliptic curve E over a finite field $\mathbb{F}_p$, a pairing $\hat{e}$ and a hash function H, this hash function associates a point of $E(\mathbb{F}_p)$ to an identity: $H : \{Identity\} \rightarrow E(\mathbb{F}_p)$. We consider that two person Alice and Bob want to exchange a common secret for use it as a key in a secure communication.

With the public data, Alice can compute $Q_B = H(Bob)$ the public key of Bob and Bob can compute $Q_A = H(Alice)$ the public key of Alice.

Alice and Bob request the trusted authority to receive their secret key. The secret key is a point of $E(\mathbb{F}_p)$.

The trusted authority chooses s, as its secret key, then it generates $P_A = [s]Q_A$ the secret key of Alice and $P_B = [s]Q_B$ the secret key of Bob.

Then, Alice (respectively Bob) can compute $\hat{e}(P_A, Q_B)$ (resp. $\hat{e}(Q_A, P_B)$), by bilinearity, Alice and Bob have calculated the same key: $\hat{e}(Q_A, Q_B)^{[s]}$. Indeed:

$$\hat{e}([s]H(A), H(B)) = \hat{e}(H(A), [s]H(B)) = \hat{e}(H(A), H(B))^{[s]}.$$

4. Mathematical optimizations

We recall here the mathematical optimizations of pairings. As a pairing is defined over an elliptic curve which is an abelian variety, the first optimization for a pairing computation comes from the mathematical background of pairings. We will use the twist of an elliptic curve, the pairing friendly elliptic curve will follow. We will consider the cyclotomic subgroup of a finite field and then how the final exponentiation in a pairing computation can be improve.

4.1. The twist of an elliptic curve

The twisted elliptic curve of E is another elliptic curve isomorphic to E. Using twisted elliptic curves (when it is possible) in pairing based cryptography is a way to avoid the denominator evaluation in Miller's algorithm. The execution of Miller's algorithm involves computation over $E(\mathbb{F}_{p^k})$, considering a twist of degree d of $E(\mathbb{F}_{p^k})$ allows some computations to be executed in $\tilde{E}(\mathbb{F}_{p^{k/d}})$, where $\tilde{E}(\mathbb{F}_{p^{k/d}})$ is the twisted elliptic curve of $E(\mathbb{F}_{p^k})$ [64].

Definition 4.1. Let E and E' be two elliptic curves, the elliptic curve E' is **a twisted elliptic curve of** E if there exists an isomorphisme Φ defined over $\overline{\mathbb{F}}_p$ mapping each point of E' to a point of E.

There is a limited number of twisted elliptic curves of E. The number of twisted curves depends on the finite field on which the elliptic curve E is defined. The Theorem 4.2 from [64] gives the classification of the possible twists.

Theorem 4.2. *Let E be an elliptic curve of equation $y^2 = x^3 + ax + b$ defined over $\mathbb{F}_{p^k}$. Following the value of k, the possible degrees d of twists are 2, 3, 4 and 6. Let E' be a twist of E, the morphism between E and E' is one of the following.*

- $d = 2$, $E' : Dy^2 = x^3 + ax + b$ defined over $\mathbb{F}_{p^{k/2}}$, where $D \in \mathbb{F}_{p^{k/2}}$ is not a quadratic residue, i.e. such that the polynomial $X^2 - D$ has no solution over $\mathbb{F}_{p^{k/2}}$. The morphism Φ_d is defined by

$$\Phi_d : E' \to E$$
$$\Phi_d(x,y) \to (x, yD^{1/2}).$$

- $d = 4$. The elliptic curve E has a twist of degree 4 if and only if $b = 0$. The equation of E' is then $y^2 = x^3 + \frac{a}{D}x$, where D is not a residue of degree 4, i.e. D is not solution in $\mathbb{F}_{p^{k/4}}$ of a polynomial $X^4 - D$. The morphism is then

$$\Phi_d : E' \to E$$
$$\Phi_d(x,y) \to (xD^{1/2}, yD^{3/4}).$$

- $d = 3$ (resp. 6), the curve E has a twist of degree 3 or 6 if and only if $a = 0$. The equation of E' is then $y^2 = x^3 + \frac{b}{D}$, where D is not a residue of degree 3 (resp. 6), i.e. D is not solution of a polynomial $X^3 - D$ (resp. $X^6 - D$). The morphism is then

$$\Phi_d : E' \to E$$
$$\Phi_d(x,y) \to (xD^{1/3}, yD^{1/2}).$$

Considering the definition above, an elliptic curve can admit a twist of degree 2, 3, 4 or 6. We will only consider here the twisted elliptic curve for an even degree. In order to simplify the notations, we will consider a twist of degree 2. The same method can be applied for twists of degree 4 and 6. The case of twist of degree 3 is a little different, but can also be considered, we refer to [31] for more details. Using a twisted elliptic curve of $E(\mathbb{F}_{p^k})$ allows to make some computation of the Miller's algorithm in a subfield of $\mathbb{F}_{p^k}$, instead of $\mathbb{F}_{p^k}$ and thus allows to simplify the computation. Using a twisted elliptic curve is the solution to avoid the denominators in the Miller's algorithm (i.e. the update of the function f_2). We will denote $\widetilde{E}(\mathbb{F}_{p^{k/2}})$ the twisted curve of $E(\mathbb{F}_{p^k})$, for an even k. We could remark that the twisted elliptic curve of E is an elliptic curve define over an extension of degree half of the initial extension ($\mathbb{F}_{p^k}$) [11]. Let $v \in \mathbb{F}_{p^{k/2}}$ a non square element in $\mathbb{F}_{p^{k/2}}$, then $\sqrt{v}$ is an element of $\mathbb{F}_{p^k} \setminus \mathbb{F}_{p^{k/2}}$. We can define $\widetilde{E}$ the twisted elliptic curve of $E(\mathbb{F}_{p^k})$ of equation $vy^2 = x^3 - 3x + b$. The morphism mapping $\widetilde{E}(\mathbb{F}_{p^{k/2}})$ to $E(\mathbb{F}_{p^k})$ is Ψ_2 define by

$$\Psi_2 : \widetilde{E}(\mathbb{F}_{p^{k/2}}) \to E(\mathbb{F}_{p^k})$$
$$(x,y) \to (x, y\sqrt{v}).$$

The probability that the point $Q = (x, y\sqrt{v})$ image of $Q' = (x,y) \in \widetilde{E}$ by Ψ_2 belongs to the subgroup generate by $P \in E(\mathbb{F}_p)$ is negligeable [11]. This assures us that the pairing is non degenerated between

$P \in E(\mathbb{F}_p)$ and $Q = \Psi_2(Q')$. As a consequence, we can consider that the coordinates of the point Q are element of $\mathbb{F}_{p^{k/2}}$ plus a multiplication by $\sqrt{v}$.

We give the formulae for Miller's algorithm with the use of a twisted elliptic curve. Let A, B, C, D, E and F be the intermediate values in the doubling and addition of a point over E (in Jacobian coordinates). These values are dependant only on the point $P = (X_P; Y_P; Z_P)$ and multiples of P: $T = (X_T; Y_T; Z_T)$; $2T = (X_{2T}; Y_{2T}; Z_{2T})$ and $T + P = (X_3; Y_3; Z_3)$. The equations of functions l_1, l_2, v_1 and v_2 are

$$
\begin{aligned}
l_1(x_Q, y_Q\sqrt{v}) &= Z_P^2(Z_{2T}Dy_Q\sqrt{v} - B(Dx_Q - X_T) - 2Y_T), \\
v_1(x_Q, y_Q\sqrt{v}) &= Z_{2T}^2 Z_P x_Q + 4Y^2(X_P D + X_T Z_P^2) - 9Z_P^2(X_T^2 - Z_T^4)^2, \\
l_2(x_Q, y_Q\sqrt{v}) &= Z_{T+P}^2(Z_T^3 Ey_Q\sqrt{v} - Z_T F(Z_T^2 x_Q) - Y_T E), \\
v_2(x_Q, y_Q\sqrt{v}) &= Z_T^3 E(Z_3^3 x_Q + E(A+B) - Z_T^2 Z_P^2 F).
\end{aligned}
\tag{5}
$$

The multiplications and additions in these formulae are made in $\mathbb{F}_p$ and $\mathbb{F}_{p^{k/2}}$. For $x_Q \in \mathbb{F}_{p^{k/2}}$, if we consider carefully the equations of v_1 and v_2, we can remark that the results $v_1(x_Q, y_Q\sqrt{v})$ and $v_2(x_Q, y_Q\sqrt{v})$ are elements of $\mathbb{F}_{p^{k/2}}$. Indeed, the y-coordinate of Q does not appear in the denominator v_1 and consequently $\sqrt{v}$ either. This simple remark allows the elimination of the denominators during the Tate pairing computation.

Property 4.3. *During the evaluation of Miller's algorithm for the Tate pairing, the evaluation of f_2 and thus the computations of v_1 and v_2 can be omited [11].*

Indeed, when using a twist, the equation shows that $v_1(Q)$, $v_2(Q) \in \mathbb{F}_{p^{k/2}}$ and then $f_2 \in \mathbb{F}_{p^{k/2}}$. By definition of the embedding degree k of the elliptic curve, $\frac{p^k-1}{r}$ is a multiple of $p^{k/2} - 1$ and $f_2^{\frac{p^k-1}{r}} = 1$ by the following proposition.

Property 4.4. *Let r be a prime divisor of $\#E(\mathbb{F}_p)$ and E be an elliptic curve of embedding degree k relatively to r. Then $\frac{p^k-1}{r}$ is a multiple of $p^{k/2} - 1$.*

Proof. The demonstration is a straight forward consequence of the construction of k as the smallest integer such that r divides $p^k - 1$. So for an even k, $p^k - 1 = (p^{k/2} - 1)(p^{k/2} + 1)$ and r a prime integer divides $p^k - 1$. Using the Gauss theorem, r divides $(p^{k/2} - 1)$ or $(p^{k/2} + 1)$. If r divides $(p^{k/2} - 1)$, then the definition of k would be wrong, thus the only possibility is that r divides $(p^{k/2} + 1)$. $\square$

For all $\xi \in \mathbb{F}_{p^{k/2}}$, we know that $\xi^{p^{k/2}-1} \equiv 1$ (from the Little Fermat's theorem). Consequently the final exponentiation of the Tate pairing kills every factor of the result belonging to a proper subfield of $\mathbb{F}_{p^k}$. The Miller's computation can be simplified by forgetting v_1 and v_2. But with the same remark, we can also simplify the function l_1 and l_2 into

$$
\begin{aligned}
l_1(x_Q, y_Q\sqrt{v}) &= Z_{2T}Dy_Q\sqrt{v} - B(Dx_Q - X_T) - 2Y_T, \\
l_2(x_Q, y_Q\sqrt{v}) &= Z_T^3 Ey_Q\sqrt{v} - Z_T F(Z_T^2 x_Q) - Y_T E.
\end{aligned}
\tag{6}
$$

This method can be applied for every pairing with a final exponentiation. In the case of the Weil pairing, we can also apply it by raising the result of Weil pairing at the power $p^{k/2} - 1$. The cost of this exponentiation will be study in Section 4.4.

In order to illustrate the simplification of the computation with the use of a pairing, we compare two computations of the doubling step in Miller's algorithm. The Miller Lite execution is the computation of the Miller's algorithm for the Tate pairing ($Miller(P, Q)$). The Miller full execution is the computation of $Miller(Q, P)$. The Table 2 compare the cost of the doubling step in Miller Lite and Miller Full with and without the use of twisted elliptic curve.

Miller	Without twist	With twist
Lite	$8S_p + (12 + 4k)M_p + 2S_{p^k} + 2M_{p^k}$	$4S_p + (7 + k)M_p + S_{p^k} + M_{p^k}$
Full	$3kM_p + 10S_{p^k} + 14M_{p^k}$	$kM_p + 5S_{p^k} + 7M_{p^k}$

Table 2. Cost of Miller Lite and Miller Full

4.2. Pairing friendly fields and elliptic curves

The computation of pairings implies computations over extension fields of the form $\mathbb{F}_{p^k}$. If the embedding degree k is smooth, than the arithmetic in $\mathbb{F}_{p^k}$ can be computed step by step. A complete an extensive nice definition of smooth number is given in [50], we recall here an intuitive naive definition.

Definition 4.5. A *smooth integer* is an integer such that its prime factor are composed only by small primes.

Example 4.6. An integer of the form $2^i 3^j$ is smooth.

We illustrate how a smooth integer k allows a construction of $\mathbb{F}_{p^k}$ with a tower field.

Example 4.7. Let l be a prime number and m an integer such that $k = lm$. The extension $\mathbb{F}_{p^k}$ of $\mathbb{F}_p$ can be constructed like an extension of degree l of $\mathbb{F}_{p^m}$. We suppose that we have already constructed the extension $\mathbb{F}_{p^m}$. Let $P(X)$ be an irreducible polynomial of degree l in $\mathbb{F}_{p^m}[X]$. Then $\mathbb{F}_{p^{lm}} = \mathbb{F}_{(p^m)^l}$ is constructed with the quotient

$$\mathbb{F}_{p^{lm}} = \mathbb{F}_{p^m}[X] / (P(X)).$$

We use the tower field construction in order to optimize the multiplication over $\mathbb{F}_{p^k}$. We will see in Section 5 that for extensions of degree 2 and 3, we can use the Karatsuba and Toom Cook multiplications. The tower field construction reduce the number of elementary operations over $\mathbb{F}_p$ to compute a multiplication in $\mathbb{F}_{p^k}$ [35].

A.Menezes and N.Koblitz [48] proposed the definition of pairing friendly elliptic curves. There are elliptic curves suitable for pairing computation. Pairing friendly fields are defined with k smooth.

Definition 4.8. A **pairing friendly field** $\mathbb{F}_{p^k}$ is an extension of a finite field $\mathbb{F}_p$ with the following property

- the characteristic p is such that $p \equiv 1 \ mod(12)$,
- the embedding degree k is such that $k = 2^i 3^j$.

Pairing friendly field are such that the polynomial reduction over the extension $\mathbb{F}_{p^k}$ is very easy to compute [50, Theorem 3.75].

Theorem 4.9. *Let $\beta \in \mathbb{F}_p$ be a neither a square nor a cube in $\mathbb{F}_p$ and $\mathbb{F}_{p^k}$ a pairing friendly field with $k = 2^i 3^j$. Then the polynomial $X^k - \beta$ is irreducible in $\mathbb{F}_p$.*

Using the definition and the above property, we construct the extension $\mathbb{F}_{p^k} = \mathbb{F}_p[X]/(X^k - \beta)$ using several extensions of degree 2 and 3. The construction is done step by step with square or cubic root of β and the results.

***Example* 4.10.** Example of possible tower field for $k = 2^2 3^1$:

$$\mathbb{F}_p \xrightarrow{2} L = \mathbb{F}_p[T]/(T^2 - \beta),$$
$$K \xrightarrow{3} M = L[U]/(U^3 - T),$$
$$L \xrightarrow{2} N = M[V]/(V^2 - U).$$

The representation of fields L, M and N are as follow

$$L = \{l_0 + l_1 \beta, \text{ with } l_0, l_1 \in \mathbb{F}_p\},$$
$$M = \{m_0 + m_1 T + m_2 T^2, \text{ with } m_0, m_1, m_2 \in L\},$$
$$N = \{n_0 + n_1 U, \text{ with } n_0, n_1 \in M\}.$$

The arithmetic in $\mathbb{F}_{p^k}$ can be composed in each floor of the tower field construction. As k is a product of power of 2 and 3, the Karatsuba and Toom Cook methods are the more suitable for improving the multiplication in $\mathbb{F}_{p^k}$. We consider that a multiplication in $\mathbb{F}_{p^k}$ with $k = 2^i 3^j$ involves $3^i 5^j$ multiplications in $\mathbb{F}_p$, which is denoted $M_{p^k} = 3^i 5^j M_p$.

4.3. Cyclotomic subgroup and squaring

A. Lenstra and M. Stam introduce in [52] an efficient method for squaring. They use the structure of a cyclotomic subgroup. They construct an extension of degree 6 with a polynomial different from $X^6 - \beta$. The cyclotomic subgroup $G_{\phi_k(p)}$ is the subgroup of order $\phi_k(p)$ of $\mathbb{F}_{p^k}^\star$, where $\phi_k(p)$ is the kth cyclotomic polynomial evaluated at p. The cyclotomic polynomials are constructed such that there roots are the primitive roots of unity.

The multiplication developed by Lenstra and Stam is interesting for computing squares in degree 6 extension of $\mathbb{F}_p$ (or a degree multiple of 6). It could be interesting to generalize it for other degree extension. They construct the degree 6 extension using the cyclotomic polynomial $\phi_k(X) = X^{k/3} - X^{k/6} + 1$. This method can be used for every degree extension multiple of 6.

Let $\alpha \in G_{\phi_k(p)}$, $\alpha = \sum_{i=0}^{k-1} a_i \gamma^i$, where for all i, $a_i \in \mathbb{F}_p$ and $\mathscr{B} = (1, \gamma, \gamma^2, \ldots, \gamma^{k-1})$ is a basis of $\mathbb{F}_{p^k}$.

We are seeking for the general expression of an element in $G_{\phi_k(p)}$. We consider that α is a polynomial in several variables in $\mathbb{F}_p$ (the a_is), with coefficients power of γ in $\mathbb{F}_{p^k}$.

As α belong to the cyclotomic subgroup $G_{\phi_k(p)}$, the order of α divides the cardinal of $G_{\phi_k(p)}$ which is $\phi_k(p)$. So, we have that $\alpha^{p^{k/3}-p^{k/6}+1} = 1$ in $G_{\phi_k(p)}$. This equality can be written $\alpha^{p^{k/3}+1} = \alpha^{p^{k/6}}$.

In order to find the decomposition of $\alpha \times \alpha^{p^{k/3}} - \alpha^{p^{k/6}}$, we can then formally compute $\alpha^{p^{k/3}}$ and $\alpha^{p^{k/6}}$

$$\alpha \times \alpha^{p^{k/3}} - \alpha^{p^{k/6}} = \sum_{i=0}^{k-1} v_i \gamma^i.$$

Where

$$
\begin{aligned}
v_0 &= a_1^2 - a_0 a_2 - a_4 - a_4^2 + a_3 a_5, \\
v_1 &= -a_0 + a_1 a_2 + a_3 - 2a_0 a_3 + a_3^2 - a_2 a_4 - a_1 a_5, \\
v_2 &= -a_0 a_1 + a_3 a_4 - a_5 - 2a_2 a_5 + a_5^2, \\
v_3 &= -a_1 - a_2 a_3 + 2a_1 a_4 - a_4^2 - a_0 a_5 + a_3 a_5, \\
v_4 &= a_0^2 + a_1 a_2 + a_3 - 2a_0 a_3 - a_4 a_5, \\
v_5 &= -a_2 + a_2^2 - a_1 a_3 - a_0 a_4 + a_3 a_4 - 2a_2 a_5.
\end{aligned}
$$

As $\alpha \in G_{\phi_k(p)}$, we have that $\sum_{i=0}^{k-1} v_i \gamma^i = 0$. With this equation, we construct a system in the α_i, the resolution of this system will give us the general form of an element in $G_{\phi_k(p)}$.

The subgroup $G_{\phi_k(p)}$ is the set of elements α such that $\forall i$, $v_i = 0$, which gives $\alpha^2 = \alpha^2 + \mathcal{B}.\Gamma.^t v$, with $\mathcal{B} = (1, \gamma, \gamma^2, ..., \gamma^{k-1})$ and with Γ a chosen matrix. As v is zero in $\mathbb{F}_p$, we can reduce the cost of a square with this method.

Denoting $\alpha^2 = \sum_{i=1}^{k} s_i \gamma^i$, we have the equality

$$\sum_{i=1}^{k} s_i \gamma^i = (\sum_{i=1}^{k} a_i \gamma^i)^2 + \mathcal{B}.\Gamma^t.v.$$

We can formally develop the right expression and for a well chosen matrix Γ, the formulae for a square in $\mathbb{F}_{p^k}$ would be simplified. For instance, for $k = 6$[52] :

$$\alpha^2 = \mathscr{B} . \begin{pmatrix} 2a_1 + 3a_4(a_4 - 2a_1) \\ 2a_0 + 3(a_0 + a_3)(a_0 - a_3) \\ -2a_5 + 3a_5(a_5 - 2a_2) \\ 2(a_2 - a_4) + 3a_1(a_1 - 2a_4) \\ 2(a_0 - a_3) + 3a_3(2a_0 - a_3) \\ -2a_2 + 3a_2(a_2 - 2a_5) \end{pmatrix} . \tag{7}$$

Granger, Page and Smart apply this method to construct the Table 3 [41].

Degree extension k	cost of a square in $\mathbb{F}_{p^k}$
6	$4,5M_p$
12	$18M_p + 12S_p$
24	$84M_p + 24S_p$

Table 3. Complexity of a square in $\mathbb{F}_{p^k}$

In the particular case where $k = 6$ and $p \equiv 2 \pmod 9$, the cost of a square with the Lenstra and Stam method is less than $0,75M_{p^k}$, which is usually the ratio of a square compare to a multiplication.

***Example* 4.11.** In $\mathbb{F}_{p^6}$, a square with Lenstra and Stam method cost $6 \times 0,75M_p \approx 4,5M_p$. With the classical ratio, a square in $\mathbb{F}_{p^6}$ costs $15 \times 0,75M_p \approx 10M_p$.

4.4. The finale exponentiation

The Tate pairing (and also the Ate, optimal Ate) is composed of two steps, first the Miller's execution and then a final exponentiation. This exponentiation is a very expensive operation as it takes place in $\mathbb{F}_{p^k}$ and the exponent $\frac{p^k-1}{r}$ is a large integer. In order to simplify this exponentiation it is split in two parts [48] using the fact that:

$$\frac{(p^k - 1)}{r} = \frac{(p^k - 1)}{\phi_k(p)} \times \frac{\phi_k(p)}{r},$$

where $\phi_k(p)$ is the evaluation in p of the k-th cyclotomic polynomial.

The first part of the exponentiation uses the twisted elliptic curve and it is equivalent to computing the Frobenius map of elements in $\mathbb{F}_{p^k}$. The second part is a reduced exponentiation in $\mathbb{F}_{p^k}$ which is performed with classical method for exponentiation.

4.4.1. First part of the exponentiation

We consider here the exponentiation to the power $\frac{p^k-1}{\phi_k(p)}$. We can first remark that if $k = 2^i 3^j$, then $\phi_k(p) = p^{k/3} - p^{k/6} + 1$ and $\frac{p^k-1}{\phi_k(p)} = (p^{k/2} - 1)(p^{k/6} + 1)$. Using a twist, the result of Miller's algorithm is something like $(X + Y\sqrt{v})$ avec $X, Y \in \mathbb{F}_{p^{k/2}}$.

The computation of $(X + Y\sqrt{v})^{p^{k/2}-1}$ can be decomposed in

$$(X + Y\sqrt{v})^{p^{k/2}} \times (X + Y\sqrt{v})^{-1}.$$

As $(X + Y\sqrt{v})^{-1} = (X + Y\sqrt{v})^{p^{k/2}}$, we have that

$$(X + Y\sqrt{v})^{p^{k/2}-1} = (X + Y\sqrt{v})^{2p^{k/2}}.$$

Raising an element of $\mathbb{F}_{p^k}$ to a power $p^{k/2}$ is a Frobenius operation, which mainly consists in shifts. The total cost of the exponentiation to the power $(p^{k/2} - 1)$ is a square in $\mathbb{F}_{p^k}$ and a Frobenius application. Let $(X' + Y'\sqrt{v})$ be the result of $(X + Y\sqrt{v})^{p^{k/2}-1}$.

We then have to compute $(X' + Y'\sqrt{v})^{p^{k/6}+1}$ which is another application of the Frobenius.

Let γ be a root of $X^k - \beta$ in $\mathbb{F}_{p^k}$. An element a of $\mathbb{F}_{p^k}$ can be decomposed in $a = \sum_{i=0}^{k-1} a_i \gamma^i$, with $a_i \in \mathbb{F}_p$.

The property of a finite field gives $a^p = \sum_{i=0}^{k-1} a_i \gamma^{ip}$ and recursively

$$a^{p^j} = \sum_{i=0}^{k-1} a_i \gamma^{ip^j}.$$

For i and j two integers let q_{ij} and r_{ij} be the quotient and the remainder of the Euclidien division of ip^j by k, we know that

$$\gamma^{ip^j} = \beta^{q_{ij} \bmod(p)} \gamma^{r_{ij}}.$$

The computation of $(X' + Y'\sqrt{v})^{p^{k/6}+1}$ can be decomposed in

$$(X' + Y'\sqrt{v})^{p^{k/6}+1} = (X'^{p^{k/6}} + Y'^{p^{k/6}} \sqrt{v}^{(p^{k/6})}) \times (X' + Y'\sqrt{v})$$

For example, if we describe what happened for the variable X' raised to the power $p^{k/6}$, we obtain the following step

$$\begin{cases} X' = \displaystyle\sum_{i=0}^{k/2-1} x_i \gamma^i, \\[2mm] X'^{p^{k/6}} = \displaystyle\sum_{i=0}^{k/2-1} x_i \gamma^{ip^{(k/6)}}, \\[2mm] X'^{p^{k/6}} = \displaystyle\sum_{i=0}^{k/2-1} (x_i \beta^{q_{i(k/6)}} \bmod (p)) \gamma^{r_{i(k/6)}}. \end{cases}$$

We have to compute the $\frac{k}{2}$ products $(x_i \beta^{q_{i(k/6)}} \bmod(p))$, with x_i and $\beta^{q_{i(k/6)}} \bmod(p)$ in $\mathbb{F}_p$. The total complexity of the first part of the exponentiation is $2kM_p + S_{p^k} + M_{p^k}$ plus shifts and multiplications by β.

Second part of the exponentiation

The second part of the exponentiation is the hard part. We use classical method of exponentiation like the Lucas sequences [16] or sliding windows [40]. In [67], more tricky method are developed.

The Lucas sequence method induces a cost of a square and a multiplication in the intermediate field $\mathbb{F}_{p^{k/2}}$ for each bit of the exponent. The sliding window method has the advantage that the squares are computed in the cyclotomic subgroup and consequently we can use the method described in Section 4.3. The complexity of the two methods is linearly related to the number of the bits in the binary decomposition of the exponent, we recall here the complexity of the methods and refer to for instance the book [25] for more details.

Let b_r be the number of bits of r, the prime number dividing the cardinal of E. Let b_{p^k} be the number of bits of p^k. The respective size of b_r, b_{p^k}, r and p^k are fixed by the security level we want to reach. We give them in the Table 4. The number of positive integers smaller than k and prime with k is $\varphi(k)$, the Euler totent function evaluated at k. The number $\varphi(k)$ is also the number of primitive k-roots of unity, then it is the degree of the polynomial $\phi_k(p)$. The exponent of the second part of the exponentiation is $(\frac{\varphi(k)}{k} b_{p^k} - b_r)$ bits.

The number of squares and multiplications involved for the computation of the exponentiation depends on $\frac{\varphi(k)}{k} b_{p^k} - b_r = (\tau_k \gamma - 1) b_r$, where

$$\gamma = \frac{b_{p^k}}{b_r},$$

$$\tau_k = \frac{\varphi(k)}{k} = \begin{cases} 1/2 \text{ si } k = 2^i, \, i \geqslant 1 \\ 1/3 \text{ si } k = 2^i 3^j, \, i, \, j \geqslant 1 \end{cases}.$$

The number γ is related to the security levels given in the Table 4 and its is a good appreciation of the total complexity of the exponentiation.

Security level in bits	80	128	192	256
Minimal number of for r	160	256	384	512
Minimal number of for p^k	1 024	3 072	7 680	15 360
$\gamma = \frac{b_{p^k}}{b_r}$	6,4	12	20	30

Table 4. Security level

The complexity of the Lucas sequance method is [16]

$$C_{Luc} = (M_{p^{k/2}} + S_{p^{k/2}}) \log_2 \left(\frac{\phi_k(p)}{r} \right).$$

The complexity of the sliding window method is [40]

$$C_{sw} = \left(\frac{\log_2(e)}{\log_2(p)} + \log_2(p) \right) S_{G_{\phi_k(p)}} + \left(\frac{\log_2(e)}{\log_2(p)} \left(2^{n-1} - 1 \right) + \frac{\log_2(e)}{n+2} - 1 \right) M_{p^k},$$

where $e = \frac{\phi_k(p)}{r}$, and n is the integer giving the size of the window in bits, generally $n = 4$.

5. Arithmetical optimisation

As the pairings computation lays on arithmetic over finite fields, a way to improve the efficiency of computation of pairings is to improve the arithmetic of finite fields and extension of finite fields.

The elliptic curve used in pairing based cryptography are constructed throught the complex multiplication method. These methods of constructions do not allow to fixe p the characteristic of the field $\mathbb{F}_p$, we can only choose the number of bits in the decomposition of p. As a consequence, the arithmetic of pairings is particular. We cannot choose p with a special structure which would provide an efficient arithmetic, like for example a sparse decomposition or a Mersenne or Pseudo Mersenne prime. A very nice overview of construction of elliptic curve for pairing based cryptography is available in the work of Freeman, Scott and Teske [33].

We then begin this section with the presentation of efficient multiplications in finite fields and extensions of finite fields. We recall the different methods for a multiplication and we will provide a comparison of efficiency of these multiplications in Section 5.2, 5.3, 5.4. In Section 5.5, we will consider the representation of elements in a finite field. Indeed, in Section 5.1 we describe the classical representation of a finite field, this classical representation is used for the description of the multiplications. But it is possible, to have original representations of finite field, which can offer opportunities for improvement in pairing based cryptography. In Section 5.6 we will consider how the choice of coordinates can be a way for improving the efficiency of computation of pairings and on the equation of the elliptic curve.

5.1. Setting

We consider in this Section the cost of operations over $\mathbb{F}_{p^k}$ in number of operations over $\mathbb{F}_p$. We give the notations for the rest of the chapter. Let $\mathbb{F}_p$ be a finite field field of prime characteristic p, with p of thousands digits. Let $\mathbb{F}_{p^k}$ be the extension of degree k of $\mathbb{F}_p$. The extension $\mathbb{F}_{p^k}$ is defined through an irreducible polynomial $P(X)$ of degree k. Let A and B be two elements of $\mathbb{F}_{p^k}$. The elements of $\mathbb{F}_{p^k}$ are described in the basis $\mathscr{B} = (1, \gamma, \gamma^2, \ldots, \gamma^{k-1})$, for γ a roots of $P(X)$ in $\mathbb{F}_{p^k}$. An element of $\mathbb{F}_{p^k}$ is a polynomial in γ with coefficients in $\mathbb{F}_p$:

$$\mathbb{F}_{p^k} = \{\sum_{i=0}^{k-1} a_i\gamma^i, a_i \in \mathbb{F}_p\}.$$

A is represented by $\sum_{i=1}^{k-1} a_i\gamma^i$ and B by $B = \sum_{i=0}^{k-1} b_i\gamma^i$. The product of A and B can be done in two steps. The first one is the the product of the polynomials, to obtain the polynomial $C(X) = A(X) \times B(X)$ of degree $(2k-2)$. The second step is the polynomial reduction modulo $P(X)$. The cost of this reduction depends on the form of $P(X)$. The more $P(X)$ is sparse, the more the reduction is efficient. As a consequence, $P(X)$ should be as possible chosen of the form $X^k - \beta$, with $\beta \in \mathbb{F}_p$ [50]. In this case, the polynomial reduction is reduced to multiplications by β and $(k-1)$ additions:

$$C(X) = C_0(X) + C_1(X)X^k \equiv C_0(X) + \beta C_1(X) \mod(P(X)).$$

with, $C_0(X), C_1(X)$ of degree $(k-1)$.

The following theorem [50, Theorem 3.75] gives us a natural construction of the extension $\mathbb{F}_{p^k}$ using a sparse representation.

Theorem 5.1. *Let k be an integer and $\mathbb{F}_{p^k}$ an extension of degree k of $\mathbb{F}_p$, for p a prime number. There exists β an element of $\mathbb{F}_p$ which is not a k-th roots in $\mathbb{F}_p$ and such that the polynomial $X^k - \beta$ is irreducible over $\mathbb{F}_p$.*

Thus, we can consider that the complexity of a product in $\mathbb{F}_{p^k}$ is highly dependent on the complexity of the product of two polynomials, neglecting the complexity of the modular reduction. We introduce above the possible multiplications of polynomials.

5.2. The school book method

As the name gives the hint, the school book multiplication is the one we learned at school. The school book method of two polynomials is the following

$$A(\gamma) \times B(\gamma) = \sum_{i=0}^{2k-1} \left(\sum_{j=0}^{i} (a_j b_{i-j}) \right) \gamma^i.$$

This simple method is very expensive, indeed its complexity is quadratic in the degree of the polynomials. The cost of this method is k^2 multiplications in $\mathbb{F}_p$ plus $k(2k-1)$ addition, thus the complexity is $k(2k-1)A_p + k^2 M_p$.

The interpolation method are an alternative to the school book method, there are efficient for k greater than a fixed value. This value depends on the method.

5.3. Interpolation method

Let $A(X) = a_0 + a_1 X + \ldots + a_{k-1} X^{k-1}$ and $B(X) = b_0 + b_1 X + \ldots + b_{k-1} X^{k-1}$ be the polynomials obtained by substitution (γ becomes X). The result $C(X)$ of $A(X) \times B(X)$ is a polynomial of degree $(2k-1)$. It is known that a polynomial of degree m is determined by its image in $(m+1)$ distinct values.

Theorem 5.2. *Let $P(X)$ be a polynomial of degree m, then $P(X)$ is determined by the image of $(m+1)$ distinct values.*

The multiplications by the interpolation method use in this theorem. The methodology is to find $(2k-1)$ images of the polynomial $C(X)$ and then to reconstruct $C(X)$ by interpolation. All multiplications by interpolation follow this scheme

1. Find $(2k-1)$ distinct values in $\mathbb{F}_p$
      denoted by $\alpha_0, \alpha_1, \ldots, \alpha_{2k-2}$.
2. Evaluate the polynomials $A(X)$ and $B(X)$ in these values
      keep in memory $A(\alpha_0), \ldots, A(\alpha_{2k-2}), B(\alpha_0), \ldots, B(\alpha_0)$.

3. Compute the evaluation of C in these $(2k-1)$ values,
$$C(\alpha_i) = A(\alpha_i)B(\alpha_i).$$
4. Use these evaluations of $C(X)$ to reconstruct by interpolation the polynomial $C(X)$.

The complexity of a multiplication by interpolation depends

1. on the evaluation of the $A(\alpha_i)$, $B(\alpha_i)$,
2. on the multiplications in $\mathbb{F}_p$ $C(\alpha_i) = A(\alpha_i) \times B(\alpha_i)$,
3. and on the reconstruction of the polynomial expression of $C(X)$.

If we compare the interpolation method with the school book method, we substitute some multiplications in $\mathbb{F}_p$ by multiplications by constants in $\mathbb{F}_p$. The constants are determined by the choice of the α_i values. The drawback is that the multiplication by interpolation need more additions, but as an addition in $\mathbb{F}_p$ is less expensive than a multiplication, for some degree k interpolation methods are more efficient than the school book method.

Let M_a the cost of a multiplication by the constant a in $\mathbb{F}_p$. The evaluations in $(\alpha_i)_{\{i=0...(2k-1)\}}$ cost

$$2(2k-1)(k-1)(A_p + CM_p),$$

when executed using the Horner scheme:

$$A(\alpha_i) = a_0 + \alpha_i(a_1 + \alpha_i(a_2 + \alpha_i[...])).$$

The computation of the $C(\alpha_i) = A(\alpha_i) \times B(\alpha_i)$ involves $(2k-1)$ multiplications in $\mathbb{F}_p$, which costs $(2k-1)M_p$.

Two classical method of interpolation exist, the Lagrange and the Newton interpolation methods.

5.3.1. Lagrange's interpolation method

We suppose that we have obtained the evaluation of the polynomial $A(X)$ and $B(X)$ in $2k-1$, denoted $(\alpha_0, \alpha_1, ..., \alpha_{2k-2})$. We then have the image of $C(X) = A(X) \times B(X)$ in these $2k-1$ points. The reconstruction of the coefficients of $C(X)$ using the Lagrange interpolation is done through the formula:

$$C(X) = \sum_{i=0}^{2k-2} \left(C(\alpha_i) \times \frac{\prod\limits_{j=0, j \neq i}^{2k-2}(X - \alpha_j)}{\prod\limits_{j=0, j \neq i}^{2k-2}(\alpha_i - \alpha_j)} \right). \tag{8}$$

The complexity of Lagrange's interpolation is

$$(2k-1)M_p + (2k-1)(4k-3)CM_p + 2(2k-1)(3k-2)A_p. \tag{9}$$

5.3.2. Newton's interpolation

As in the Lagrange's interpolation, we dispose of the $C(\alpha_i)$s and we want to find the coefficients of $C(X)$. The Newton's interpolation needs the construction of intermediates values.

The first step is the computation of the values c'_i

$$
\begin{cases}
c'_0 = C(\alpha_0) \\
c'_1 = (C(\alpha_1) - c'_0)\frac{1}{(\alpha_1 - \alpha_0)} \\
c'_2 = \left((C(\alpha_2) - c'_0)\frac{1}{(\alpha_2 - \alpha_0)} - c'_1\right)\frac{1}{(\alpha_2 - \alpha_1)} \\
\vdots = \vdots \\
c'_{2k-2} = \left((C(\alpha_{2k-2}) - c'_0)\frac{1}{(\alpha_{2k-2} - \alpha_0)} - c'_1\right)\frac{1}{(\alpha_{2k-2} - \alpha_1)} - \ldots
\end{cases}
$$

With the c'_is, the expression of $C(X)$ is

$$
\begin{aligned}
C(X) = {}& c'_0 + c'_1(X - \alpha_0) + c'_2(X - \alpha_0)(X - \alpha_1) \\
&+ \ldots + c'_{2k-2}(X - \alpha_0)(X - \alpha_1)\ldots(X - \alpha_{2k-2}).
\end{aligned}
$$

The reconstruction of the coefficients of $C(X)$ can be done using the Horner's scheme

$$
\begin{aligned}
C(X) = {}& c'_0 + (X - \alpha_0)[c'_1 + (X - \alpha_1)(c'_2 + (X - \alpha_2)(\ldots \\
&\ldots + (X - \alpha_{2k})[c'_{2k-1} + (X - \alpha_{2k-1})c'_{2k-2}]))].
\end{aligned}
$$

The efficiency of the multiplication by interpolation depends on the choice of the α_is. The Newton's interpolation involves divisions be the differences of the α_is, these elements can be precomputed once for all as the α_is are fixed. Furthermore, the divisions by $(\alpha_i - \alpha_j)^{-1}$ can be transformed in multiplication by constants, as we work in a finite field.

The complexity of Newton's interpolation is the sum of the complexity of the computation of the $C(\alpha_i)$, the c'_i and the reconstruction of the coefficients of $C(X)$.

The complexity of Newton's interpolation is

$$
4(2k^2 - 3k + 1)A_p + 4(2k^2 - 3k + 1)CM_p + (2k - 1)M_p.
$$

5.3.3. Comparison between the two methods

The two methods involves the same number of multiplications in the base field $\mathbb{F}_p$: $(2k - 1)$, for polynomials of degree $(k - 1)$.

The Lagrange's interpolation is very important when computations can be parallelised. Indeed, the computation of the $C(\alpha_i) \times \dfrac{\prod\limits_{j \neq i}(X - \alpha_j)}{\prod\limits_{j \neq i}(\alpha_i - \alpha_j)}$ are independent. The Newton's interpolation involves less additions and multiplications by constants than the Lagrange's one, but we cannot parallelise the computation. The c_i' must be computed one after another.

Operation \ Method	Lagrange	Newton
A_p	$12k^2 - 14k + 4$	$8k^2 - 12k + 4$
CM_p	$8k^2 - 10k + 3$	$8k^2 - 12k + 4$
M_p	$(2k - 1)$	$(2k - 1)$

Table 5. Complexity in number of operation over the base field

The Lagrange's interpolation should be privileged when computations can be parallelised and Newton when the size of the device is limited, typically for smart cards.

5.4. Karatsuba and Toom Cook methods

5.4.1. Karatsuba's method

The Karatsuba multiplication is a straightforward application of the Newton's method, for polynomials of degree 1. The result of the multiplication is a polynomial of degree 2, then we need $2 + 1 = 3$ points of interpolation. These values are $\{0, 1, \infty\}$. The Karatsuba multiplication provide the product of two polynomials of degree 1 in 3 multiplications in the base field, instead of 4 using the school book method. The multiplication by constants in the Newton multiplication are free, because of the choice of the interpolation values. Let $A(X) = A_0 + A_1 X$ and $B(X) = B_0 + B_1 X$ be two polynomials of degree 1 and $C(X) = A(X) \times B(X)$.

We evaluate the polynomial $C(X)$ in the point $\{0, 1, \infty\}$ using equations 10.

$$
\begin{aligned}
C(0) &= (A_1 X + A_0)(B_1 X + B_0) \bmod(X), \\
&= A_0 \times B_0, \\
C(1) &= (A_1 X + A_0)(B_1 X + B_0) \bmod(X - 1), \\
&= (A_0 + A_1) \times (B_0 + B_1), \\
C(\infty) &= (A_1 X + A_0)(B_1 X + B_0) \bmod(X - \infty), \\
&= A_1 \times B_1 \times X^2 \bmod(X - \infty).
\end{aligned}
\tag{10}
$$

The evaluation of polynomial $C(X)$ in the 3 values involves $2A_p + 3M_p$ operations in the base field $\mathbb{F}_p$.

Then, we use the formulas in the Newton interpolation to reconstruct the polynomial $C(X)$.

$$\begin{cases}
c_0' = C(0), \\
\quad = A_0 B_0, \\
c_1' = (C(1) - c_0')\frac{1}{(1-0)}, \\
\quad = (A_0 + A_1)(B_0 + B_1) - A_0 B_0, \\
c_2' = \left((C(\infty) - c_0')\frac{1}{(\infty - 0)} - c_1'\right)\frac{1}{(\infty - 1)}, \\
\quad = \left((A_1 B_1 X^2 - A_0 B_0)\frac{1}{(X-0)} - ((A_0 + A_1)(B_0 + B_1) - A_0 B_0)\right)\frac{1}{(X-1)} \bmod (X - \infty), \\
\quad = \frac{A_1 B_1 X^2}{X^2} - \frac{A_0 B_0}{X^2} - \frac{((A_0 + A_1)(B_0 + B_1) - A_0 B_0)}{X} \bmod (X - \infty), \\
\quad = A_1 B_1.
\end{cases}$$

$$\begin{aligned}
C(X) &= c_0' + c_1' X + c_2' X(X - 1), \\
&= A_0 B_0 + ((A_0 + A_1)(B_0 + B_1) - A_0 B_0)X + A_1 B_1 X(X - 1), \\
&= A_0 B_0 + ((A_0 + A_1)(B_0 + B_1) - A_0 B_0 - A_1 B_1)X + A_1 B_1 X^2.
\end{aligned}$$

We can resume the computation of the polynomial $C(X)$ using Karatsuba's multiplication by the following equation

$$\begin{cases}
c_0 = A_0 \times B_0, \\
c_1 = (A_0 + A_1) \times (B_0 + B_1), \\
c_2 = A_1 \times B_1, \\
C(X) = c_0 + (c_1 - c_0 - c_2)X + c_2 X^2.
\end{cases} \tag{11}$$

For polynomials of degree 1, the complexity of Karatsuba's multiplication is $3M_p + 4A_p$.

The Karatsuba's multiplication can be recursively applied for polynomials of degree greater than 1. Let $A(X) = A_0 + A_1 X + \ldots A_m X^m$, we can split $A(X)$ in two parts of degree smaller or equal to $\lfloor \frac{m}{2} \rfloor$:

$$A(X) = A_0 + A_1 X + \ldots A_{\lfloor \frac{m}{2} \rfloor - 1} + X^{\lfloor \frac{m}{2} \rfloor}\left(A_{\lfloor \frac{m}{2} \rfloor} + A_{\lfloor \frac{m}{2} \rfloor + 1}X + \ldots A_m X^{\lfloor \frac{m}{2} \rfloor}\right),$$

$$= \widetilde{A_0} + Y\widetilde{A_1}, \text{ where we denote } Y = X^{\lfloor \frac{m}{2} \rfloor}.$$

Then, we apply the Karatsuba's multiplication to the two parts. Each of the three multiplications can also be done using the Karatsuba's multiplication. The recursive application of Karatsuba's multiplication is the most efficient method for the computation of polynomials of degree a power of 2. The asymptotic complexity of Karatsuba's multiplication is $O(m^{\log_2(3)})$ multiplications and $O(m)$ additions, with m being the degree of the polynomials we want to multiply.

5.4.2. Toom Cook 3 multiplication

Exactly like the Karatsuba's multiplication, Toom Cook 3 multiplication is an application of Newton's interpolation. The Toom Cook 3 method provide the product of polynomials of degree 2 with 5 multiplications of coefficients, instead of 9 using the school book method multiplication. The values for the interpolation are $\{0, 1, -1, 2, \infty\}$. Unlike the Karatsuba's method, there are few multiplications and divisions by constants that we cannot avoid.

Let $A(X) = A_0 + A_1 X + A_2 X^2$ and $B(X) = B_0 + B_1 X + B_2 X^2$ be polynomials of degree 2 and $C(X) = A(X) \times B(X)$ obtained using the Toom Cook method. The evaluation part of Toom Cook 3 multiplication involves 10 additions of A_i and B_i, for $i = 0, 1, 2$. The evaluation of $A(X)$ needs 5 additions.

$$
\left\{
\begin{array}{l}
A(0) = A_0, \\
Sp_1 = A_0 + A_2, \\
A(1) = Sp_1 + A_1, \\
A(-1) = Sp_1 - A_1, \\
A(2) = A_0 + 2A_1 + 4A_2, \\
A(\infty) = A_2 X^2 \bmod (X - \infty).
\end{array}
\right.
$$

We begin with the evaluation of $C(X)$ in the α_i pour $i = 0, 1, 2, 3, 4$.

$$
\left\{
\begin{array}{l}
C(0) = A(0) \times B(0) = A_0 B_0, \\
C(1) = A(1) \times B(1), \\
C(-1) = A(-1) \times B(-1), \\
C(2) = A(2) \times B(2), \\
C(\infty) = A(\infty) \times B(\infty) = A_2 B_2 X^4 \bmod (X - \infty).
\end{array}
\right.
$$

We apply the Newton's method to find the coefficients c_i'

$$
\left\{
\begin{array}{l}
c_0' = C(0), \\
c_1' = C(1) - c_0', \\
c_2' = \frac{1}{2} \left(C(-1) - c_0' + c_1' \right), \\
c_3' = \frac{1}{6} C(2) - \frac{1}{6} c_0' - \frac{1}{3} c_1' - \frac{1}{3} c_2', \\
c_4' = A_2 B_2.
\end{array}
\right.
$$

The reconstruction of $C(X)$ is then

$$
C(X) = c_0' + c_1' X + c_2' X(X-1) + c_3' X(X-1)(X+1) + c_4' X(X-1)(X+1)(-2).
$$

This step can be resume by the formula

$$C(X) = c_0' + (c_1' - c_2' - c_3' - 2c_4')X + (c_2' - c_4')X^2$$
$$+ (c_3' - 2c_4')X^3 + c_4'X^4.$$

Which gives

$$\begin{cases} C_0 = c_0', \\ C_1 = c_1' - c_2' - c_3' - 2c_4', \\ C_2 = c_2' - c_4', \\ C_3 = c_3' - 2c_4', \\ C_4 = c_4', \\ C(X) = C_0 + C_1 X + C_2 X^2 + C_3 X^3 + C_4 X^4. \end{cases}$$

For polynomials of degree 2, the complexity of Toom Cook 3 is $5M_p + 11CM_p + 11A_p$. As for Karatsuba's method, the Toom Cook 3 method can be recursively applied. The asymptotic complexity of Toom Cook 3 multiplication is $O(m^{\log_3(5)})$ multiplications and $O(m)$ additions, where m is the degree of the polynomials we want to multiply.

5.4.3. Extensions to other extensions

The Toom Cook 3 method can be extended to Toom Cook 5, this multiplication is suited for polynomials of degree 3. Few works deal with the multiplication of polynomials of degree greater than 3. For polynomials of degree 4, we can use the Karatsuba's method. As a consequence, in pairing based cryptography, field with extension degree of the form $2^i 3^j$ are called pairing friendly because we can use tower fields and for each stage of the tower we use the Karatsuba or Toom Cook 3 multiplication. However in pairing based cryptography (and in cryptography in general) there are some cases where it is more interesting to use fields with degree extensions different from 2 and 3. We can cite the problem of compression (i.e. representing elements in a finite field subgroup with fewer bits than classical algorithms) for extension fields in terms of *algebraic tori* $T_n(\mathbb{F}_q)$ [63] or applications based on $T_{30}(\mathbb{F}_q)$, such as El Gamal encryption, El Gamal signatures and voting schemes in [69].

Let $\mathbb{F}_p$ be a finite field of characteristic greater than 5. For instance for polynomials of degree 5, we can begin with Karatsuba's method and then use Karatsuba and Toom Cook 3 for each part. This construction gives an efficient multiplication for polynomials of degree 5, but not the most efficient. For degree 5 extensions, Montgomery [58] has proposed a Karatsuba-like formula for 5-terms polynomials performed using 13 base field multiplications. This work was improved by El Mrabet et all in [30] using Newton's interpolation.

We recall here Montgomery's method for an extension of degree 5. Let $A = a_0 + a_1 X + a_2 X^2 + a_3 X^3 + a_4 X^4$ and $B = b_0 + b_1 X + b_2 X^2 + b_3 X^3 + b_4 X^4$ in $\mathbb{F}_{p^5}$ with coefficients over $\mathbb{F}_p$. Montgomery constructs the polynomial $C(X) = A(X) \cdot B(X)$ using the following formula $C = (a_0 + a_1 X + a_2 X^2 + a_3 X^3 + a_4 X^4)(b_0 + b_1 X + b_2 X^2 + b_3 X^3 + b_4 X^4)$

$$\begin{aligned}
&= (a_0+a_1+a_2+a_3+a_4)(b_0+b_1+b_2+b_3+b_4)(X^5-X^4+X^3)\\
&+(a_0-a_2-a_3-a_4)(b_0-b_2-b_3-b_4)(X^6-2X^5+2X^4-X^3)\\
&+(a_0+a_1+a_2-a_4)(b_0+b_1+b_2-b_4)(-X^5+2X^4-2X^3+X^2)\\
&+(a_0+a_1-a_3-a_4)(b_0+b_1-b_3-b_4)(X^5-2X^4+X^3)\\
&+(a_0-a_2-a_3)(b_0-b_2-b_3)(-X^6+2X^5-X^4)\\
&+(a_1+a_2-a_4)(b_1+b_2-b_4)(-X^4+2X^3-X^2)\\
&+(a_3+a_4)(b_3+b_4)(X^7-X^6+X^4-X^3)\\
&+(a_0+a_1)(b_0+b_1)(-X^5+X^4-X^2+X)\\
&+(a_0-a_4)(b_0-b_4)(-X^6+3X^5-4X^4+3X^3-X^2)\\
&+a_4b_4(X^8-X^7+X^6-2X^5+3X^4-3X^3+X^2)\\
&+a_3b_3(-X^7+2X^6-2X^5+X^4)\\
&+a_1b_1(X^4-2X^3+2X^2-X)\\
&+a_0b_0(X^6-3X^5+3X^4-2X^3+X^2-X+1).
\end{aligned}$$

The cost of these computations is $13M_q+22A_q$. Note that in order to recover the final expression of the polynomial of degree 8, we have to re-organize the 13 lines to find its coefficients. We denote the products on each of the 13 lines by u_i, $0 \le i \le 12$ (i.e. $u_{12} = (a_0+a_1+a_2+a_3+a_4)(b_0+b_1+b_2+b_3+b_4)$, $u_{11} = (a_0-a_2-a_3-a_4)(b_0-b_2-b_3-b_4)$ etc.) By re-arranging the formula in function of the degree of X, we obtain the following expression for C

$$\begin{aligned}
C = &\ u_3 X^8\\
&+(-u_2-u_3+u_6)X^7\\
&+(u_0+2u_2+u_3-u_4-u_6-u_8+u_{11})X^6\\
&+(-3u_0-2u_2-2u_3+3u_4-u_5+2u_8+u_9-u_{10}-2u_{11}+u_{12})X^5\\
&+(3u_0+u_1+u_2+3u_3-4u_4+u_5+u_6-u_7-u_8-2u_9+2u_{10}+2u_{11}-u_{12})X^4\\
&+(-2u_0-2u_1-3u_3+3u_4-u_6+2u_7+u_9-2u_{10}-u_{11}+u_{12})X^3\\
&+(u_0+2u_1+u_3-u_4-u_5-u_7+u_{10})X^2\\
&+(-u_0-u_1+u_5)X\\
&+u_0.
\end{aligned}$$

Considering this expression, hidden additions must be taken in account. Once every simplification is done, the total complexity of Montgomery's method is $13M_p+62A_p$.

In [30], the Newton's interpolation gives a better result for the multiplication of 5-terms polynomials. The interpolation values are $\alpha_0 = 0$, $\alpha_1 = 1$, $\alpha_2 = -1$, $\alpha_3 = 2$, $\alpha_4 = -2$, $\alpha_5 = 4$, $\alpha_6 = -4$, $\alpha_7 = 3$, $\alpha_8 = \infty$. With these values, the evaluations of A and B are only composed of shifts and additions. Details are provide in [30], the evaluations of $A(X)$ and $B(X)$ have a total complexity of $48A_p$. The evaluation of $C(X)$ in the α_is costs $9M_p$. The computation of the c'_is is not straightforward. Indeed, there are few divisions by 3, 5 and 7 that appear in the formula Section 5.3.2. To avoid the computation of a division which is an expensive operation over a finite field, using a trick on the binary decomposition of integers, they perform very efficiently the divisions. The complexity for these divisions is smaller than

$2A_p$. The global complexity for the computation of the c_i's is then $64A_p$. Finally, the reconstruction of the polynomial $C(X)$ using the Horner's scheme has a complexity of $28A_p$. And the total complexity of the 5-terms polynomials is $9M_q + 137A_q$.

The comparison with Montgomery's result is not evident, but implementations in [30] shows that the results are more efficient than the Montgomery's one.

In the two articles, the authors give also results for 6-terms and 7-terms polynomials.

The fact that we can compute efficiently the multiplication for extensions greater than 2 and 3 gives the opportunity to consider pairing computation over elliptic curve with an embedding degree k different from $2^i 3^j$ and can improve the implementation of pairings. But this work is still to be made.

5.5. Original representation of finite fields

In the previous section we consider efficient multiplications for a classical representation of finite fields and extension of finite fields. But they are many ways to represent a finite field. In [22], the authors use an original representation of finite field to provide a very efficient implementation of a pairing. This original representation is the Residue Number System (RNS) representation and it was developed in [7, 8]. The RNS representation relays on the Chinese remainder theorem. Let $\mathscr{B} = \{m_1, \ldots, m_n\}$ be a set of co-prime natural integers, $M = \prod_{i=1}^{n} m_i$ and $0 \leq X < M$. There exists a unique representation $X_{\mathscr{B}}$ of X in the basis $\mathscr{B}$, $X_{\mathscr{B}} = \{X \mod m_1, \ldots X \mod m_n\} = \{x_1, x_2, \ldots, x_n\}$. Given $X_{\mathscr{B}}$, we can reconstruct X using the Chinese Remainder theorem:

$$X = \left(\sum_{i=1}^{n} (x_i \times b_i^{-1} \mod m_i) \times b_i \right) \mod M, \text{ where } b_i = \frac{M}{m_i}.$$

The RNS representation is obviously very interesting for parallel computations. An efficient multiplication in RNS representation is described in [7, 8]. This multiplication is based on the Montgomery modular multiplication. In [22], the authors present two very efficient implementation of a pairing algorithm on an FPGA, in RNS representation. They implement the optimal Ate pairing at several security levels over Altera and Xilinx FPGA. They compare there result with previous work and obtaint very nice results.

5.6. The arithmetic of Pairings

The complexity of a computation of a pairing depends on the finite field and the arithmetic underlying, but also of the model and the equation of the elliptic curve and the choice of the coordinates. Usually, an elliptic curve is represented using the short Weierstrass equation which is on the form $E : y^2 = x^3 + ax + b$, with a and b elements of the finite field $\mathbb{F}_p$. In [20], Brier and Joye show that the value a can be chosen to be -3. This value contributes to improve the computation of pairings. But, even on a short Weierstrass equation, several cases exist, we can have $b = 0$, $a = 0$ with b a square or not just an integer. For each option, the coordinates have also an influence on the efficiency of the computation of a pairing. The coordinates are usually chosen between affine, Projective and Jacobian. The affine coordinates are often put aside. Indeed, the operations over the elliptic curve in affine coordinates involves inversion over finite fields. As inversion over a finite field is an expensive operation, one try to avoid them so far as possible. To achieve this aim, the Projective or Jacobian coordinates are suitable, as by construction, the Projective and Jacobian coordinates substitute inversions in affine coordinates into multiplications. The fact that the affine coordinates involves inversions was a drawback to their use in pairing based cryptography. In [51], the authors analyzed the use of affine coordinates for pairing based cryptography. They adapt two known techniques for speeding up field inversion to the pairing based cryptography case. They found out that for high security levels, an implementation in affine coordinates of a pairing will be much faster than an implementation in projective coordinates. The first technique to improve the inversion consists in computing inverses in extension fields by using towers of extension field and transform inverse computation to subfield computations via the norm map. Using this technique, the authors reduce drastically the ratio of the costs of inversions to multiplications in extension fields. This is very interesting for the computation of pairings over a large extension field, typically at high level security such as 256 bits. The second trick is to take advantage of the inversion-sharing, a standard trick whenever several inversions are computed at once. This method involves the lecture of the binary expansion from right to left, instead of left to right. This second method is very interesting when multi-core processors are used, indeed, it can be easily parallelized. We can find in [51] detailed performance numbers with timing for base field and extension field arithmetic. For security level more reasonable, the Projective and Jacobian coordinates are for now more suitable.

In [24], the authors resume, compare and improve several works dealing with the optimizations of pairings, considering all the possibilities for the Weierstrass equation. They give efficient computations in Jacobian and Projective coordinates. We resume there work in Table 6.

Curve Curve order Twist deg.	Doubling Addition Result of [24]	Prev Result	Doubling Addition
$y^2 = x^3 + ax$ any $d = 2,4$	$M_a + (2k/d + 2)M_p + 8S_p$ $(2k/d + 12)M_p + S_p$ New coord.	[2]	$M_a + (2k/d + 1)M_p + 11S_p$ $(2k/d + 10)M_p + 6S_p$ Jacobian
$y^2 = x^3 + c^2$ $3 | \sharp E$ $d = 2,6$	$(2k/d + 3)M_p + 5S_p$ $M_c + (2k/d + 3)M_p + 5S_p$ Projective	[23]	$(2k/d + 3)M_p + 5S_p$ $M_c + (2k/d + 3)M_p + 5S_p$ Projective
$y^2 = x^3 + b$ $3 \nmid \sharp E$ $d = 2,6$	$M_b + (2k/d + 2)M_p + 7S_p$ $M_b + (2k/d + 2)M_p + 7S_p$ Projective	[2]	$(2k/d + 3)M_p + 8S_p$ $(2k/d + 3)M_p + 8S_p$ Jacobian
$y^2 = x^3 + b$ any $d = 3$	$M_b + (k + 6)M_p + 7S_p$ $(k + 16)M_p + 3S_p$ Projective	[31]	$M_b + (2k + 8)M_p + 9S_p$ not reported Projective

Table 6. Comparaison of pairings considering Weierstrass models

There exists several model of elliptic curves, for instance

- Short Weierstrass: $y^2 = x^3 + ax + b$, for a, b in $\mathbb{K}$.
- Legendre coordinates: $y^2 = x(x - 1)(x - \lambda)$, for $\lambda \in \mathbb{K}$.
- Montgomery: $by^2 = x^3 + ax^2 + x$, for a, b in $\mathbb{K}$.
- Edwards coordinates: $x^2 + y^2 = c(1 + x^2y^2)$ over $\mathbb{K}$.
- Huff's coordinates: $aX(Y^2 - Z^2) = bY(X^2 - Z^2)$ for $a^2 \neq b^2 \neq 0$ over $\mathbb{K}$.

Several works study the efficiency of an implementation of pairing over some of these models of elliptic curves. The Edwards elliptic curves were recently introduced in cryptographie. In [32], Edwards demonstrates that every elliptic curve E defined over an algebraic number field is birationally equivalent over some extension of that field to a curve given by the equation:

$$x^2 + y^2 = c^2(1 + x^2 y^2).$$ (12)

Edwards curves became interesting for elliptic curve cryptography when it was proven by Bernstein and Lange in [18] that they provide addition and doubling formulas faster than all addition formulas known at that time. The advantage of Edwards coordinates is that the addition law can be complete (i.e. the formulas for adding or doubling two points are the same) and thus the exponentiation in Edwards coordinates is naturally protected against side channel attacks. Recently, the Edwards elliptic curves were used to compute pairings [3, 44]. In [46], the authors study the Huff's model of an elliptic curve, they provide explicit formulae for fast doubling and addition and also for Tate pairing computation. Another example is the work in [72], in this work the authors consider the Selmer elliptic curves, they present formulae for doubling, addition and pairing computations. They compare there results to various elliptic curve models such as Weierstrass, Edwards, Hessian. There is many choices for the equation/model of the elliptic curve and of the coordinates, the website [17] regroups every new result on this subject. It is a very nice overview of this topic of research.

6. Conclusions

We presented the various pairings available for cryptographic use. As the pairing are aimed to be implemented in smart cards, the efficiency of a pairing implementation is a subject of several research. We presented optimizations developed for the improvement of a pairing implementation. We introduced the twisted elliptic curve which leads to the denominator elimination. We constructed the extension field $\mathbb{F}_{p^k}$ using tower fields and the method for an efficient multiplication over each step of the tower. We described efficient squaring method combine with the cyclotomic subgroup. We also highlighted the fact that the choice of the model of the elliptic curve and the choice of the coordinates is important for an efficient implementation. We saw that the representation of an element in the base field $\mathbb{F}_p$ with original definition can leads to very efficient implementation. To conclude, the optimizations of pairing are a very interesting point of research and a lot of scientists work hardly to find new optimizations. Further research can follow the presented optimizations and adapt to the case of pairings over hyperelliptic curves, or find any other point of optimizations in the implementation.

Author details

Nadia El Mrabet

LIASD, University Paris 8, Saint Denis, France

References

[1] Ahmadi O., Hankerson D., Menezes A.: Software Implementation of Arithmetic in $\mathbb{F}_{3^m}$, WAIFI Conference, Madrid Spain 2007.

[2] C. Arene, T. Lange, M. Naehrig and C. Ritzenthaler Faster pairing computation   Cryptology ePrint Archive, Report 2009/155, 2009

[3] C. Arène and T. Lange and M. Naehrig and C. Ritzenhaler, Faster Pairing Computation of the Tate pairing, Cryptology ePrint Archive, Report 2009/155, http://eprint.iacr.org/2009/155, 2009

[4] J.C.Bajard and N.El Mrabet: Pairing in cryptography: an arithmetic point de view, In *Advanced Signal Processing Algorithms, Architectures and Implementations XVI*, part of SPIE, August 2007.

[5] Bajard J.C., Imbert L., Negre Ch.: Arithmetic Operations in Finite Fields of Medium Prime Characteristic Using the Lagrange Representation, IEEE Transactions on Computers, September 2006 (Vol. 55, No. 9) p p. 1167-1177

[6] Bajard, J.C., Meloni, N., Plantard, T.: Efficient RNS bases for Cryptography IMACS'05, Applied Mathematics and Simulation, (2005)

[7] J-C. Bajard, L-S. Didier and P. Kornerup, Modular Multiplication and Base Extensions in Residue Number Systems, 15th IEEE Symposium on Computer Arithmetic (Arith-15 2001), p. 59–65, 2001.

[8] J-C. Bajard, L-S. Didier and P. Kornerup,   An RNS Montgomery Modular Multiplication Algorithm, IEEE Trans. Computers, vol. 47, p. 766–776, 1998.

[9] Barreto, P.: The Pairing-Based Crypto Lounge
http://paginas.terra.com.br/informatica/paulobarreto/pblounge.html

[10] P.D. Barrett. Implementing the Rivest Shamir and Adleman Public Key Encryption Algorithm on a Standard Digital Signal Processor. In *Advances in Cryptology (CRYPTO)*, LNCS 263, 311–323, 1986.

[11] Barreto P., Lynn B., Scott M.: On the Selection of Pairing-Friendly Groups Selected Aeras in Cryptography SAC 2003, LNCS 30006, 2004,17-25

[12] P.S.L.M. Barreto, S.D. Galbraith, C. O'hEigeartaigh and M. Scott. Efficient Pairing Computation on Supersingular Abelian Varieties, In *Designs, Codes and Cryptography*, 42 (3), 239–271, 2007.

[13] Barreto P., Kim H., Lynn B., Scott M.: Efficient algorithms for pairing-based cryptosystems, Advances in Cryptology CRYPTO 2002, Lecture Notes in Computer Science, 2442 (2002), 354-368.

[14] Barreto P., Naehrig M.: Pairing-friendly elliptic curves of prime order, Selected Areas in Cryptography (SAC 2005), LNCS 3897 (2006), 319-331.

[15] Barreto P., Lynn B., Scott M.: Efficient implementation of pairing-based cryptosystems, Journal of Cryptology, 17 (2004), 321-334

[16] Barreto P., Scott M.: Compressed pairings, Advances in Cryptology I Crypto 2004, LNCS 3152, 140-156, http://eprint.iacr.org/2004/032.

[17] D. J. Bernstein and T. Lange Explicit-formulas database. http://www. hyperelliptic.org/EFD.

[18] D. J. Bernstein and T. Lange, Faster additions and doubling on elliptic curves, In Advances in cryptology - ASIACRYPT 2007, LNCS, vol. 4833, p. 29–50,2007

[19] Boneh D., Franklin M.: Identity-based encryption from the Weil pairing. SIAM Journal of Computing, 32, 586?615, 2003

[20] Brier E., Joye M.: Point multiplication on elliptic curves through isogenies, AAECC 2003, LNCS., vol. 2643, 2003, 43–50.

[21] Blake F., Seroussi G., Smart N. (editors): Advances in Elliptic Curve Cryptography, Series: London Mathematical Society Lecture Note Series (No. 317),Cambridge University Press,2005

[22] R. C. C. Cheung, S. Duquesne, J. Fan and, N. Guillermin, I. Verbauwhede and G. Xiaoxu Yao, FPGA Implementation of Pairings Using Residue Number System and Lazy Reduction, Cryptographic Hardware and Embedded Systems - CHES 2011 LNCS vol. 6917, p. 421–441, 2011.

[23] C. Costello, H. Hisil, C. Boyd, J-M. Gonz?alez Nieto and K. Koon-Ho Wong. Faster pairings on special Weierstrass curves Pairing2009, LNCS, vol. 5671, p. 89–101, 2009

[24] C. Costello, T. Lange and M. Naehrig. Faster pairing computations on curves with high-degree twists. Progress in Cryptology ? PKC 2010 (13th International Conference on Practice and Theory in Public Key Cryptography LNCS, vol. 6056, p. 224–242, 2010.

[25] Cohen, H., Frey, G. (editors): Handbook of elliptic and hyperelliptic curve cryptography. Discrete Math. Appl., Chapman & Hall/CRC (2006)

[26] Diffie W., Hellman M.: directions in cryptography, IEEE Transactions on Information Theory, 22 (1976), 644-654.

[27] I. Duursma and H. Lee. Tate Pairing Implementation for Hyperelliptic Curves $y^2 = x^p - x + d$. In *Advances in Cryptology (ASIACRYPT)*, Springer-Verlag LNCS 2894, 111–123, 2003.

[28] Duquesne S., Frey G. Background on Pairings, Chapter 6 of Cohen, H., Frey, G.: Handbook of elliptic and hyperelliptic curve cryptography. Discrete Math. Appl., Chapman & Hall/CRC (2006)

[29] Duquesne S., Frey G. Implementation of Pairings, Chapter 16 of Cohen, H., Frey, G.: Handbook of elliptic and hyperelliptic curve cryptography. Discrete Math. Appl., Chapman & Hall/CRC (2006)

[30] N. El Mrabet, A. Guillevic and S. Ionica, Efficient Multiplication in Finite Field Extensions of Degree 5. Progress in Cryptology-Africacrypt 2011, Springer-Verlag LNCS 6737, p. 188–205, 2011.

[31] N. El Mrabet, N. Guillermin and S. Ionica. A study of pairing computation for elliptic curves with embedding degree 15 Cryptology ePrint Archive, Report 2009/370, 2009.

[32] H. Edwards , A normal Form for Elliptic Curve Bulletin of the American Mathematical Society, vol. 44, nř 3, p. 393–422, July 2007

[33] D. Freeman, M. Scott and E. Teske, A Taxonomy of Pairing-Friendly Elliptic Curves, Journal of Cryptology, vol. 23, nř 2, p. 224–280, 2010

[34] Frey G., Müller M., Rück H.G.: The Tate Pairing and the Discrete Logarithm Applied to Elliptic Curve Cryptosystems, IEEE Transactions Inf. Theory, 45, 1717-1719;1999

[35] Fleischmann P., Paar C., Soria-Rodriguez P.: Fast Arithmetic for Public-Key Algorithms in Galois Fields with Composite Exponents, IEEE Transactions on Computers, vol. 48, no. 10, pp. 1025-1034, October, 1999.

[36] Frey G., Rück H.G.: A Remark Concerning m-divisibility Constructions and the Discrete Logarithmic problem in the Divisor Class Group of Curves, in Math. comp., 62, 865-874, 1994.

[37] Galbraith S.: K.G.: Pairings, Chapter IX, Advances in Elliptic Curve Cryptography, F. Blake and G. Seroussi and N. Smart editors, Series: London Mathematical Society Lecture Note Series (No. 317),Cambridge University Press,2005

[38] S.D. Galbraith, C. O'hEigeartaigh and C. Sheedy. Simplified Pairing Computation and Security Implications, In *Journal of Mathematical Cryptology*, 1 (3), 267–282, 2007.

[39] S.D. Galbraith, F. Hess and F. Vercauteren. Aspects of Pairing Inversion In *IEEE Transactions on Information Theory*, 54 (12), 5719–5728, 2008.

[40] Granger R., Page D., Stam M.: Hardware and Software Normal Basis Arithmetic for Pairing-Based Cryptography in Characteristic Three. IEEE Transactions on Computers,volume 54(7): 852–860, July 2005

[41] R. Granger and M. Scott, Faster Squaring in the Cyclotomic Subgroup of Sixth Degree Extensions, Practice and Theory in Public Key Cryptography 2010, LNCS vol. 6056, p. 209–223, 2010

[42] F. Hess, Pairing Lattices, Pairing 2008, LNCS vol. 5209, p. 18–38, 2008

[43] F. Hess, N. Smart and F. Vercauteren The Eta Pairing Revisited, IEEE Transactions on Information Theory, vol. 52, p. 4595–4602, 2006

[44] S. Ionica and A. Joux , Another Approach to Pairing Computation in Edwards Coordinates, INDOCRYPT '08, LNCS,vol. 5365, p. 400–413,2008

[45] Joux A.: one round protocol for tripartite Diffie-Hellman, Algorithmic Number Theory: Fourth International Symposium, Lecture Notes in Computer Science, 1838 (2000), 385-393. Full version: Journal of Cryptology, 17 (2004), 263-276

[46] M. Joye, M. Tibouchi and D. Vergnaud Huff's Model for Elliptic Curve Algorithmic Number Theory (ANTS-IX), LNCS vol. 6197, p. 234–250, 2012

[47] Koblitz N.: Elliptic curve cryptosystems, Mathematics of Computation, Vol. 48, 1987, 203-209.

[48] N. Koblitz and A. Menezes, Pairing-Based Cryptography at High Security Levels, Cryptography and Coding 2005, LNCS vol. 3796, p. 13–36, 2005

[49] S. Kwon. Efficient Tate Pairing Computation for Supersingular Elliptic Curves over Binary Fields. In *Cryptology ePrint Archive*, Report 2004/303, 2004.

[50] R. Lidl and H. Niederreiter Finite Fields Cambridge University Press, 1994, 0-521-39231-4

[51] K. Lauter, P. L. Montgomery and M. Naehrig An Analysis of Affine Coordinates for Pairing Computation, Pairing 2010, LNCS, vol. 6487, p. 1–20, 2010

[52] Lenstra A., Stam M.: Efficient Subgroup Exponentiation in Quadratic and Sixth Degree Extensions, Cryptographic Hardware and Embedded Systems, CHES 2002, LNCS 2523 pp. 318-332.

[53] MenezesA., Okamoto T. and Vanstone S.A.: Reducing Elliptic Curve Logarithms to Logarithms in a Finite Field, IEEE Trans. Inf . Theory 39, numéro 5, pages 1639-1646, 1993.

[54] Miller V.: The Weil pairing and its efficient calculation, J. Cryptology, 17 (2004), 235-261.

[55] Miller V.: Use of Elliptic Curves in Cryptography Advances in Cryptology-Crypto 85 pages 417-426 Vol. 218 of LNCS 1986.

[56] Miller V.: Short Programs for Functions on Curves, IBM, Thomas J. Watson Research Center, 1986 http://crypto.stanford.edu/miller/miller.pdf

[57] P.L. Montgomery. Modular Multiplication Without Trial Division. *Mathematics of Computation*, 44, 519–521, 1985.

[58] P. L. Montgomery Five, Six and Seven-terms Karatsuba-Like Formulae, IEEE Transactions on Computers 2005, vol. 54, p. 362–369.

[59] C. O'hEigeartaigh. Pairing Computation on Hyperelliptic Curves of Genus 2. PhD Thesis, Dublin City University, 2006.

[60] Pairing 2005 in Dublin Ireland, http://pic.computing.dcu.ie/
Pairing 2007 in Tokyo Japan, http://www.pairing-conference.org/
Pairing 2008 Egham UK,
Pairing 2009 Palo Alto Ca, USA
Pairing 2010 Yamanaka Hot Spring, Ishikawa, Japan
Pairing 2012 Darmstadt, Germany http://2012.pairing-conference.org/

[61] PARI/GP, version 2.1.7, Bordeaux, 2005, http://pari.math.u-bordeaux.fr/

[62] Paterson K.G.: Cryptography from Pairings, Chapter X, Advances in Elliptic Curve Cryptography, F. Blake and G. Seroussi and N. Smart editors, Series: London Mathematical Society Lecture Note Series (No. 317),Cambridge University Press,2005

[63] K. Rubin and A. Silverberg, Torus-Based Cryptography, Advances in Cryptology CRYPTO 2003, Springer-Verlag, LNCS 2729, p. 349–365, 2003.

[64] J.H. Silverman The arithmetic of elliptic curves, Graduate Texts in Mathematics, Springer Verlag, vol. 106, 1992

[65] Shamir A.: Identity BasedCryptosystems and Signature Schemes, Advances in Cryptology Crypto '84, LNCS, Vol. 196, pp 47-53, 1984

[66] M. Scott. Computing the Tate Pairing. In *Topics in Cryptology (CT-RSA)*, Springer-Verlag LNCS 3376, 293–304, 2005.

[67] M. Scott, N. Benger, M. Charlemagne, L. J. Dominguez Perez and E. J. Kachisa, On the Final Exponentiation for Calculating Pairings on Ordinary Elliptic Curves, Pairing 2009, LNCS vol. 5671, p. 78–88,2009

[68] M. Scott, N. Costigan and W. Abdulwahab. Implementing Cryptographic Pairings on Smartcards. In *Cryptographic Hardware and Embedded Systems (CHES)*, Springer-Verlag LNCS 4249, 134–147, 2006.

[69] M. Van Dijk and R. Granger and D. Page and K. Rubin and A. Silverberg and M. Stam and D. Woodruff Practical cryptography in high dimensional tori, Progress in Cryptography Eurocrypt'2005

[70] F. Vercauteren, Optimal pairings, IEEE Trans. Inf. Theor., vol. 56, nř1,p. 455–461, Jan 2010

[71] C. Whelan and M. Scott. The Importance of the Final Exponentiation in Pairings When Considering Fault Attacks. In *Pairing-Based Cryptography*, Springer-Verlag LNCS 4575, 225–246, 2007.

[72] L. Zhang, K. Wang, H. Wang and D. Ye, Another Elliptic Curve Model for Faster Pairing Computation, ISPEC 2011, LNCS vol. 6672, p. 432–446, 2011.

Permissions

The contributors of this book come from diverse backgrounds, making this book a truly international effort. This book will bring forth new frontiers with its revolutionizing research information and detailed analysis of the nascent developments around the world.

We would like to thank Professor Jaydip Sen, for lending his expertise to make the book truly unique. He has played a crucial role in the development of this book. Without his invaluable contribution this book wouldn't have been possible. He has made vital efforts to compile up to date information on the varied aspects of this subject to make this book a valuable addition to the collection of many professionals and students.

This book was conceptualized with the vision of imparting up-to-date information and advanced data in this field. To ensure the same, a matchless editorial board was set up. Every individual on the board went through rigorous rounds of assessment to prove their worth. After which they invested a large part of their time researching and compiling the most relevant data for our readers. Conferences and sessions were held from time to time between the editorial board and the contributing authors to present the data in the most comprehensible form. The editorial team has worked tirelessly to provide valuable and valid information to help people across the globe.

Every chapter published in this book has been scrutinized by our experts. Their significance has been extensively debated. The topics covered herein carry significant findings which will fuel the growth of the discipline. They may even be implemented as practical applications or may be referred to as a beginning point for another development. Chapters in this book were first published by InTech; hereby published with permission under the Creative Commons Attribution License or equivalent.

The editorial board has been involved in producing this book since its inception. They have spent rigorous hours researching and exploring the diverse topics which have resulted in the successful publishing of this book. They have passed on their knowledge of decades through this book. To expedite this challenging task, the publisher supported the team at every step. A small team of assistant editors was also appointed to further simplify the editing procedure and attain best results for the readers.

Our editorial team has been hand-picked from every corner of the world. Their multi-ethnicity adds dynamic inputs to the discussions which result in innovative outcomes. These outcomes are then further discussed with the researchers and contributors who give their valuable feedback and opinion regarding the same. The feedback is then collaborated with the researches and they are edited in a comprehensive manner to aid the understanding of the subject.

Apart from the editorial board, the designing team has also invested a significant amount of their time in understanding the subject and creating the most relevant covers. They scrutinized every image to scout for the most suitable representation of the subject and create an appropriate cover for the book.

The publishing team has been involved in this book since its early stages. They were actively engaged in every process, be it collecting the data, connecting with the contributors or procuring relevant information. The team has been an ardent support to the editorial, designing and production team. Their endless efforts to recruit the best for this project, has resulted in the accomplishment of this book. They are a veteran in the field of academics and their pool of knowledge is as vast as their experience in printing. Their expertise and guidance has proved useful at every step. Their uncompromising quality standards have made this book an exceptional effort. Their encouragement from time to time has been an inspiration for everyone.

The publisher and the editorial board hope that this book will prove to be a valuable piece of knowledge for researchers, students, practitioners and scholars across the globe.

List of Contributors

Xiaoqing Tan
Dept. of Mathematics, Jinan University, Guangzhou, Guangdong, China

Jaydip Sen
Department of Computer Science, National Institute of Science & Technology, Odisha, India

Kim Fook Lee and Yong Meng Sua
Department of Physics, Michigan Technological University, Houghton, Michigan, USA

Harith B. Ahmad
Department of Physics, University of Malaya, Kuala Lumpur, Malaysia

Masa-aki Fukase
Graduate School of Science and Technology, Hirosaki University, Hirosaki, Japan

Nadia El Mrabet
LIASD, University Paris 8, Saint Denis, France

Printed in the USA
CPSIA information can be obtained
at www.ICGtesting.com
JSHW011334221024
72173JS00003B/149